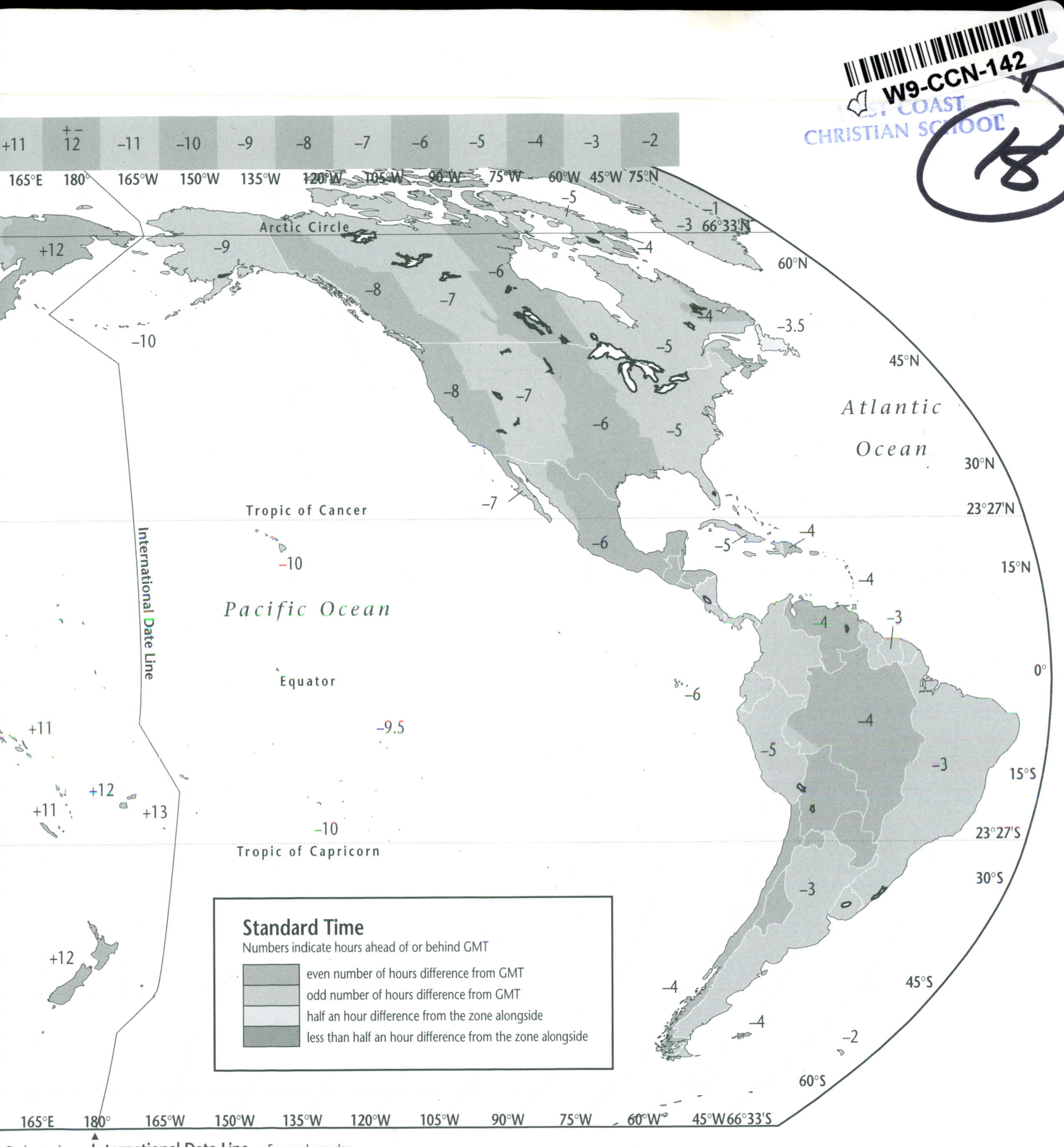

Back one day ← **International Date Line** → Forward one day

On either side of the 180°longitude line the time differs by one whole day – across the International Date Line.
A traveller crossing from east to west moves forward one day. Crossing from west to east the calender goes back one day.

West Coast Christian School

Name	Date Borrowed	Date Returned
Michael	9/2/03	
Jared	October/05	

Global Citizens

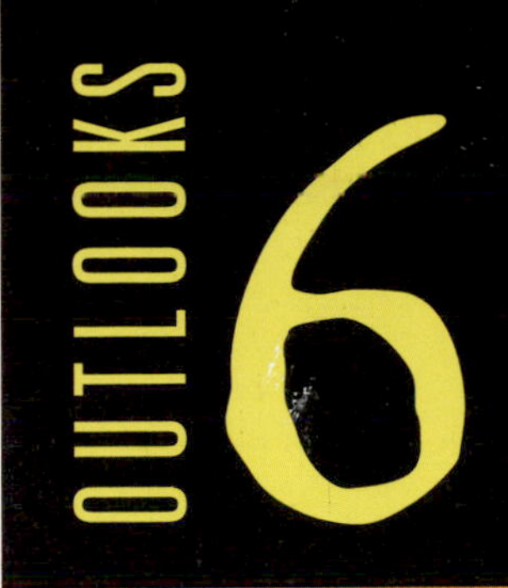

SHARON STERLING
STEVE POWRIE

OXFORD
UNIVERSITY PRESS

70 Wynford Drive, Don Mills, Ontario M3C 1J9
www.oupcan.com

Oxford University Press is a department of the University of Oxford.
It furthers the University's objective of excellence in research, scholarship, and education by publishing worldwide in

Oxford New York

Athens Auckland Bangkok Bogotá Buenos Aires Calcutta Cape Town Chennai Dar es Salaam Delhi Florence Hong Kong Istanbul Karachi Kuala Lumpur Madrid Melbourne Mexico City Mumbai Nairobi Paris São Paulo Shanghai Singapore Taipei Tokyo Toronto Warsaw

with associated companies in Berlin Ibadan

Oxford is a registered trade mark of Oxford University Press
in the UK and in certain other countries

Published in Canada
by Oxford University Press

First published 2001

Canadian Cataloguing in Publication Data

Sterling, Sharon, 1955-
Global citizens
(Outlooks ; 6)
Includes index.
ISBN 0-19-541-433-0

1. Human geography – Juvenile literature. 2. Civilization, Modern – 1950– Juvenile literature. I. Powrie, Steven. II. Title. III. Series.

GF43.S73 2000 304.2 C99-932393-8

3 4 04 03 02 01

This book is printed on permanent (acid-free) paper ∞.

Printed in Canada

Contents

Acknowledgements

The authors would like to thank Loralee Case for her excellent editorial work, creative problem-solving, and great patience during the writing of this book.

The authors and the publisher wish to thank the following consultants for their guidance and advice:

Darlene Gordon
David Cameron Elementary School
Victoria, BC

Sheila Borman
Kitchener Elementary School
Burnaby, BC

The authors and the publisher also extend their thanks to the following people for reviewing the manuscript:

Donna Anderson
Coal Tyee Elementary School
Nanaimo, BC

Wade Blake
Rutherford Community School
Nanaimo, BC

Pat Horstead
Maple Ridge Primary School
Maple Ridge, BC

Credits

Cover Design: Brett Miller

Text Design: Brett Miller

Layout: Ibex Communications Inc.

Cartography: Dave McKay, Visutronx, Paul Sneath

Technical Art: Dave McKay

Illustrations: Heather Graham

Cover Image: First Light/Glenn McLaughlin

Introduction

Global Citizens is a social studies textbook that invites you to investigate the world!

Global means to do with the world. *Citizen* means to be a member of a community. So a global citizen is anyone who lives on planet earth—and that means you! This year in social studies, you can find out what it takes to be a good global citizen.

Part of being a good global citizen is finding out as much as you can about the lives of people in other countries in the world. Once we understand each other's point of view, it is easier for people to get along. So in this text, you'll read about the environment and way of life in a variety of countries, including Japan, Australia, China, Mexico, India, and the United States. You'll also learn about some of the many ways in which Canada is connected to other parts of the world.

Another part of being a good global citizen is to understand the challenges facing the world today. Some of the issues you will investigate this year include human rights, world poverty, managing our natural resources, and child labour. You'll find out why these issues affect all of us in one way or another, and learn about people your age who are working to make the world a better place.

The best way to be a good global citizen, though, is to take action yourself. So this text suggests some steps you can take to find out what needs to be done and ways you can get organized to do it. So go ahead—make a difference. After all, it's your world!

Chapter 1

A Global View

A **global view** is a way of looking at things that includes every person and every place on earth. This may seem like a very big picture to keep in your head. It's an important one, though!

People around the world are connected in many ways. For example, the shoes you are wearing might have been made in Thailand—13 000 kilometres away! Your community might have the same concerns about protecting your culture as a community in Mexico. The pollution we put into the air in British Columbia can travel as far away as South America or Asia.

Because of these connections, you can think of yourself as a **global citizen**—an important member of a worldwide community. This gives you the right to have a say in how the world works and the responsibility to make a change for the better when you can.

Can people your age *really* make a difference? Yes! In this chapter, you can find out what some students have done to make the world a better place to live.

The Global Village

A village is a small community where people work and play together. People in a village depend on one another in good times and bad. Today people all over the world are so closely connected that it is almost as though we are all living in the same village. This world community is often called the **global village**.

The global village is possible because of **technologies** that were developed during the twentieth century.

Technologies such as the Internet, telephones, and faxes make it easy for people who are thousands of kilometres apart to share ideas and information. Television and movies are another way we share ideas about culture. Airplanes allow us to send goods across the world in a few hours. Larger goods can be transported by ship. People can also travel easily from place to place as tourists, or they can choose to move to new countries.

These close connections give us the chance to benefit from the ideas of billions of people. Close connections also mean we have to learn how to work together to find information, solve problems, and investigate issues.

The Big Picture

This year in social studies you can investigate four main topics that all work together to make the world the place it is: **cultures**, **governments**, **environments**, and **economies**.

Pages 4 and 5 show some of the questions we need to ask to investigate these topics.

Reading Hint

When you see a word in **boldface**, pay attention! This is an important word. The explanation of what it means will be nearby on the same page or on the next page.

Technologies are the tools we use and the things we do to get what we need to survive. Computers, hammers, and knowing how to dry fish are all examples of technology.

Cultures

Your **culture** is your way of life. There are many different cultures in the world.

Questions to Investigate

- What do we need to know to understand cultures?
- How can we show respect for our differences?
- How can we make sure that solutions to global problems work for people of all cultures?

These children of Greek heritage are dressed in traditional costumes for a special parade in Montreal. What special cultural celebrations do you take part in?

Governments

Each country has a **government** that makes its laws and helps people meet their needs and wants.

Questions to Investigate

- What are the different systems of government in the world?
- Do people have the same rights and responsibilities in all countries?
- What organizations besides governments help people meet their needs and wants?

In 1998, over 200 students marched through the streets of Ottawa to try to convince the government to spend more money on education. This is called a **protest**. What other protests have you heard about?

Environments

The **environment** is the physical world we live in—land, water, and air. It is our home, and the source of everything we need to live.

These children are planting bog plants to restore the creek near their school. What environmental projects could your school become involved in?

Questions to Investigate

- How do our environments affect us?
- How do our actions and technologies affect our environments?
- What is the best way to manage **natural resources** such as soil and water?
- How can we make sure everyone takes care of the environment?

Economies

Economic systems are the ways we exchange the natural and human-made resources we want and need.

These students are selling tulip bulbs as part of a fund-raising campaign at their school. What types of fund-raising activities have you been involved in?

Questions to Investigate

- What are the economic systems we use to share resources?
- Why aren't resources shared equally?
- Who is going without? Who is taking too much?
- How can we share equally?

Try This

The photographs on pages 4 and 5 show you examples of young people working to make a difference in the world.

1. With a partner, pick one photograph and look at it closely. Make sure you read the **caption**—the words that go with the picture. In point form, describe what you see in the picture and answer the question in the caption.
2. Explain one way the actions of the young people shown in the picture could make a difference in the world.

Think For Yourself

The questions on pages 4 and 5 are **powerful questions**. It takes research and thinking to answer a powerful question.

For each topic on pages 4 and 5, try to think of one powerful question of your own. If a topic interests you a lot, you may have more questions. Keep your questions in your social studies journal or notebook to check later in the year.

HOW TO... Ask Powerful Questions

A powerful question is one that gets you the information you need. Sometimes it also gets you information that makes you see things in a whole new way. You can never answer a powerful question with just "yes" or "no."

When you ask questions, first decide whether you want information on facts or big ideas.

Questions About Facts

Powerful questions about facts get you the details you need to understand the topic.

Weak Questions

- Is there much poverty in Canada?
- Does it get hot in France?

Powerful Questions

- What per cent of Canadians get all they need to eat each week?
- What's the average summer temperature in the capital city of France?

Questions About Big Ideas

Sometimes you want to ask questions about big ideas. These types of questions don't have one answer, and they don't have "easy answers." They're great for getting your brain thinking, though!

Weak Questions

- Is there anything people can do to protect the environment?
- Is Japanese culture different from Canadian culture?

Powerful Questions

- What can we do here at our school to protect the environment?
- In what ways are Japanese and Canadian cultures similar or different?

Global Citizens

Canada is one country that took part in writing the Universal Declaration of Human Rights. Now we also have laws protecting human rights. You might know that many of these laws are explained in the **Canadian Charter of Rights and Freedoms**.

In the year 2000, 185 countries belonged to the United Nations. One of the main purposes of the UN is to help countries settle their differences without going to war. You can learn more about the UN in Chapter 2.

A **citizen** is a person who is part of a community. We usually use this word to describe belonging to a particular country. For example, Canadians are people who are citizens of Canada.

It is the job of a country to decide on the **rights** and **responsibilities** of its citizens. Your rights are the things that it is fair for you to have or be able to do. Your responsibilities are the things *you* should do in order to be fair to others.

Every person on earth is also a citizen of the global village—this means you, your family, and all your friends! Being a **global citizen**, just like being a citizen of any country, means you have certain rights and responsibilities.

Human Rights

Back in 1948, an organization called the **United Nations (UN)** thought about what rights all people in the world should have. They wrote out their ideas in the **Universal Declaration of Human Rights**. Since then, many governments and other organizations in the world have used these ideas when making up their laws.

There are 30 different **articles**, or main points, in the Universal Declaration of Human Rights. A summary of some of these points is shown on the next page. The United Nations says these rights apply to all people on earth, no matter what colour their skin is, what language they speak, what opinions they have, or what beliefs they practice. These rights apply equally to males and females, to rich people and poor people, and to people of all countries and cultures.

Try This

With a partner, look at the drawings on page 9. For each one, decide which right is being shown. Discuss why this right is important to all people in the world. Ask yourselves: *How would people's lives change if they didn't have this right?*

After your discussion, work on your own to make a picture showing one of the other rights in the Universal Declaration of Human Rights.

The Universal Declaration of Human Rights

Everyone has the right to:

- live in freedom and safety
- be treated fairly and equally by laws
- meet their basic needs for food, shelter, and clothing
- take part in their governments
- get an education
- have a job, or get help if that's not possible
- move within their countries and visit other countries
- marry whom they please and have a family
- own things that others cannot take from them
- follow their beliefs
- express their opinions
- have some time for fun!

Making your community a better place helps to make Canada a better place. Making Canada a better place helps improve the whole world.

Your Responsibilities

Human rights don't happen all by themselves. It's the responsibility of every global citizen to respect the rights of others. This doesn't always happen, though. So it is the responsibility of global citizens to find out what problems there are and to help solve them.

There is a common saying that we all need to "think globally but act locally." This means that you should find out what challenges the world faces—that's the *global* part. Then you should do something in your own life to help change things for the better—that's the *local* part.

Being a responsible global citizen takes curiosity, common sense, and action!

Being a Responsible Global Citizen

Curiosity

Keep an **open mind**—listen to new ideas and find out as much as you can about the world. Ask questions and share what you know.

Common Sense

Don't believe everything you read or hear about other places or people. If something doesn't make sense to you or seems unfair, look for more information.

Action

If you think there is a problem, figure out what you can do to change things. Sometimes you might want to find others who agree with you. This way you can work together to make a difference.

Think For Yourself

One way to make a difference is to help other people learn about their rights and responsibilities.

Make a poster to tell people at your school one important idea about being a global citizen. Here's one way to do it.

1. Choose one right or one responsibility that you think is important for global citizens.
2. Think of what you want to say in words. Write a title for your poster, then two or three points to explain it.
3. Think about how to show your ideas in a picture. You could make a drawing or cut a picture from a magazine.
4. Put your words and picture together in a poster that will get people's attention.

The Business of Caring

Kids in Action!

Each year the students in Mr. Williamson's Grade 6 class in Whitby, Ontario, Canada show the world just what kind of a difference a group of kids can make.

Along with learning subjects like math and language arts, each year Mr. Williamson's class creates and runs a **foundation**. This is an organization that raises money for good causes. Most years the class raises $3000 to $5000. Once they've raised the money, they decide which causes they want to support. These causes are usually groups that work to help children or to protect the environment.

The class also takes action in other ways besides raising money. For example, one year they produced a video letter in support of a local Outdoor Education Centre. They sent their video to the board of directors, and their interest helped keep the centre going.

This is the class of 1998/99 in their foundation T-shirts. What was the foundation called this year? What does the name mean to you?

David Cotroneo (left) and Ryan Bennett (right) are preparing to sell their baskets of chocolate Easter eggs in real grass!

A charity is an organization that works to help others.

Fundraising

Over the years, students have come up with many different fundraising ideas. These include selling candy, running the milk program, having special dances, and holding used-toy auctions. Each student also sets up a small personal business. Some students sell handmade products such as candles, refrigerator magnets, and dog biscuits. Others offer services such as house cleaning and **origami** [or-ih-GAM-ee] classes. The profits of the businesses go into the foundation.

Origami is the Japanese art of folding paper into decorative figures and shapes.

Organization

Running a foundation takes organization and planning. First the class elects an **executive committee** that includes a president, a vice president, a **treasurer** (to handle money), and a **secretary** (to take notes). At meetings, all members vote on important decisions, such as what fundraising projects they should run.

The executive committee makes sure that for each fundraising activity there is a group to plan it and do the work. Each group has to decide on the people, resources, and skills they'll need. Then they have to make a detailed plan of what has to happen and when. After each event, they review everything to see what worked well and what should be done differently next time.

Making Decisions

After midwinter break, the class invites people from different **charities** to speak to them about how their organizations help people or the environment. They usually invite nine or ten speakers.

At the end of the year, the class adds up the money they have collected and decides which organizations they will donate it to. They always give at least $100 to each organization that sends a speaker.

These students are putting on a skit to tell people about the Kenya Wildlife Fund. The class adopted three animals that year. Can you guess what species of animal?

What the Kids Say

What's it like to run a foundation? Here's what some of the kids from Mr. Williamson's classes have to say.

Even though we kind of knew that we could do something (to make a difference), it was much more eye-opening when we actually did it.

David Burling

I think it is amazing we could raise so much money!

Ashley Duttmann

It makes me feel really proud.

Hailey Agnew

This class kept a graph to record how much money they raised. How can setting goals help when you want to raise money?

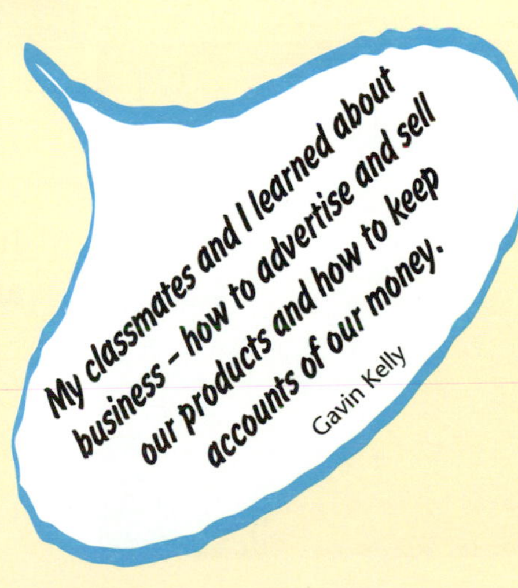

Some of the Organizations Mr. Williamson's Class Has Helped

Kids Help Phone

This is an organization that provides advice to kids over the phone or on the Internet. Kids can call with any type of problem and the call won't appear on their phone bill. A counsellor talks to the caller and suggests how to handle the problem. One year Mr. Williamson's class donated $500 to help the organization get more phone lines.

Sleeping Children Around the World

This is an organization that provides bed kits to children who have no homes and must sleep on the streets. Each kit includes blankets and a few other things children might need, depending on the climate where they live. These children may live in any country in the world. Each kit costs $30. One year Mr. Williamson's class contributed enough money to buy 16 kits.

Horizons of Friendship

This is a Canadian organization that helps people in Central America and Mexico meet their basic needs. One year Mr. Williamson's class contributed to a Learning Development Centre in Honduras. This centre teaches local farmers how to take care of the soil. This helps the farmers and the environment.

Try This

Answer these questions with a partner or in a group.

- *In what way does Mr. Williamson's class "think globally but act locally"?*
- *How do organizations such as charities help make a difference in the world? What other charities do you know about?*
- *What are two things you could learn from this project that might help you with your own projects?*

Looking Back

In this chapter, you read about two important ideas: the global village and what it means to be a global citizen.

What do you think these ideas have to do with your everyday life?

Chapter 2

The United Nations and You

Until you are 18 years old, most governments in the world consider you a child. Sometimes you might think this isn't so great—there are a lot of things you aren't allowed to do until you're an adult.

There are usually some benefits in being a child, though. If you're lucky, somebody else takes care of your basic needs while you learn and grow. Some children aren't so lucky, though. They have to work hard just to survive.

In 1990, the United Nations decided that in addition to the human rights that everyone deserves, children have special needs. Because of this they also have special rights. The UN wrote down what rights children should have in the **Convention on the Rights of the Child**. Canada is one of the countries that agreed to give its children the rights described in this document.

Are you curious to know what these rights are? Read on to find out!

The United Nations

The symbol for the United Nations is the world seen from the North Pole. This is surrounded by olive branches, an ancient Greek symbol for peace. Why do you think the world is shown from the top?

The United Nations is an important link between countries in the global village. Because the UN is responsible for the Convention on the Rights of the Child, it is especially important to young people. In this section, you can learn more about this organization.

Joining the Club

The UN is like a big club of countries. Countries who join the club agree to work towards certain goals. The main purpose of the UN is to prevent wars. The UN believes the best way to do this is to work towards three goals:

- to make sure that the basic human rights of all people are respected
- to help people from different cultures understand one another
- to work together to solve global problems such as poverty and environmental destruction

The UN believes that if all people were treated fairly and the earth's resources were shared equally, then people would have fewer reasons to fight.

The headquarters for the UN is in New York City in the United States. Although this site is in the US, the land is an international zone that is owned by all member countries. The UN also has offices in countries around the world.

The Rules

Members of the United Nations are expected to follow certain rules. In the UN **charter**, these rules are written in legal language. If they were written for a kids' club, though, they might look something like this:

- Treat everyone as an equal.
- Work towards the goals.
- No fighting.
- No bullying.
- Once the club agrees to do something, help to make it happen.
- Don't interfere with the private matters of club members.

Dealing with Problems

The United Nations can't force its members to follow the rules. If a country breaks the rules, what can the United Nations do about it?

One thing that might happen if a country breaks a really *big* rule—such as attacking another country—is that it might be **expelled** from the UN. (This means it can no longer belong to the organization.) Another way to punish a country for breaking the rules is for other countries to refuse to trade with it.

The UN tries to get people to settle their differences by talking. If a war breaks out, though, the UN often sends soldiers to stop the fighting or to keep the peace once the war is over. Canadian soldiers are famous for their work as peacekeepers.

A charter is the written description of an organization's rules and goals. Governments of countries sometimes also have charters.

Kids in Action!

To celebrate the UN's 50th anniversary in 1995, 115 young people from around the world contributed poems, art, and articles to a book about the work the UN does. This painting is by Roksalana Stošić [roks-uh-LAH-nuh STOSH-its] from Yugoslavia, age 13. What do you think this picture is showing?

Think For Yourself

In a group, read the list of rules for members of the UN on page 17. Discuss these questions:

- *Which of the UN rules could also help us work together in groups?*
- *What other rules might we want to have?*
- *What can we do if group members don't follow the rules?*

You might want to write out your own list of Rules for Good Group Work.

Human Rights

There are many different organizations in the United Nations. Each one has certain responsibilities. All of these organizations respect human rights and help governments work towards giving human rights to all of their citizens.

There is one organization that is especially concerned with human rights, though. This is the **Commission on Human Rights**. This group studies human rights around the world and helps countries make laws to protect human rights. The Commission also writes conventions and declarations on human rights. Much of their work is done at the **Centre for Human Rights** in Geneva, Switzerland.

The Commission on Human Rights also investigates complaints from people who think their rights are being ignored. The Centre for Human Rights has a fax "hot line" that operates 24 hours a day so that people can get help in an emergency. For example, if a person has been arrested without a good reason, and her or his life is in danger, the Human Rights Centre can look into the situation right away.

UNICEF

Thousands of people in many different organizations in the UN work to make a difference in the world. The **United Nations Children's Fund (UNICEF)** is one organization that helps protect the rights of the world's children. It does this by telling people about children's rights and by helping families get what they need to care for their children.

Projects

UNICEF has different kinds of projects, depending on what people in communities want and need. For example, people in a community might get together with the help of a UNICEF worker to discuss what rights children have. In another community, people might use UNICEF equipment to work together to stop pollution in a stream and make their water safe to drink. Or the women in a community might use a small loan from UNICEF to set up a business together.

Emergencies

During emergencies such as floods, **famines**, and wars, UNICEF sends supplies such as blankets and food. (A famine is when there isn't enough food and people are starving.)

Sharing Ideas

UNICEF encourages people to see the value in all world cultures. For example, the greeting cards they sell to raise money feature young artists from a variety of cultures and countries. They also have a Web site where young people from all countries can discuss issues, such as children's rights and world poverty, and learn more about one another.

Image courtesy of UNICEF Canada/Richard Ponsonby

Kids in Action!

Some of the money for UNICEF's projects comes from governments. Some comes from donations from individuals. Each Halloween Canadian young people raise approximately $4 million for UNICEF when they go trick-or-treating!

Try This

Write the three goals of the UN in your own words. (Check back to page 16 for information.) Give one example of how UNICEF works towards each goal. Then think of one thing you could do in your own life to work towards each goal.

Here's a chart you could use to present your work.

UN Goals	How UNICEF Helps	What I Can Do

Needs and Wants

The UN believes that children have specials **needs**. Needs are the things that you have to have to survive and grow. They are different from **wants**. Wants are the things that you would like to have but could do without.

Think For Yourself

Use two circles to sort the things shown on this page into *needs* and *wants*. How did you decide which circle to put each thing in? Think of two more needs and two more wants to add to your circles

Your World, Your Issues

The United Nations believes that children have the right to have all their needs met.

Most people agree with this. The problem is that many families are poor and cannot meet their basic needs for food, shelter, and clothing. They may live in areas involved in war, where the environment is damaged, or where the economy is just so poor there are no jobs. Some children are also part of cultural groups that are not treated fairly by others. In all of these situations, children suffer a great deal because the adults in their lives cannot give them what they need.

The UN and other organizations are doing many things to help children, and the lives of children around the world are improving all the time. In this book you can find out ways you can help. The first step in helping, though, is to understand what some of the problems are.

Some Data

The UN and other organizations collect data about children in all countries. These numbers are only approximate—things change all the time and in some countries it is not easy to collect information. Still, the data in the box below might give you an idea about why some children need help to make sure they get what they need.

Around the World

- **35 000 children** die each day from diseases caused by not having enough food to eat
- **120 million children** between the ages of 5 and 14 work full time to support themselves and their families; they often work 10 hours a day, 6 days a week

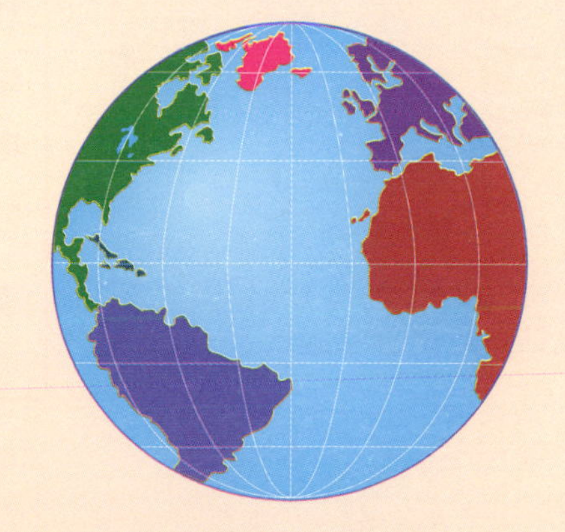

- **130 million children** do not have the chance to go to school
- **2 million children** were killed in wars from 1985 to 1995; 12 million children had to leave their homes because of war

Sources: UNICEF and the International Labour Organization.

"Sita's Day"

This is a description of a day in the life of an 11-year-old girl who lives with her family on a small farm in Nepal [ne-POL]. In this part of Nepal, rice is the main food. It is grown in fields called ***paddies****.*

Sita [SEE-tuh] gets up at sunrise. She begins her day by feeding the chickens and oxen and collecting eggs. This takes about half an hour. She also makes two trips to a nearby stream to get water for the animals and her family. This takes about 45 minutes.

After half an hour for breakfast, Sita spends about two hours gathering **fodder** (green plants used to feed the oxen). To do this, she walks a few kilometres from the farm and cuts grass or small bushes to bring back to the animals. She saves some fodder for the next morning's feed.

Sita eats an early lunch before beginning work planting in the paddy. One of her jobs is to take small rice plants from where they were first planted and replant them in a larger paddy where they will finish growing. After about eight hours of work in the paddy, she again takes care of the animals and fetches water. After dinner, Sita is tired and goes to bed around 7:30.

Nepal is very mountainous, so farmers have to make small fields on the sides of hills. In this picture you can see two oxen pulling a plough, with rice growing in the paddies below.

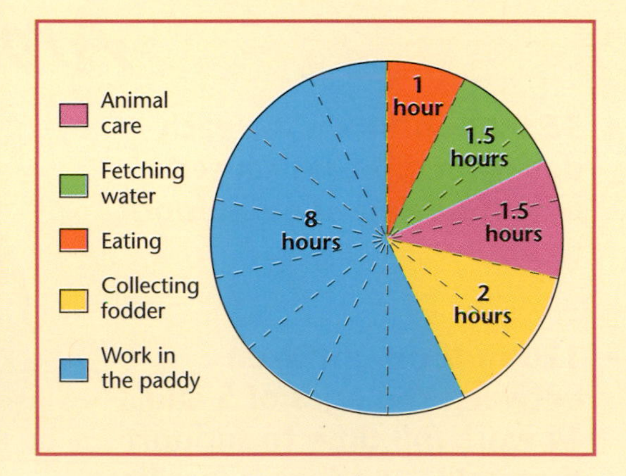

Sita's day is about 14 hours long. This circle graph shows how the hours are divided.

Try This

1. For one school day, keep track of what you do from the time you get up until the time you go to bed. For each hour, record one of these activities:
   - work (for example, helping at home or having a paper route)
   - play (free time with your friends or on your own)
   - school
   - recreation (for example, a soccer practice or music lesson)
   - other
2. Make a circle graph that shows how your time was spent. Begin by dividing a circle into the number of hours you were awake. Add up all the hours for each type of activity. Decide on a colour for each type of activity, then colour in the right number of hours on your graph.
3. Write a paragraph describing "My Day." Then write a few sentences comparing your day to Sita's day.

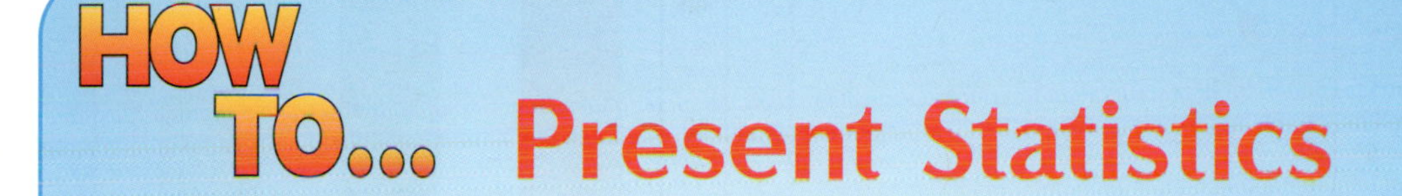

HOW TO... Present Statistics

Statistics are information that can be described in numbers. They are often presented in different types of **graphs** so that it is easier to see the main ideas and patterns. Here are four ways to present statistics.

A **circle graph** is good for showing what part of the whole something is. When you show percentages, the circle is made up of 100 parts.

Favourite T-shirt Colours

- 10% of students chose yellow
- 10% of students chose green
- 80% of students chose red

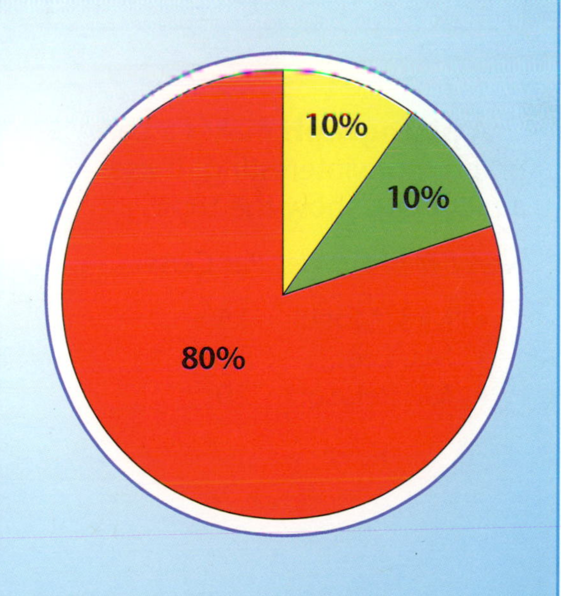

A **line graph** is good for showing how something changes over time.

Temperature During the Day

- 8:00 a.m. (08:00 h): 10°C
- 12:00 noon (12:00 h): 20°C
- 8:00 pm (20:00 h): 15°C

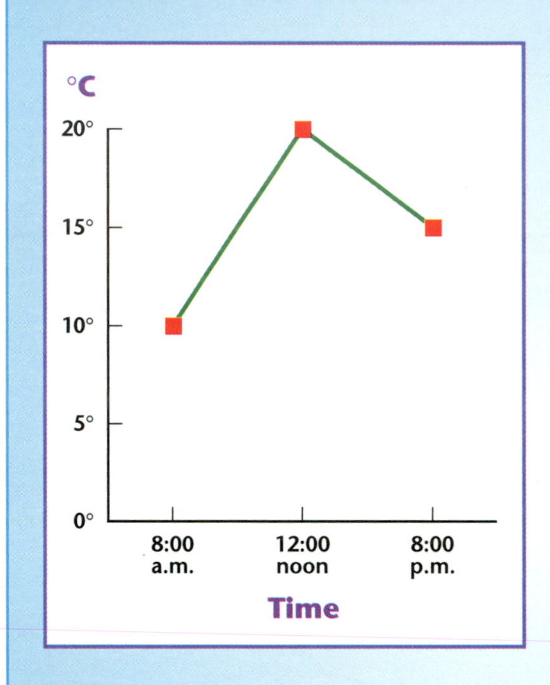

A **bar graph** is good for comparing two or more sets of statistics.

Money Raised by Activities

- Bake Sale: $25
- Bottle Drive: $80
- Talent Night: $60

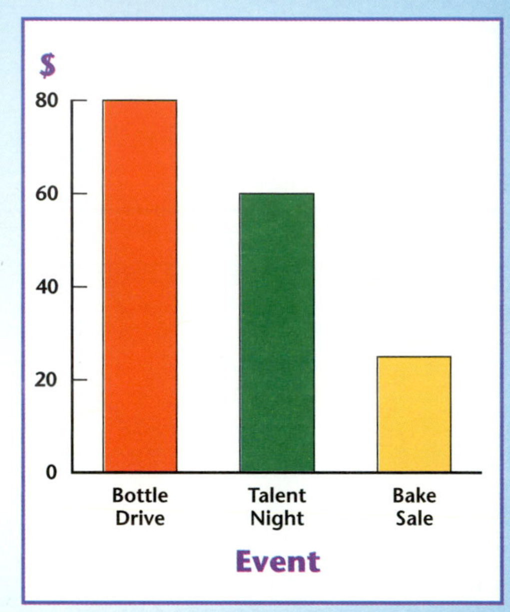

A **pictograph** makes a bar graph more interesting. It uses a picture to show the topic.

Number of Bicycles Per Class

- Mrs. Moehl: 15
- Ms. Lee: 10
- Mr. Peluso: 20

Investigate

Use the map section at the back of this book to find out more about Nepal. Work with a partner to record your answers to these questions. You might want to start by reading "Reading Maps" on page 205.

1. Turn to the Countries of the World map on page 208. This map shows you all the countries in the world.
    - *Between which lines of **longitude** shown on the map does Nepal fall?*
    - *Which is the closest line of **latitude** to Nepal shown on the map?*
    - *What large country is south of Nepal?*
2. Use the other world maps in the map section to answer these questions. Record your answer and the title of the map that gave you the information.
    - *In which continent is Nepal?*
    - *What is the name of the big mountain range that runs through Nepal?*
    - *What two climate regions are found in Nepal?*

Lines of latitude run north and south of the Equator. Lines of longitude run east and west of the Prime Meridian.

Your Rights

The UN Human Rights Commission decided that when families aren't able to give their children what they need, governments should help.

To protect the rights of children, the Human Rights Commission wrote the **Convention on the Rights of the Child**. This document describes children's needs and explains that every child has the right to have these needs met.

When a country signs the Convention on the Rights of a Child it is making a legal promise to give the children of the country all the rights in the convention. This means the Convention on the Rights of the Child is even stronger than the Declaration of Human Rights!

The document on the next page summarizes the main points of the Convention. The rights of children can be grouped under four main topics.

The United Nations defines child as any person under the age of 18, unless national laws say you are an adult at a younger age. In Canada, a child is any person under 18.

What About Adults?

Does having rights mean you should still clean up your room when your parents or guardians ask you to? Yes!

Adults have rights, too. The United Nations says that parents are usually the best people to make decisions about their children's lives. If parents cannot do this, then another responsible adult can take this role. The idea is that children and adults should respect each other and work together to make the world a good place to live for everyone.

Who are the adults who help you in your life? What do you do to help them?

The Convention on the Rights of the Child

The Right to Survive

You have the right to:

- food, water, shelter, and clothing to meet your needs
- medical services
- equal opportunities if you have a disability
- live with your parents or be given good care if this is not possible

The Right to Live in a Safe World

You have the right to:

- a clean environment
- protection from being physically harmed or made to feel badly by what people say
- special care during times of war and not be used as soldiers or **hostages** (A hostage is a person who is being held captive and whose life is threatened unless certain demands are met.)
- special care if you are a **refugee** (A refugee is a person who has to leave her or his country because of war or unfair treatment.)
- fair treatment if you break the law

The Right to Learn and Enjoy Life

You have the right to:

- an education that helps you develop to your greatest ability
- opportunities for recreation and "fun time"
- freedom to practice your culture
- freedom to practice your beliefs
- protection from being forced to work long hours or being sold into slavery

The Right to Be Heard

You have the right to:

- a name and a nationality (This gives you the benefits of being a citizen of a country.)
- have people listen to your opinions, especially about decisions that affect you and your community
- participate in peaceful gatherings
- take action to change things for the better (as long as your actions are not illegal)

Why might the rights of children with special needs need extra protection?

In 1999, refugees from the region of Kosovo [KOH-suh-voh] in Europe found safety in countries around the world, including Canada. Why might child refugees need extra protection?

Think For Yourself

In a group, decide on the seven most important rights from the Convention on the Rights of the Child. List them in order, beginning with the most important.

You might find that people have different **perspectives** on this issue. If you can't agree on all seven rights, make more than one list. One list can show what you agree on, then other lists can show different ways people think the rights should be listed.

HOW TO... Discuss Different Perspectives

Your *perspective* is the way you look at things. It includes what you know and your opinions. It's another word for *point of view*. When people have different perspectives, a discussion can quickly turn into an argument!

When people **discuss**, they listen to the ideas of others and may learn more about the topic. When people **argue**, they usually listen only to themselves and don't learn anything new. Here's how to have a good discussion.

- Give everyone a chance to speak.
- Listen to what other people say and try to understand their ideas. Find out the reasons they have for their opinions.
- Don't make up your mind too quickly. If an idea seems interesting, ask for more information.
- Express your own ideas and opinions. Give reasons for what you think.
- Look for a **compromise**—an idea that combines more than one perspective.

Investigate

The UN helps protect children's rights around the world. What organizations are there to help children in your community? These might be organizations right in your community, or ones that can be reached by phone.

1. In a group, brainstorm what you already know. You could record your ideas on a chart like this.

Organization	Need or Want it Fills	How to Contact
Softball League	Recreation	Phone: 458-0987

2. Do some research to check that your information is correct. See if you can find two or three more organizations to add to your list.
3. Think of a way to share the information you have collected with others. You might want to make a poster, a directory, or a bulletin board.
4. Look over the list of organizations you gathered. Is there an organization your community needs but doesn't have? If so, write a letter explaining your idea to a local paper or make a presentation at a community meeting.

Looking Back

This chapter described the United Nations and the work UN organizations are doing to protect human rights and to help people meet their needs and wants around the world.

How do you think knowing about your rights can help you become a responsible global citizen?

Chapter 3

Celebrating People and Places!

One of the best things about living in the global village is getting to know your neighbours—no matter where in the world they live!

When you learn about other cultures and other places, though, it is important to make sure you get reliable information. Remember what we said in Chapter 1 about being a responsible global citizen? One important point was *Don't believe everything you hear about other places or people. If something doesn't make sense to you or seems unfair, look for more information.*

In this chapter, you can learn some ways to make sure you don't believe everything you read, hear, or see about the world.

Keeping an Open Mind

Culture is how people live their lives. People in a culture share similar ways of meeting their basic needs, expressing their thoughts and feelings, and organizing themselves in their homes and communities. **Heritage** includes all the cultures in a person's family, past and present.

Reading Hint

If you come to a word you don't know, try to figure it out. Sound out the first three letters, then start the sentence over. When you come to the word again, think about the beginning sound and what word might make sense.

One way to protect yourself against getting poor information is to keep an open mind about other **cultures**.

When you grow up in a culture, it is **familiar** to you. You understand it, so the things you and your family do seem "normal." When cultures are not familiar to us, we may find them difficult to understand. When this happens, we can shut our minds and not even try to learn about others. We might even begin to believe that our culture is better than everyone else's.

When people think their culture is better than others, they are being **ethnocentric**. Today in the world, ethnocentrism is one of the main causes of **civil wars**. These are wars within a country. People of different cultures might live together for some time, accepting that they have some differences. If times become difficult, though, people can start to blame others for their problems. This can lead to violence between groups and maybe even to war.

Multiculturalism

Multiculturalism is a way of looking at the world that is the opposite of ethnocentrism.

Multi means "many," so *multicultural* describes any group that includes people from a variety of cultures. People also use the word *multicultural* to describe the attitude of respect for and appreciation of the contributions of people from many different cultures. We live in a multicultural world, so this attitude is important if we're all going to get along.

One of the benefits of multiculturalism is that it gives us contributions from many different people. How could this help if you were brainstorming ideas for a project?

A Closer Look

A World of Great Ideas

Hot Chocolate

The Aztec people of Mexico introduced chocolate drinks to the world. Cacao beans grew wild where the Aztecs lived, but the beans were considered so valuable they were used as money.

Democracy

Democracy—the idea that people should vote for their governments—was first thought up by the ancient Greeks.

Circle Graphs

The English nurse and mathematician Florence Nightingale invented circle graphs to show statistics on the reasons why soldiers were dying from diseases. Her information helped people to see that fresh air, nutritious food, and cleanliness helped reduce diseases and deaths.

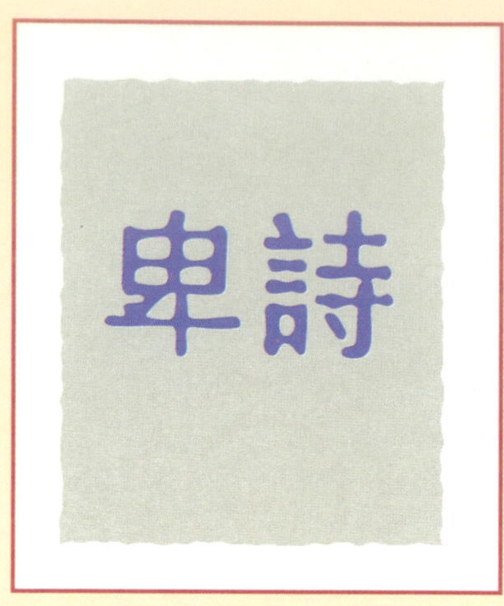

Paper
The Chinese invented paper around 105 CE.

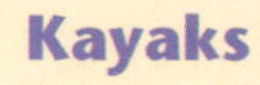

Kayaks
The kayak is a type of boat invented by the Inuit of Canada's north.

Astronomy
The Islamic countries of the Middle East made great contributions to the early study of the stars. One famous observatory, the Marāghela [mah-rah-GE-lah], was built in Iran in 1260.

Bicycles
The first bicycle was built by a Scot, but Pierre and Ernest Michaux [mee-SHOH] of France made improvements that really got this new form of transportation rolling!

Music
Drum rhythms from many different African groups were introduced to the United States when African people were taken there as slaves to work on plantations. Today, those rhythms are the base of most popular music.

Think For Yourself

Here's a question to discuss in a group:

- *How can you tell the difference between someone who respects other cultures and someone who does not?*

At the end of your discussion, complete these phrases in your social studies journal or notebook:

- *I know I'm being respectful of other cultures when . . .*
- *I know I'm not being respectful of other cultures when . . .*

Investigate

Work in a group to present a **multimedia show** on one of the "Great Ideas of the World." (Refer to "How to Organize a Multimedia Presentation" on page 36 for tips.)

You'll have to start by doing some research on great ideas. Some of these are listed below. See if you can find three more. Look at the library, search the Internet, or talk to your Elders. The Research and Report organizer at the end of this text can help you plan your work.

HOW TO... Organize a Multimedia Presentation

Multimedia means using more than one form of presentation. For example, in an oral report, you might also show pictures to help your audience understand your main points. Maybe you've done this in reports before. Here are some other forms of presentation you could combine:

- written information
- music
- skits
- collages
- cartoons
- models
- overheads, slides
- videos
- poetry
- art
- short stories
- computer graphics or Web pages
- maps
- graphs
- tables of statistics

Here are some pointers to make sure all the pieces fit together.

1. Think about the best way to present each type of information. For example, a picture would be the best way to show art, but a graph would be the best way to show climate. Make sure what you show is big enough for people to see!
2. Write out all the steps in your presentation. For example, if you are going to show a picture, decide whether you will show the picture first and then talk about it or first talk about the picture and then show it.
3. Practice!

Stereotypes

Sometimes people get an idea about a culture or country that seems to stick in their minds. For example, many people in other countries think that it snows in Canada all year round and that all Canadians wear parkas to keep warm! Like some Canadians, you might think that living on a tropical island is a paradise where you swim at the beach and eat tropical fruit and fresh fish every day!

Neither of these ideas is true, though. They are **stereotypes**. A stereotype makes it seem that all people from a certain place look and act exactly the same. If you look at the many people in your own culture and community, you can tell right away that this isn't true. All people are different.

The biggest problem with believing stereotypes is that they stop us from truly understanding others. Then we become ethnocentric. To see beyond stereotypes, you have to use your *questioning brain* to find out about people for yourself.

Use Your Questioning Brain

When you do research in social studies, make sure you don't just repeat stereotypes you see or read.

Instead, look for **reliable information**. This is information that is based on facts. Reliable information will give you the *real* picture.

When you are researching information, use your questioning brain to make sure what you read or see is reliable. For example, if you read this sentence—"People in Canada live in wooden houses"—stop to think about what you already know, then ask yourself:

- *Canada is a big place. Does this mean* ***all*** *people live in the same type of house in* ***all*** *parts of the country?*
- *Aren't there any stone or brick buildings or high-rise apartments?*

What are the clues that tell you that you're reading or hearing a stereotype?

A few questions like these can help you spot the fact that the statement "People in Canada live in wooden houses" isn't reliable information. There is some truth in it—some people *do* live in wooden houses—but it doesn't tell you about the other types of housing in Canada. The statement would be more reliable if it said, "*Some* people in Canada live in wooden houses."

Think For Yourself

Give a written description or make a picture to show how you think the person from each country listed below would dress and act:

- a teenager from Canada
- a woman from Japan
- a man from Mexico

Now compare your ideas with a partner. What did each of you base your ideas on? Can you spot any stereotypes in your ideas? What sources do you know about that could give you more reliable information?

HOW TO... Find Reliable Information

Reliable information is based on up-to-date facts that are presented in a way that gives a true and complete picture of the situation or topic. Here are some ways to find reliable information.

1. Use sources that you trust. Atlases and encyclopedias are good places to start. On the Internet, choose sites by organizations you know about, such as the United Nations.
2. Use the most recent information you can find.
3. Check to see if the information gives facts and examples to support the main ideas. Look out for these danger signs:
   - **exaggeration** (something is made to seem much worse or much better than it is)
   - weak **generalizations** (a generalization is a main idea that summarizes the facts; a weak generalization is one based on too few facts)
   - opinions presented as facts
4. Compare information from different sources and different perspectives. If a piece of information doesn't fit, think hard before you trust it.
5. If you are researching a culture or place, talk to a person who is a member of that culture or to someone who has spent some time in that place.
6. Use your questioning brain. Ask yourself, *Does this make sense?* If it doesn't, check with another source.

Advertisements often use exaggerations and generalizations to try to persuade you that a product is something you need. Advertisers also get famous people to give an opinion about a product, hoping that you will believe that what that person says are the facts.

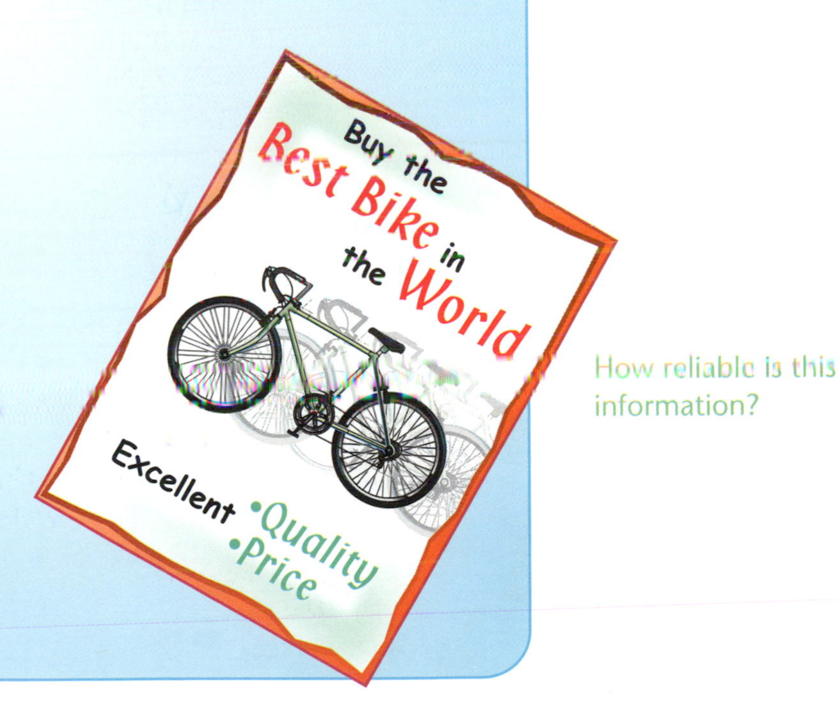

How reliable is this information?

Media Messages

Media is what we call forms of information that many people see every day. Media includes television, newspapers, magazines, movies, and the Internet.

One of the challenges we face in the world today is that a lot of the information we get about other people and places comes from the advertising and entertainment we see in the media. You can't always trust these types of information. To the people who make television programs and advertisements, true facts and honest opinions aren't as important as keeping you interested long enough to sell you something!

Where do you get your information about people and places in the world?

Better Than It Was

In the past, the messages we received from television programs, advertisements, and movies were full of stereotypes. For example, some cultural groups were often portrayed as gangsters, while others were usually shown as the "good guys" who arrested them. Even places were presented as stereotypes. European cities, such as Paris and Venice, were usually shown as beautiful and romantic. Cities in Africa and Asia, such as Cairo and Calcutta, were often shown as poor and overcrowded.

Something Is Still Missing

Today, people know that it isn't fair to show stereotypes. Most movies and television programs do a much better job of telling us what people and places are really like. There are still things to watch out for, though. Sometimes it isn't what is *in* the movie or television program that's the problem. Sometimes it's what you *don't* see. Here are some more questions for your questioning brain:

- *How many Aboriginal heroes have you seen in recent movies?*
- *If a story takes place in a tropical climate, how often do you see ordinary people instead of "jungle adventurers"?*

- *In the news, how often do you hear about good things happening in Asia or South America?*

The most likely answer to all of these questions is "Not often"! So although the media might not show a lot of stereotypes, by leaving things out they are showing you a **biased** view of the world.

Can You See Yourself?

What about your own culture in the media?

People in every culture look for examples to tell them what they should look and act like. We can get this information from our friends, our family, and the media. Friends and family can be reliable sources of information. The media, though, can really get you into trouble!

If you looked at the media for advice on what you should look and act like, you might think everyone should follow the examples of the Spice Girls, Puff Daddy, or whomever is popular this year!

The truth is, very few people *really* look, act, or live like the people we see in the media. These people are actors—in real life they have the same kinds of problems as the rest of us. When they are performing, actors have a team of photographers, make-up artists, and clothing designers to make sure you see only what they want you to see. In other words, it's biased information!

A **bias** is a one-sided view of a situation, culture, or country. It is often based on stereotypes. **Racism** is an especially strong form of bias. People who are racist judge others based on their nationality, culture, or skin colour.

PERSPECTIVES

Are Images in Advertising Harmful to Young People?

Manu
Yes! Advertising shows you all these "cool" people having a great time using a particular product, such as a soft drink or running shoes. Seeing these images makes young people feel badly about themselves because they don't look and act like the people in the advertisements. They start to believe that if they have a certain product they'll fit in. But the person ends up disappointed because these products don't really improve your life.

Morgan
No! Young people these days aren't so easily fooled by advertising. We know companies are trying to sell us things. We might think an ad is fun, but we don't believe a particular chewing gum will make us popular! Sure, all young people feel a bit insecure sometimes. That's part of growing up. But advertising doesn't cause this. Advertising just tells us what products are out there. It's up to us to decide what we really need and what we can afford.

Think For Yourself

The question about advertising in the Perspectives feature on page 41 raises an **issue**. An issue is a complicated situation—there isn't a single "right" answer. Your job when you investigate an issue is to consider *all* perspectives amd decide what you think.

Read and discuss the Perspectives feature with a partner or in a group. Afterwards, write your own perspective on this question in your notebook or social studies journal. You might agree with Morgan or Manu, or you might have another perspective entirely.

Investigate

Keep a media journal for three days. For each day, record one example of a stereotype and one example of reliable information about cultures or places. For each entry, make a note to explain why you think it is or isn't reliable information.

If you find examples in newspapers and magazines, include them with your journal. If you find something on the Internet, print out the page. If you include movies and television programs, write descriptions of them.

After you have collected your examples, pick one example of a stereotype and suggest one or two ways it could give a truer picture of a culture or place. You might need to do some research to find reliable information about your topic.

Date	**Culture or Place**	**Example** (include a description and where you found it)	**Category** (either *reliable* or *stereotype*)	**Reasons** (why you chose the category)

After you have kept a media journal for a few days, you might want to reconsider your perspective in the Think For Yourself activity.

Growing Up Canadian

The land we live in has always been multicultural.

First there were many different Aboriginal groups who lived here. Then when Europeans came, French and English people began to live here, too. In the twentieth century, people from every continent in the world have come to live here. It's no wonder Canada has always been a hard-working member of the United Nations!

In this section, you can think about what it means to be a citizen of a multicultural country.

Cultural Identity

You have two types of **identity**. One is your identity as an individual —who you are as a person. The other is your identity as a member of the groups to which you belong—your family, your community, and your culture.

In Canada, multiculturalism is the law. Here are some of the highlights of the Canadian Multiculturalism Act.

The Canadian Multiculturalism Act

It is hereby declared to be the policy of the Government of Canada to:

1. *recognize and promote the understanding that multiculturalism reflects the cultural and racial diversity in Canadian society [as well as] the freedom of all members of Canadian society to preserve and share their cultural heritage;*
2. *recognize and promote the understanding that multiculturalism is [an important] characteristic of the Canadian heritage and identity, and that it provides an invaluable resource in the shaping of Canada's future;*
3. *ensure that all individuals receive equal treatment and equal protection under the law, while respecting and valuing their cultural differences.*

GLOBAL VISIONS GLOBAL VOICES

One way people express their culture is in the **arts**—music, dance, painting, and storytelling. The arts in Canada are as varied as the people! Here are two Canadian painters' views of British Columbia.

Michael Tickner grew up in England and came to Canada as an adult. In *Sunstruck* he is showing a roadside scene near Whistler, BC. Michael Tickner says "My style expresses the joy and energy of life I see around me. I like to show how individual colours come together to make the landscape."

Roy Henry Vickers grew up in a Nisga'a [NIS-gaa] community in British Columbia. He is of Tsimshian [sim-she-an], Heiltsuk [HEL-sic], and British heritage. *A Meeting of Chiefs* shows the legendary village of Temleham. In stories, this village was so beautiful and spiritual that chiefs from many nations travelled there to meet and form friendships and to settle differences.

Knowing Who You Are

Many Canadians feel they have two or more cultural identities. For example, some people whose families have come from India call themselves *Indo-Canadians*. Sometimes it's difficult to blend two or more cultures, but a lot of Canadians are very good at it!

How would you describe your cultural identity?

This New Westminster police officer is of the Sikh faith. For religious reasons, he wears a turban instead of the hat non-Sikh members of the police force wear. Why is respect for different faiths an important part of multiculturalism?

Try This

With a partner, answer these questions to help you check that you understand the Multiculturalism Act on page 43.

1. **Diverse** means "many different." In what ways does "cultural and racial diversity" describe Canada?
2. How do you think multiculturalism could be a "valuable resource" for the future?
3. Is it possible for people to be "equal but different"? Explain.

Kids From Kanata

The Kids From Kanata computer project is one way students in classes all across Canada are working to understand each other better.

In this project, each class is linked through the Internet with two other classes of the same grade level. At least one community in each group includes children of Aboriginal heritage. Students exchange information about themselves and their communities. They also investigate three issues that are especially important in Aboriginal communities: land, language, and ancestral connections.

To investigate these issues, students read the actual agreements made long ago between Aboriginal

How do you think a project like this can help all Canadians feel that they belong?

peoples and others, use special computer software to send messages in their **heritage languages**—the first language of their cultures, and share information about their family and community histories. It's a great way to learn, and a great way to make friends!

Ka-na-ta is an Iroquoian [IR-uh-kwun] word used to describe a group of huts or a community. The first European to hear the word was Jacques Cartier in 1535. He used it to refer to the whole country—and so the name *Canada*.

Think For Yourself

Do something to help Canadians appreciate cultural differences. Some ideas include:

- In a group, create a series of posters showing the work of Canadian artists of different cultural backgrounds. Ask for permission to display your posters at a community centre.
- Write to your local newspaper, radio station, or television station to voice your concerns about stereotypes and bias in the media. Include information about what you don't see that you would like to see.
- Start an online or print-based *Cultural Connections* newsletter in which people can exchange information about their cultures, cultural events, and so on.

Use the Action Organizer at the back of this text to help you plan your project.

Looking Back

In this chapter, you investigated the challenge of how we can keep what is special about our cultures, but still learn to get along with others. You found out that this is a challenge in Canada and in the world.

How can you be proud of your own culture and country and still be a good global citizen?

Chapter 4

Investigating Cultures

One of the *really fun* parts of social studies is finding out what life is like in different cultures.

In this chapter, you can investigate the culture of Japan. Japan is an interesting country for Canadians to study. When it comes to culture, it is almost the opposite of Canada! Instead of many cultures, Japanese people have one strong cultural tradition that is hundreds of years old. Although this culture is changing with the times, the way all cultures do, it is still very *Japanese*.

To investigate the culture of Japan, you'll have to think about what culture is and how it develops and changes. These ideas can help you investigate other cultures, including your own.

Thinking About Culture

Reading Hint

When you start a new section, begin by looking at all the headings and pictures. This will give you an idea of what the section is all about. Then go back and read in detail.

What are the main parts of all cultures? What basic facts should you know about a place when you start investigating its culture? Read on to find out!

Cultures and Countries

When we think about cultures, we often think about what makes them different from one another, such as clothing styles and celebrations. Even though each culture is special in its own way, all cultures have ways of meeting basic needs, expressing thoughts and feelings, and keeping organized.

There are hundreds of different cultures in the world. Every culture started in a particular place. For example, Japanese culture started in one part of Asia; Spanish culture started in one part of Europe.

As people moved around over the years, though, cultures moved with them. Sometimes one culture became an important part of many countries. For example, Spanish culture is part of the heritage of some countries in Central and South America, such as Mexico and Peru. Other times, people of many different cultures moved to a particular country. Canada is an example of a multicultural country.

Cultures and Environments

One reason that there are many cultures in the world is that there are different **physical environments**.

Which words and ideas in this chart have you seen before? Which raise questions in your mind? Which part of culture do you most look forward to learning about?

The Parts of Culture

Meeting Basic Needs	Expressing Thoughts and Feelings	Keeping Organized
• *Patterns of daily life and work:* what people do to make sure they have food, shelter, clothing, and water • *Technology:* the tools and knowledge people use to get what they need and want	• *Language* • *Beliefs* • *Ideas about the roles of men, women, and children* • *Ideas about the environment* • *Ideas about rights and responsibilities* • *The arts:* paintings, sculpture, music, dance, drama • *Sports* • *Special celebrations*	• *Politics:* government and laws for the community or country • *Economics:* ways of buying or exchanging the things people need or want • *Family structures:* the ways people organize themselves to raise and care for their children

The physical environment is the natural world of the land, sea, and air. It includes living things such as plants and animals. It also includes non-living things such as soil, water, and minerals. The first job of any culture is to figure out a way to live safely in its environment and to provide people with their basic needs of food, shelter, water, and clothing.

As people live and work in their environments, they figure out the best ways to do things. After awhile, many of these ways of doing things become traditions in the culture. People's traditions help them feel they belong to a group. So even when the environment changes or new ways of doing things are possible, people still keep many of their traditions.

To study a culture, it helps to study the environment where the culture started.

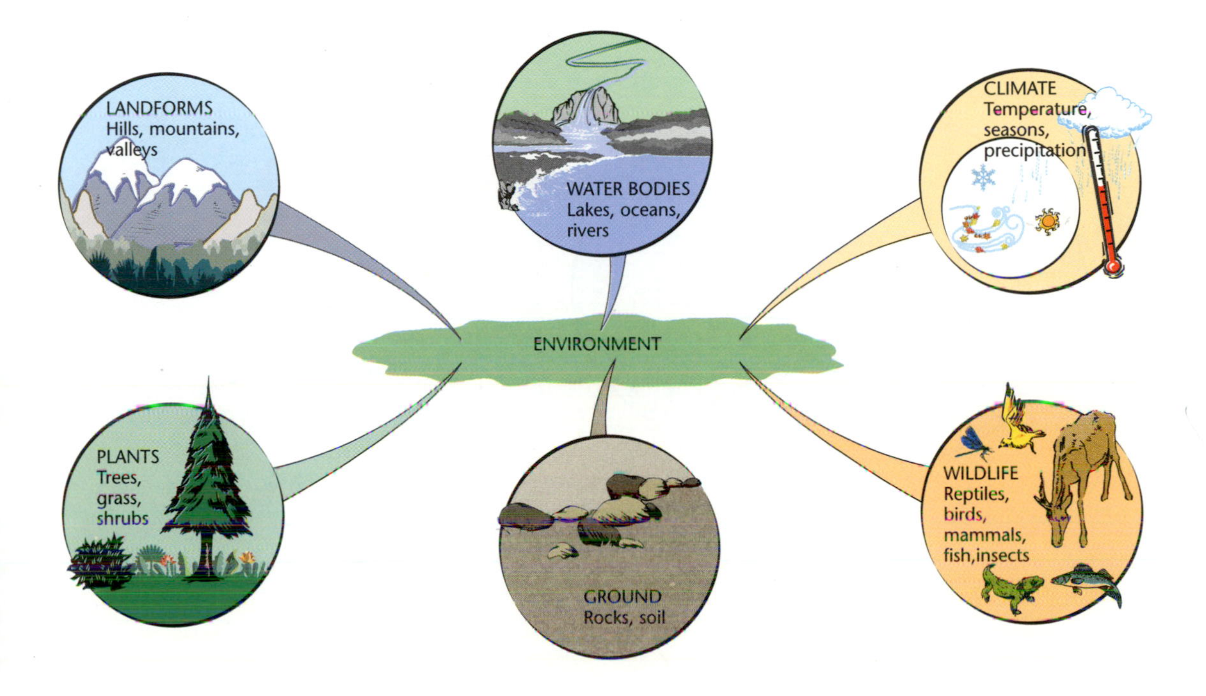

This web shows the different parts of a natural environment. What are the names of some of the trees that grow where you live? What wild animals might you find? How would you describe your climate?

Try This

When you investigate a culture or a country, it's a good idea to start by researching some basic facts.

1. With a partner, read the "Snapshot: Japan" feature on page 50. Sort the facts into these categories:
   - Facts About the Physical Environment
   - Facts About Culture
2. In your social studies journal or notebook, write one powerful question that you have about Japanese culture that you hope you will be able to answer by the end of this chapter. If you need some ideas, check back to "The Parts of Culture" chart on page 48.

CAPITAL CITY
Tokyo

LARGEST CITY
Tokyo, population 26 863 000

LOCATION
Asia, 35°68′N/139°77′E
(Based on the location of Tokyo, the largest city)

HEAD OF GOVERNMENT
Elected prime minister.
(There is a traditional emperor who inherits his position, but a government elected by the people makes the important decisions.)

MAIN LANGUAGE
Japanese

CURRENCY
Yen (¥)

CLIMATES
Continental, coastal, high mountain

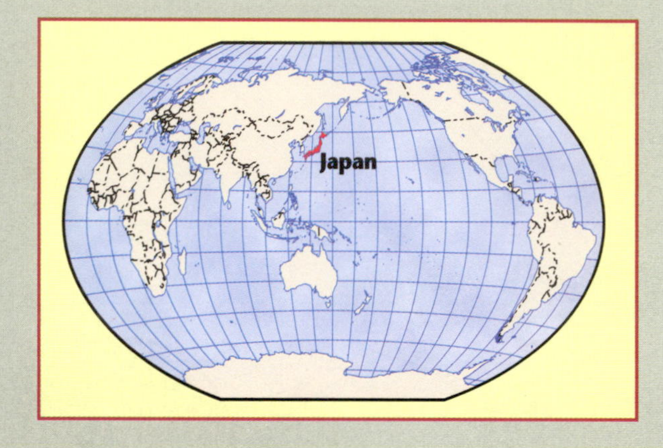

The red circle in the flag of Japan symbolizes the sun. The Japanese call their country *Nihon* [NEE-hon] or *Nippon* [NEE-pon]—"the source of the sun." A traditional story tells how Japan was the first place the sun shone.

One famous landform in Japan is *Fujisan* [FOO-jee-sahn]—known in English as Mount Fuji. Mount Fuji is a **dormant** volcano—it hasn't erupted since 1707 and isn't likely to. It's the tallest mountain in Japan, and it is an important symbol to the Japanese of the beauty of their country.

Landforms and Climate

Landforms (features of the land such as hills and valleys) and **climate** (the general pattern of weather in an area) are two important parts of an environment. In this section, you can find out about Japan's landforms and climate and how these compare to British Columbia.

Climate

Climate includes **temperature** (how hot or cold it gets) and **precipitation** (how much rain or snow falls). Four main things determine a region's climate:

- **altitude** (higher regions are colder)
- nearness of water (areas near water don't get as warm or as hot)
- direction of the winds (winds blowing across water bring rain to an area)
- latitude (average temperatures are lower the farther away a place is from the Equator)

This is a **relief map**. Relief maps are used to show landforms. What information can you gather from this map?

Typhoons and Snowstorms

Japan is in the **temperate zone**, so it has four seasons: spring, summer, autumn, and winter. The north has a **continental climate**—very cold winters and warmer summers. The south has a **coastal climate**—warm summers and mild winters. The island of Kyushu, which is the furthest south, is **subtropical**—hot summers and warm winters.

Altitude is how high a place is from **sea level**—where the ocean meets the land.

Between late August and early October, storms called **typhoons** bring heavy rains and strong winds to Japan. These storms sometimes cause flooding and damage buildings. In winter, cold winds from northern Asia blow down across Japan, bringing snow. In fact, Japan gets some of the heaviest snowfalls in the world!

Climate Zones of the World

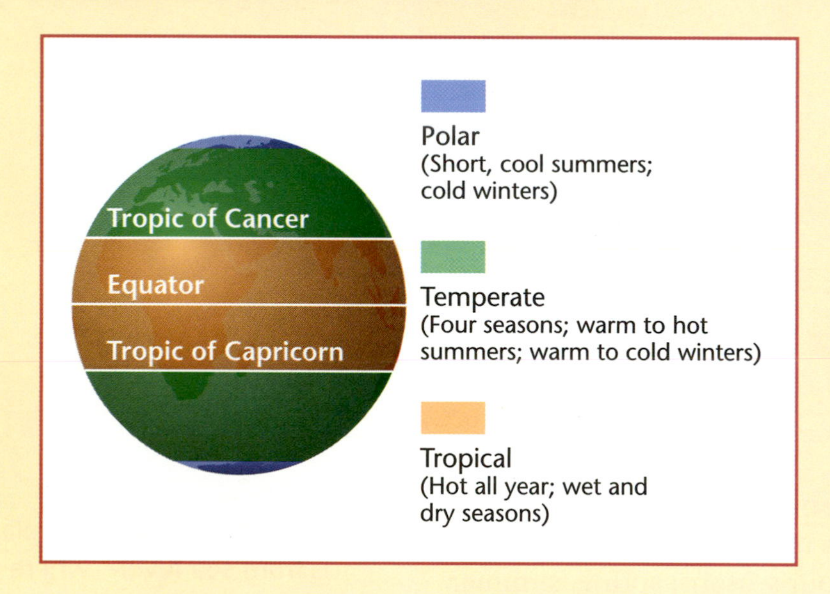

The Four Seasons

As the earth rotates around the sun, temperate zones move toward and away from the sun. This creates four seasons in the year: spring, summer, autumn, and winter.

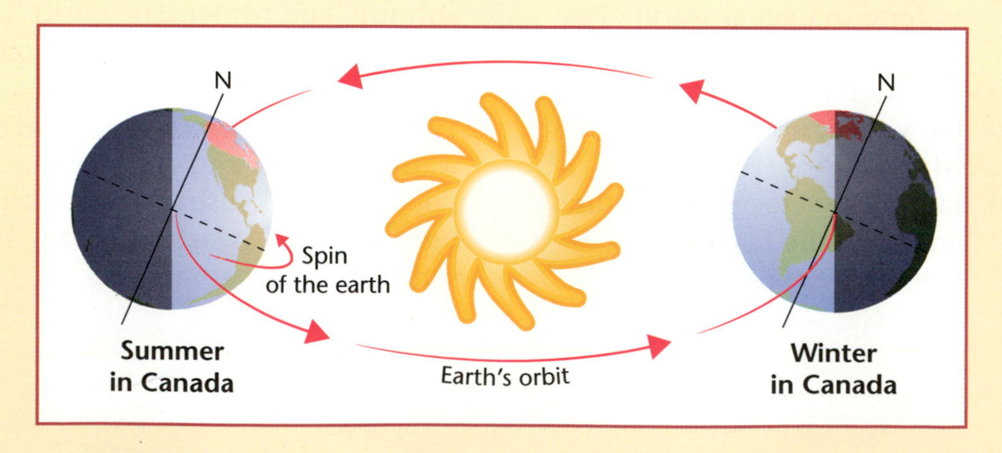

Natural Vegetation

Temperature and precipitation affect the **natural vegetation**—the plant life that grows in an area. In general, forests grow where there is high precipitation, grasslands grow where there is moderate precipitation, and desert plants grow where there is light precipitation. The species of plants are different, depending on the temperature. For example, pine trees grow in colder regions, while palm trees grow in warmer climates.

Japan's climate is ideal for forests. This is a mixed forest in northern Honshu. What is the natural vegetation where you live?

Investigate

Here are some questions to help you compare the environments of Japan and British Columbia. Write short answers in your notebook. You might want to work with a partner.

1. On the World Land Heights and Rivers map on pages 210 to 211, compare the landforms of Japan and British Columbia. What similarities do you see?
2. Use the World Environments map on pages 212 to 213 to compare the environments of Japan and British Columbia. What similarities and differences do you see?
3. A **climate graph** combines a line graph to show temperature with a bar graph to show precipitation. Compare these climate graphs of Tokyo and Vancouver. What similarities and differences do you see?

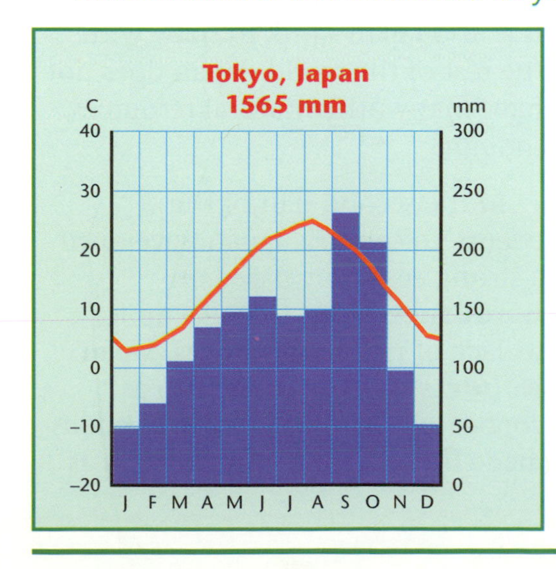

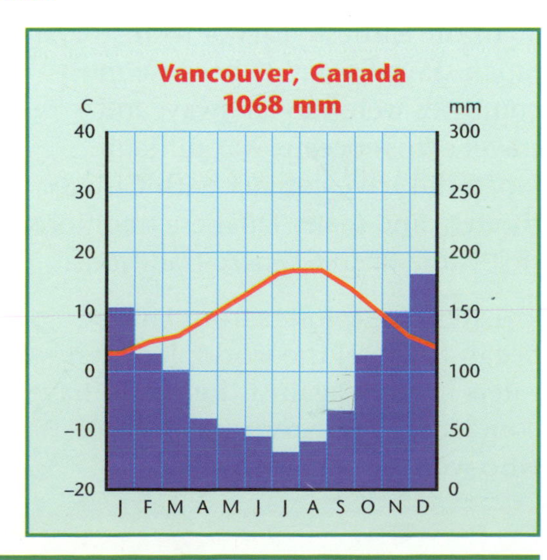

Meeting Nature's Challenges

If you add up all the physical challenges presented by Japan's environment, you might wonder how a culture developed there at all! In this section, you can learn some of the ways the environment has **influenced** Japanese culture.

Influence is when one thing partly causes another thing to happen.

An Island Nation

When you see a map of Japan, the most obvious physical feature is that the country is made up of islands. In the past, when people didn't have **communications technologies** such as television and the Internet, it was easy for the people of an island nation to keep themselves separate from others.

Japan began trading with foreigners only when four ships of the American Navy showed up in Tokyo Harbour demanding to land. The Americans wanted a base from which to trade with the Chinese. The Japanese didn't have powerful enough weapons to defend themselves, so they agreed.

In the earliest years of its history, Japan stayed separate because most countries were too far away, and travel across oceans was difficult. Japan did have contact with China, though, and many Japanese traditions first came from Chinese traditions.

Later, as explorers from Europe began to travel the world, Japanese rulers made it against the law to have contact with **foreigners**—people who were not Japanese. They believed this was the best way to keep control of the people. From the 1630s to the 1850s, it was illegal for Japanese people to travel to other countries. Only a few foreigners were allowed to trade with the Japanese, and they had to stay anchored offshore in their boats. During this time the Japanese cultural identity grew stronger and stronger. Because of this, today 98.4 per cent of people in Japan are of Japanese heritage.

Few Natural Resources

Natural resources are the parts of the environment that are useful to people, such as minerals, farmland, and fresh water.

Japan's main **natural resource** is the ocean. It provides food in the form of fish, shellfish, and seaweed. It is also Japan's link to trade with the rest of the world. Japan does not have many other natural resources, though.

In the second half of the twentieth century, Japan developed a strong economy based on **manufacturing** to make up for its lack of natural resources. Japan **imports** raw materials such as copper and iron and **exports** goods made from these materials, such as computers and cars. Today, Japanese factories use all the latest computer-controlled technologies to help with their work.

Because of the importance of manufacturing, most of the people in Japan live in cities and towns where they are close to the factories and businesses. A "city lifestyle" is the most common in Japanese culture today.

Little Farmland

In a traditional Japanese diet, rice and fish are two of the main food items. With the ocean nearby, you can probably guess why fish is so important, but what about rice?

The steep mountains in Japan mean that only 15 per cent of the land is good for farming. So the Japanese farm in **terraces**—small fields carved into the hillside. Rice paddies are an efficient use of these small spaces.

The climate in southern Japan is warm, with a lot of rain. This creates good conditions for growing rice. In fact, more than half of Japan's farmland is used to grow this grain.

Imported goods are those things a country buys from other countries. Exported goods are those things a country sells to other countries.

This is Toyko. How can you tell that this is a *Japanese* city?

Sushi [SOO-shee] is a traditional Japanese dish made with ingredients such as rice, raw fish, vegetables, and seaweed. Today, sushi is popular in many parts of the world. How would you describe the way this food is presented?

Coastal British Columbia is also in the ring of fire. What do you know about being ready for an earthquake? Do you think Japanese children learn similar things?

The crust is the outer layer of the earth's surface.

The Ring of Fire

Japan is part of an area around the edges of the Pacific Ocean called the **ring of fire**. In this area, the movement of the earth's **crust** causes many earthquakes and volcanic eruptions. The islands of Japan are actually the tips of underwater volcanoes! About 50 of them are **active**—this means they could erupt at any time. The country also gets about 1500 minor earthquakes each year.

The Japanese developed a practical yet beautiful style of housing. Light wood was used for the outside and frame, and paper walls or dividers were used to create the rooms inside. This type of house reduced the danger to the people who lived in it in case it collapsed in an earthquake. The Japanese also made their houses small so that they could rebuild them quickly. To make the most of the small space, a mattress called a **futon** [FOO-ton] was placed directly on the floor. Then the mattress and the blankets could be rolled up and put away during the day. People sat on straw mats called **tatami** [tah-TAH-mee], so there was no need for tables or chairs.

Today, Japanese people live in many different types of homes. Many people live in apartment buildings that are built with the latest earthquake-proof technologies. Many Japanese families also have some European-style furniture in addition to Japanese furniture.

The populations in Japanese cities are growing every day. To make sure everyone has a place to live, houses and apartments are quite small. Traditional furniture styles such as futons and screens are still popular ways of making the best use of small spaces.

Try This

Make a **fishbone chart** that shows some of the ways in which the environment in Japan influenced Japanese culture. You could complete your presentation by drawing one or two pictures showing the environment or culture of Japan.

To gather the information you need, you will have to **skim** the words and pictures in this section and the section "Landforms and Climate." When you skim, you don't reread every word. Instead, look for words or headings that signal there might be information about your topic.

This fishbone chart has been started for you. How do you think this type of chart got its name?

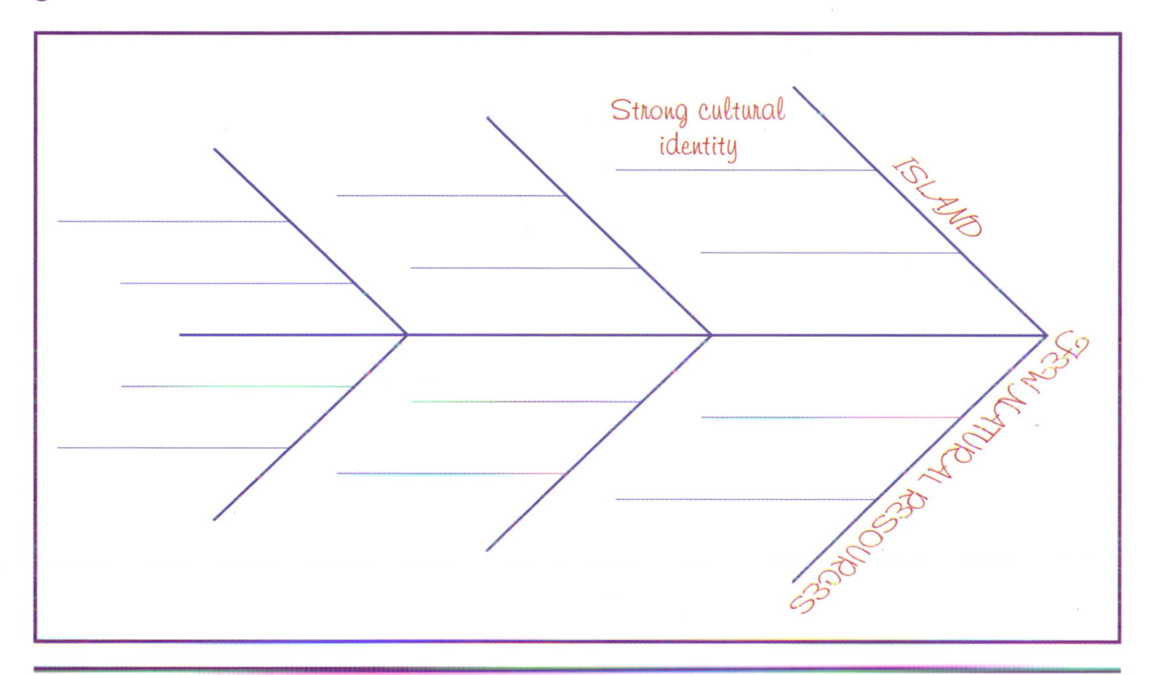

Rights and Responsibilities

On "The Parts of Culture" chart on page 48 there is a column for "Expressing Thoughts and Feelings." This part of culture includes how people see the world around them and how they show what they think and feel in their daily lives and in their arts. In this section, you can learn about the traditional Japanese view of this topic:

- *Ideas about rights and responsibilities*

The traditional Japanese view of the importance of rights and responsibilities is common in many cultures around the world. What view would you say is held by your family?

Responsibility to the Group

In traditional Japanese culture, a person's individual rights are not as important as her or his responsibility to the group. In school, work, and daily life, a person is expected to fit in and do her or his share to make things better for everyone. For example, Japanese workers usually work for one company all their lives. People are more often rewarded for being loyal to the company than for doing especially good work.

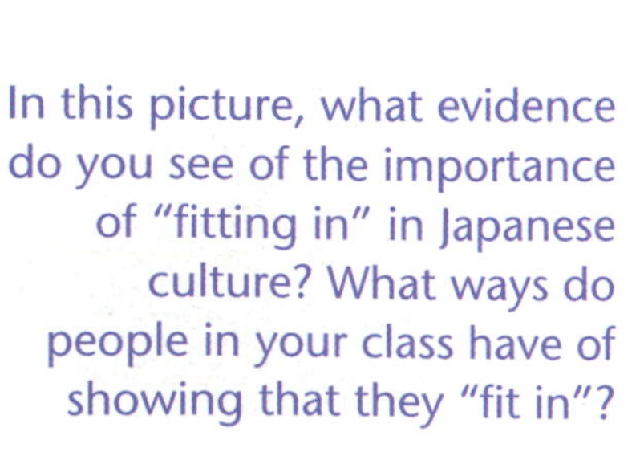

In this picture, what evidence do you see of the importance of "fitting in" in Japanese culture? What ways do people in your class have of showing that they "fit in"?

In Japan, people greet each other by bowing. To show respect, a student would bow lower than a teacher. What ways of showing respect for others do you have in your classroom?

Another way to think of it is that the Japanese have a good "team spirit"! Boasting, asking for special privileges, or wanting to be "different" are considered bad manners.

There is also a strong **social order** in Japan. This means that each person knows his or her "place" in the community. For example, it is important to show respect for your elders and for people in positions of authority, such as teachers. On the other hand, people who have powerful positions are expected to treat those with less power in kind and generous ways.

Children, especially, must always show respect and not speak out about what they want or think. For their part, adults treat children kindly, preferring to show the right thing to do by good example rather than by punishment.

Changing Times

Although traditions are still very important to many Japanese, contact with other citizens of the global village is bringing changes to Japanese culture. Some Japanese young people admire North American styles in clothing, music, and food that they see in the media. They are also interested in ideas from other cultures, such as the idea that you might want to change jobs several times in your life.

In what ways are these young people breaking away from traditional Japanese culture? What kinds of problems might this cause in the community? How might this be good for the community?

PERSPECTIVES

Should the Needs of the Group or the Individual Come First?

Kayla
In my opinion, it is very important to put the needs of the group first when you make a decision about what to do. People need to work together to get things done. If everybody works towards the same goal, then there is a greater chance of reaching that goal. Just think of people in a lifeboat—if everyone pulls together there is a better chance of getting to safety. Working as a group makes sure we survive!

Lindy
In my opinion, always putting the needs of the group first means that a person doesn't get a chance to think for herself or himself. Sometimes people who don't "fit in" come up with creative solutions to problems. If Florence Nightingale had just done her job as a nurse it might have taken us a lot longer to find out how to help patients get well. Instead, she thought for herself and spoke out against the plans of the people in charge. I say "Hooray for individuals!"

Think For Yourself

1. Read and discuss the Perspectives feature on this page. You could use a chart like this to record the main ideas.

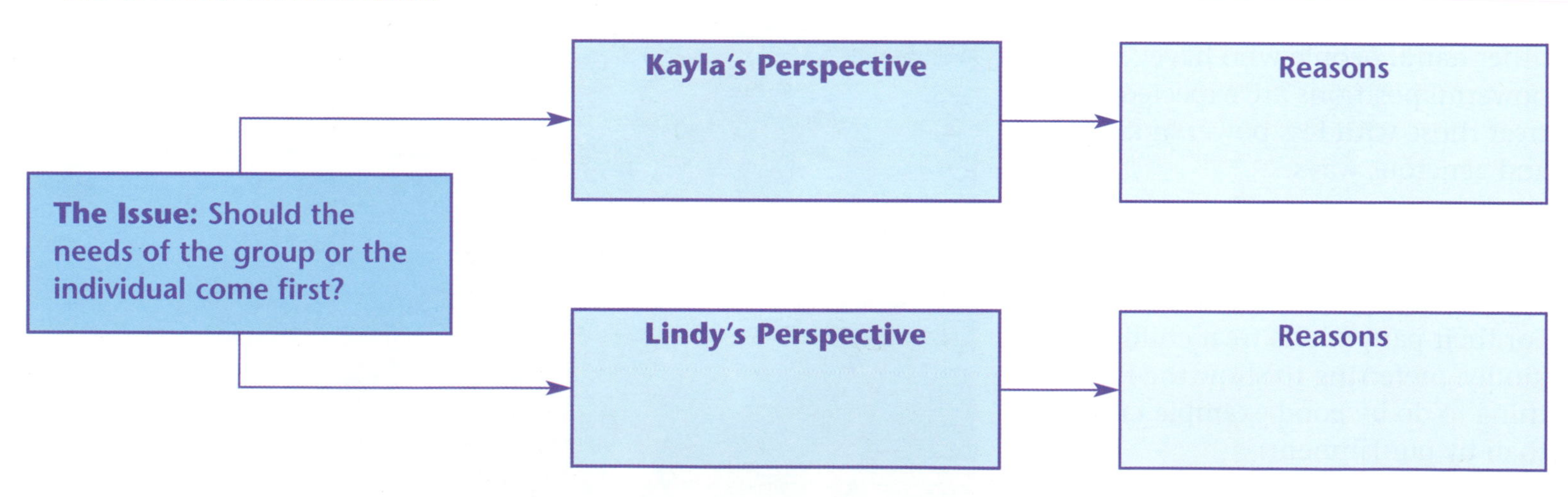

2. In a group, describe a situation in which putting the group first would be the best thing to do. Then describe a situation in which it would be important to respect a person's individual rights. Write down your ideas in point form. Then perform two skits to show your two ideas.

The Arts in Japan

The arts, such as dance, drama, music, and writing, are all highly valued in Japanese culture. Every person tries to make studying some form of art part of her or his life. This is a tradition that goes back many hundreds of years. In the past, even warriors were expected to be skilled painters and poets.

In traditional Japanese culture, it is also considered important to make "a work of art" of every part of life. For example, Japanese homes traditionally have a **tokonoma** [toh-kuh-NOH-muh], which is a place set aside in the main room of the house for a flower display and a painting on a **scroll**—a long, narrow piece of paper. The painting is changed each season to help keep a connection with nature.

Arranging flowers, making tea, wrapping gifts, and preparing box lunches are other examples of everyday tasks that are done with great care for special occasions. All of these are forms of art. While they may appear to be simple, they take great skill to do well. For example, it can take several years to all the movements in the traditional tea ceremony.

Historians think the first novel in the world was written by a Japanese woman called Lady Murasaki Shikibu [MOO-rah-sah-ki SHEE-kee-boo] around the year 1000. It is called *Tale of the Genji* and it describes the adventures of a Japanese prince.

Noh theatre is the oldest form of drama in Japan. The actors wear wooden masks to show their inner feelings. This actor is wearing a smiling mask to show that he is happy.

GLOBAL VISIONS GLOBAL VOICES

The power of nature and the look of the countryside at different times of the year have traditionally been favourite topics for Japanese artists and writers. The forces of nature can even be seen in Japanese letter characters.

Literature

Literature is the art of writing stories and poems. One of the most famous forms of Japanese literature is **haiku** [HY-koo]. In these three-line poems, the writer tries to help you imagine the sights, sounds, feel, smell, or taste of something in a small scene or event. These haiku are by the poet Basho (1644–1694). He was the first poet to write this style of haiku.

A crow
has settled on a bare branch—
autumn evening.

A petal shower
of mountain roses,
and the sound of the rapids.*

Haiku usually tells about a particular season. What images do you see in your mind when you read these haiku?

Art

This painting from the nineteeth century, called *Pontoon Bridge at Sano*, is by the artist Katsushika Hokusai [kah-TSOO-shee-kah hoe-KOO-sy]. In paintings such as this, the artist hopes to give you a feeling about nature and the moment in time being shown. How would you describe the feeling in this painting?

Writing

When the Japanese first started to write their language, they began with characters borrowed from the Chinese. These characters are called **kanji** and are still one of the ways of writing Japanese today. Many kanji characters take the form of the things they represent. Can you see the natural forms in these characters?

*Pages 12, 13, 20, 21 from *The Essential Haiku: Versions of Basho, Buson and Issa*, edited and with an introduction by Robert Hass. Introduction and selection copyright © 1994 by Robert Hass. Unless otherwise noted, all translations copyright © 1994 by Robert Hass. Reprinted by permission of Harper Collins Publishers, Inc.

Think For Yourself

Haiku is still a popular form of poetry for people of all ages in Japan. Young people read haiku magazines and post their haiku on Web sites. Do some research to find out the rules for haiku, then pick a season in your environment and write a haiku to describe it.

Investigate

Pick a topic that interests you and find out more about Japanese culture. Here are some topics to consider:

- reading and writing Japanese
- beliefs in modern Japan
- sports (try sumo wrestling or baseball!)
- festivals and holidays (what about special festivals for children?)
- Japanese traditional drama

After you have done your research, make an **artifacts** box to show the main ideas about your topic. Your objects could be made by you or gathered from home. Write a few sentences to describe each artifact in your box.

Or you might want to check back to the powerful question about Japan that you wrote in your notebook at the beginning of this chapter. If your question hasn't been answered yet, you might prefer to research that topic. Use the Research and Report organizer at the end of your text to plan your work.

An artifact is an object made by people. It tells you something about their culture.

Daily Life

Fukuoka [foo-KOO-oe-kah] is a lively and important international port with many businesses and shops. There are many lovely beaches along the shore.

When we talk about the big ideas of culture we can make generalizations such as "the Japanese traditionally value people who participate as part of a group." When it comes to describing people's daily lives, it is harder to make generalizations. Each family is different.

Just imagine if you had to describe a "typical" Canadian family's life. There are so many **variables**—things that could be different—that your generalizations probably wouldn't be very accurate. Is a typical Canadian family one that lives in Nunavut or British Columbia? Is it a farm family or a family living in Vancouver? Is it a family with one parent living in the home or two? The list could go on and on.

So to take a peak at daily life in Japan, this section presents information about one Japanese family—the Tagawa family. They live in Fukuoka, a large city on Kyushu Island.

A Japanese Home

The Tagawa [TAH-gah-wah] family's home is a modern two-story house in Nagao [nahg-AH-oe], a district that is a 15-minute drive from the centre of Fukuoka. There are many other houses, apartments, and small businesses spaced closely together in the neighbourhood.

The house has a small garden. Inside, there are two European-style bedrooms, a small kitchen, a medium-sized living/dining area, and a Japanese-style room. The Japanese-style room has a tokonoma, a **butsudan** [boo-TSOO-don] (Buddhist family altar), and a low table called a **horigotatsu** [hoe-EE-go-ta-tsoe]. There is a space beneath the table so that when you sit on the floor your legs have someplace to go.

There are four people in the family: Mr. and Mrs. Tagawa, Yumi [YOO-mee] (12), and Yuki [YOO-kee] (10). In this photo, Yumi is on the left. Can you see the tokonoma on the wall?

Daily Life in the Tagawa Family

Mr. Tagawa works for a computer company called IBM. Mrs. Tagawa is an agricultural research assistant at a local university. Yuki is in Grade 5, while Yumi is in Grade 6.

Starting the Day

On a typical weekday, Mrs. Tagawa makes breakfast, and the family eats together. Mr. Tagawa leaves for work around 7:30 a.m. It takes him an hour to get to work by bus. The girls leave around 8:00 a.m. It only takes them about 10 minutes to walk to school. Mrs. Tagawa leaves at 9:00. It takes her about 45 minutes by bus and subway to get to work.

Yuki and Yumi eat lunch in the school cafeteria. Mr. and Mrs. Tagawa may take a packed lunch, eat in a restaurant, or buy a special packed lunch called a **cabento** [kah-BAYN-toe].

After School

After Yuki and Yumi finish class work about 4:00 in the afternoon, they usually join their school club activities. Yuki is in the music club, while Yumi is in the drama club. They also have English, swimming, and piano lessons each week. They usually get home around 7:00 p.m. and eat dinner with their mother. Their father often stays late at work.

Helping Out

Mrs. Tagawa is responsible for the housework and cooking. The girls help prepare the dinner, and Mr. Tagawa helps clean up when he is home. Yumi and Yuki also take care of their cat, Pamba, and make offerings to butsudan every day. On the weekend, Mr. Tagawa helps with the shopping and housework.

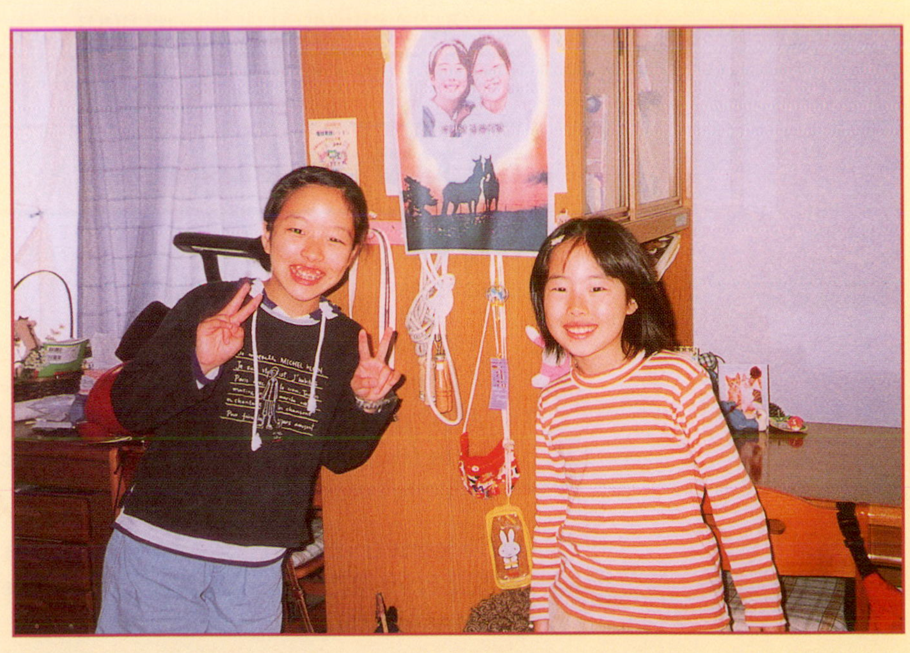

Here are Yuki and Yumi in their bedroom at home. What do you see that is similar to your way of life? What is different?

Having Fun

The Tagawas often go out together once errands are done on the weekend. Like many Japanese, they enjoy watching the change of seasons. They travel to different places to see plum and wisteria blossoms in the spring, wisteria and fireflies in the summer, and cosmos flowers and coloured leaves in the fall. They also have fun visiting museums, going hiking, and watching movies together on Sundays.

Try This

1. Use an organizer like this one to record one or two facts about each of these topics for the Tagawa family.

Family Members	Typical Weekday
Work	Roles of Men and Women

2. Circle something that surprised you. In another colour, circle something that was what you expected about Japan.
3. Look back at "The Parts of Culture" chart on page 48. What parts of culture have you investigated in this section?

Investigate

Do a study of a family in your community. Research information to answer these questions:

- *Who are the family members and how are they related to each other?*
- *What is a typical weekday like for the family?*
- *What kind of work do family members do?*
- *In the family, are there special jobs for men and women or boys and girls? If so, what are they?*

Present the results of your research in a written report. Include a cover page and at least one picture. You might find it helps to use an **outline** to organize your presentation.

HOW TO... Make an Outline

An outline is a point-form description of your presentation. This is a useful way to organize your work for oral presentations or written reports.

Introduction
- description of the topic

Body
Subtopic 1
- main idea
- facts and examples to explain it

Subtopic 2
- main idea
- facts and examples to explain it

Subtopic 3
- main idea
- facts and examples to explain it

Conclusion
- summary of the main ideas

A **topic** is the general subject you want to talk about. A **subtopic** is an important idea connected to the topic. Each subtopic should answer a question you have about the topic. You can have many subtopics in a report, but between three and five is a good number.

Looking Back

In this chapter, you had a chance to think about what cultures are and how to investigate them.

Why is learning about other cultures an important part of being a global citizen?

Chapter 5

Sharing the Wealth

Imagine you're halfway through a long hike. You're tired and hungry. If you had two sandwiches and your friend had none, would you share? What if you had only half a sandwich and your friend had none? Would you still share?

Most people believe that it is good to share with others who have less. When it comes to actually giving up something that you really need or want, though, it can be hard to do the right thing.

Learning how to share the earth's resources is one of the big challenges facing the world today. Although the world's population is increasing at a fast rate, the earth is still quite rich in resources. Many people think there are plenty of resources to go around if we'd only try harder to share.

In this chapter, you can investigate the connections between poverty and population. You'll also learn a little about the country of India and find out why some Canadians need to quit being so greedy!

The Pattern of Poverty

Poverty is when people have difficulty meeting their basic needs.

There are poor people in every country in the world. When we look at all the statistics for all countries, though, we can see that some countries have more problems than others. In this section, you can find out what patterns these statistics show.

Gross National Product

One way to investigate global poverty is to look at the **Gross National Product (GNP) per capita** for different countries. The GNP per capita tells you the average income for each person in a country. This is the amount of money each person would get if all the country's money were shared equally.

An organization called the World Bank helps countries with their money problems. The World Bank has collected information on GNP per capita for most countries in the world. They have used this information to categorize countries into **high-**, **middle-**, and **low-income** groups. According to research by the World Bank, many people in low- and middle-income countries are barely able to meet their basic needs—they are poor.

Per capita means "for each person."

Sometimes it's obvious when people are poor. Sometimes you can't tell just by looking.

The North/South Pattern

This is a **thematic map**. Thematic maps use colours to show patterns about a particular theme or topic. You have to recognize countries by their shapes. Can you locate Canada, Japan, and India? (Check the Countries of the World map on pages 208–209 if you're not sure.)

When you look at the GNP Per Capita map, you can see that most of the low- and middle-income countries are in the southern part of the world. The people in these countries noticed the pattern, too! They also found out that although only 20 per cent of the world's population live in high-income countries, those countries have 80 per cent of the world's wealth.

In 1992, 128 countries with low and middle incomes held a conference to talk about how they could get their share of the world's resources. They decided to form a group called the **Global South**. This group works towards making sure the United Nations and other organizations try to solve the problem of sharing the world's resources.

For this reason, when we talk about global issues in this text we use the term **North** to refer to high-income countries and **South** to refer to middle- and low-income countries.

GNP Per Capita

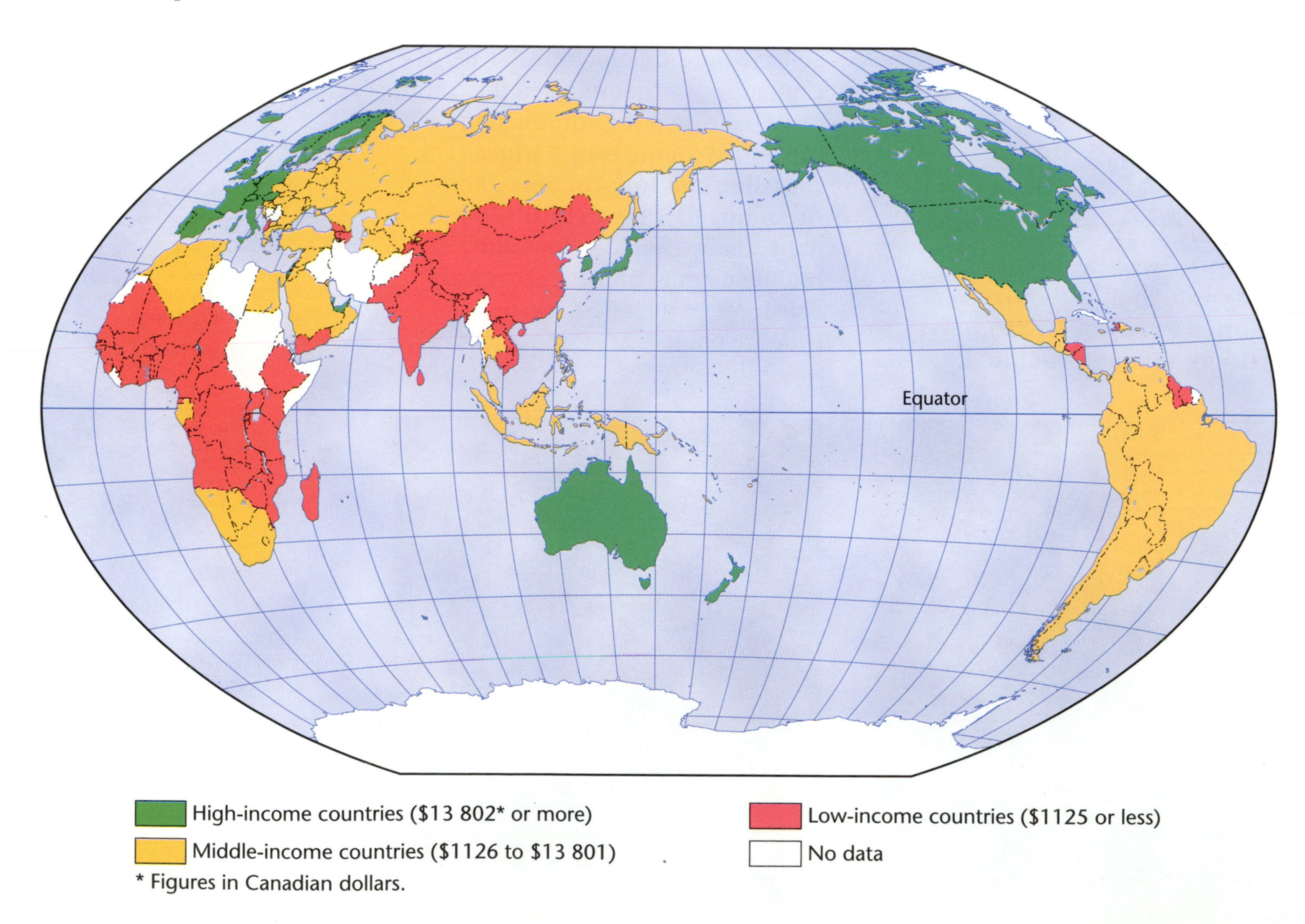

Quality of Life

Quality of life is all of the benefits a country can give a person in order to become the best she or he can be.

Each year the United Nations uses statistics to rank 174 countries in the world. They call this ranking the **Human Development Index**. The country ranked "number 1" is the country that offers a person the best chance for a good life. The country ranked "number 174" is the country where things are the most difficult for people.

GNP is one of the important statistics the UN looks at—a high GNP is usually a sign most people in the country can meet their basic needs. But the UN also considers many other factors, such as how well people's human rights are respected and how well the environment is protected. Because of this, the country with the highest GNP isn't always first on the Human Development Index. Table 1 shows you just three of the many types of statistics the UN uses to draw its **conclusions** about countries.

A conclusion is the idea you have about something after thinking about all the evidence.

What Does It Mean?

People often use statistics to draw conclusions about the world. When you do this, be sure you base your conclusions *only* on the information shown in the statistics. You might have some ideas about why the statistics are the way they are, but unless you can prove

Table 1: Quality of Life

	Life Expectancy	Children in Elementary School	GNP Per Capita
Top Five			
1. Canada	79.0 years	99.9%	$29 263
2. Norway	78.1 years	99.9%	$53 789
3. United States	76.7 years	99.9%	$43 329
4. Japan	80.0 years	99.9%	$56 858
5. Belgium	77.2 years	99.9%	$39 827
Bottom Five			
170. Burundi	42.4 years	35.6%	$208
171. Burkina Faso	44.4 years	32.3%	$372
172. Ethiopia	43.3 years	35.2%	$154
173. Niger	48.5 years	24.4%	$298
174. Sierra Leone	37.2 years	44.0%	$238

Life expectancy: how long most people live
Children in elementary school: the percentage of children who attend elementary school
GNP per capita: converted to Canadian dollars

Source: United Nations Development Program, *UN Human Development Report, 1999* (New York: Oxford University Press, 1999). The figures used are from 1997.

Reading Hint

A table is a list of statistics organized to help you see a pattern. In books, tables are sometimes given numbers. The title tells you the topic. Look for "notes" at the bottom to tell you what the headings mean.

This shows the five highest-ranked countries and the five lowest-ranked countries in the Human Development Index for 1999. How do you feel when you see Canada's ranking? Do you think Canada is still ranked number 1 today? Why or why not?

these ideas with the statistics, you shouldn't state them as facts.

For example, in Table 1 you might notice that the countries with low GNPs have lower life expectancies. So you might conclude that having a low GNP per capita *causes* the people in a country to have poor health. In fact, though, you can't know for sure that this is true just by looking at the statistics. There *could* be another reason for poor health in the country. You would have to do some more research to find out.

Think For Yourself

1. Which of these conclusions could you draw from the statistics in Table 1? You can pick more than one.
    - Life expectancy is lower in Sierra Leone than in Niger.
    - Countries with a low GNP per capita also have a lower life expectancy.
    - People in countries with a low GNP per capita are not as happy as people are in countries with a high GNP per capita.
    - Children in Niger don't like to go to school.
    - Everyone in Canada lives longer than everyone in Ethiopia.
    - More than half the children in Sierra Leone do not go to school.
2. For each conclusion you pick, write down the statistics that support the conclusion. Give the date and source of the statistics.

HOW TO... Choose Statistics

Here are two things to remember when you choose statistics to support your conclusions.

Date

Use the most recent statistics you can find. For statistics about large groups, such as the whole world, the most recent information might be several years old. This is because it takes a long time to gather and sort the numbers.

Source

Make sure the source is one you can trust. There should be some information telling you who collected the information and what the different categories mean.

Understanding Poverty

Once people are poor, it is difficult for them to improve their quality of life. In this section, you can find out how the **poverty cycle** works and what can be done to break it.

Causes of Poverty

There are many different reasons why one country has more poverty than another. Here are some of the main reasons.

History

Sometimes poverty is the result of a country's history. Many countries that are poor today were once **colonies** of European countries. (A colony is a place claimed by a country in another part of the world.) Usually, the colony was seen only as a source of natural resources.

For example, India was a colony of England for about 350 years. During this time, India was an important source of resources, such as cotton and tea, that could not be grown in England. The profits from the sale of these resources went to the English owners of the businesses. The people of the colony were paid very low wages for their labour.

When India became **independent**—its own country—in 1947, most of the English businesses left the country.

INDIA

This chapter includes examples from the country of India. India is a low-income country, but that doesn't mean everybody is poor. Although life is hard for about half the population, many Indians have a good quality of life, and some Indians are very rich. Remember—don't get stuck thinking in stereotypes!

Today, Bangalore, India, is an important world centre for the computer industry. How could having a strong computer industry help a country improve its GNP?

Countries of the North and the South both have problems with resource management. You can find out more about managing natural resources in Chapter 6.

Because they had been making such low wages for so long, few Indian people had enough money to set up their own businesses. People had to get by with very little while they built up Indian-owned businesses. The people of India worked very hard, and over the years their economy has become stronger.

Forces of Nature

Sometimes forces of nature can cause poverty. For example, just one or two years with too little rain or with too much rain can destroy farmers' crops. If the farmers haven't been able to sell anything, then they can't afford to buy new seeds. Without seeds, farmers have no way to plant crops again once the weather improves.

In high-income countries, people may lose their homes and businesses when a natural disaster like this happens. In a country like India, where many people rely on the land they live on to provide them with food, a problem like this may mean that people starve.

This part of Rajasthan [RAHJ-us-thon] in north-west India was once farm land. After several years with little rain, the soil has dried up and much of it has blown away. How do you think this might affect the lives of the families in the area?

Poor Resource Management

All the world's natural resources are created by a system of cycles in the environment. If people manage natural resources poorly by using too much or by polluting resources like air, water, and soil, these cycles break down and the environment can be damaged. If an environment is damaged badly enough, it may no longer be able to provide what people need to survive.

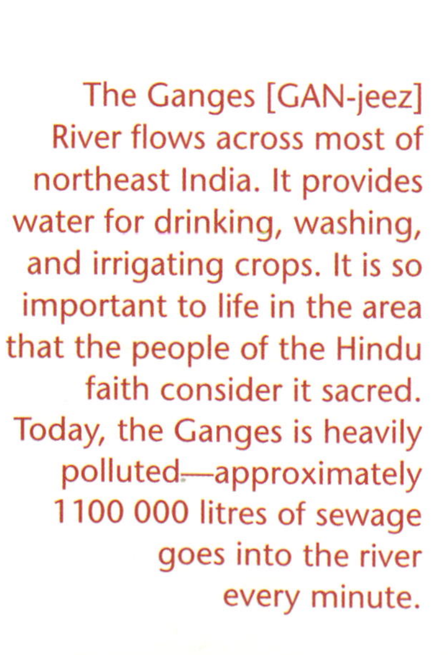

The Ganges [GAN-jeez] River flows across most of northeast India. It provides water for drinking, washing, and irrigating crops. It is so important to life in the area that the people of the Hindu faith consider it sacred. Today, the Ganges is heavily polluted—approximately 1100 000 litres of sewage goes into the river every minute.

The Poverty Cycle

Whatever the cause, the problems created by poverty make it difficult for people to help themselves. This is called the **poverty cycle**.

The cycle goes like this. If there is a lot of poverty in a country, the government doesn't have enough money to provide health care and education for everyone. If people aren't healthy, they can't work. If they don't have an education, there are fewer jobs they can do. If people aren't working, they can't make money. If people aren't making money, the country remains in poverty.

Breaking the Cycle

People in low-income countries often work together to help those who need it. Many countries, though, need help to break the poverty cycle.

Providing aid to low-income countries is one way people in high-income countries such as Canada can help share the world's resources. Some aid comes from governments. Other aid comes from people working together in **aid organizations**.

Short-term aid, in the form of food and other basic needs, helps people during emergencies such as floods, hurricanes, and earthquakes. **Long-term aid** helps people improve their community in ways that last for many years.

Aid organizations ask people what they think will help their communities the most. A long-term project might be getting a business started, building a school, or putting in a water pump to irrigate crops. By making it possible for people to help themselves in the future, long-term aid helps people break out of the poverty cycle.

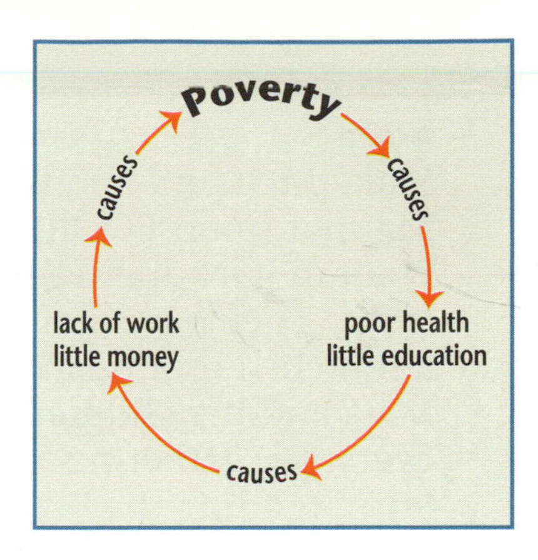

The Poverty Cycle

Some individuals break out of the poverty cycle without the help of others, but it is very difficult.

A Cow and a Goat

One problem for low- and middle-income people is that they don't have the money they need to start businesses. To get a loan from a regular bank you must own something big, like a house or land, that you can promise to give up if you don't repay the money. Most low- and middle-income people don't own these types of things.

In recent years, many communities in low-income countries have been setting up small "banks" for people who can't get regular loans. The money to start the bank usually comes from an aid organization. SHARE is one organization that provides this service in India. Here you can read how one woman used this type of loan to help her family.

Mala

Mala [MOL-uh] and her family live in Manpur [mon-POOR], in the state of Andhra Pradesh [ON-drah PRAY-desh] in southern India. They have a mud-walled house with a thatched roof (made of woven grass). Mala and her children spent many hours every day gathering firewood or dung to burn, tending the fire, or hauling water from the village well.

In the past, Mala and her husband only had work when landowners hired them to plant or harvest crops. For much of the year, there was little Mala could do to earn money. Farm work pays less than $1 a day, so it wasn't possible to save for the other times of the year when there wasn't any work.

The SHARE Program

When workers from the SHARE program came to the village, Mala and three other women arranged for a loan. Each put in a little money to begin with, then promised to pay back their share of the loan with **interest**. Interest is when you pay back a little bit more than you borrowed.

Mala used her loan of about $150 to buy a cow and a goat and to pay for their feed. She sold the animals' milk, as well as cheese and butter she made from the milk. For the first time, Mala and her family had money all year round. This meant everyone could have a little more to eat. Mala could also repair the roof of their house and buy shoes for the children.

These women are buying fish. How do you think they agree on a price?

More Cows and Goats

Recently Mala decided to use some of her income to buy two more cows and two goats. Her husband has seen what a difference her business makes, so he is now helping to care for the animals. In the future, they hope to get a cement floor in their house.

Mala and the other women make weekly payments on their loans. In time, they will have paid back the loan plus the interest. This money goes into a fund that other people in the community can borrow from.

Based on "Microenterprise Making It Possible," from the World Bank Group, 1998.

Try This

Use words and pictures to summarize how Mala used the SHARE program to break out of the poverty cycle. Be creative, but make sure your work answers these three questions:

- *What was Mala's problem?*
- *What did she do to solve it?*
- *Why is it a long-term solution?*

Think For Yourself

In 1995, 1.5 million Canadians under the age of 18 lived in poverty. This means that the families of these children live on less than half of what most families in Canada live on.

1. In a group, write down "reasons to agree" and "reasons to disagree" with this statement in a chart like the one below.
   - Canada should not send aid to other parts of the world when many of our own children live in poverty.

Reasons to Agree	Reasons to Disagree

2. On your own, think about this issue. Decide whether you mostly agree with the statement, mostly disagree, or aren't sure. Write down your reasons in your notebook or social studies journal.

Population Growth

India is one country that has been dealing with the challenge of population growth. India's economy has grown a lot in the past years, but the population has grown faster. In 2000, the population of India was about 1 billion people.

One of the reasons countries in the South have trouble breaking the poverty cycle is because their populations are increasing at a very fast rate. This means that each country has more people to feed and clothe all the time. Even if the GNP of a country increases, the population often increases even faster. So the benefits of a higher GNP are lost because there are more people for the country to support.

What are the reasons for rapid population growth today? Let's first look at patterns in the past.

Patterns in the Past

For thousands of years, population growth and human activity didn't affect the environment very much. There were few people and lots of space and resources. In time, people discovered better ways to stay healthy and grow food. This meant people lived longer and could have more children. The world's population increased only gradually.

Around the middle of the twentieth century, though, really big changes began to happen.

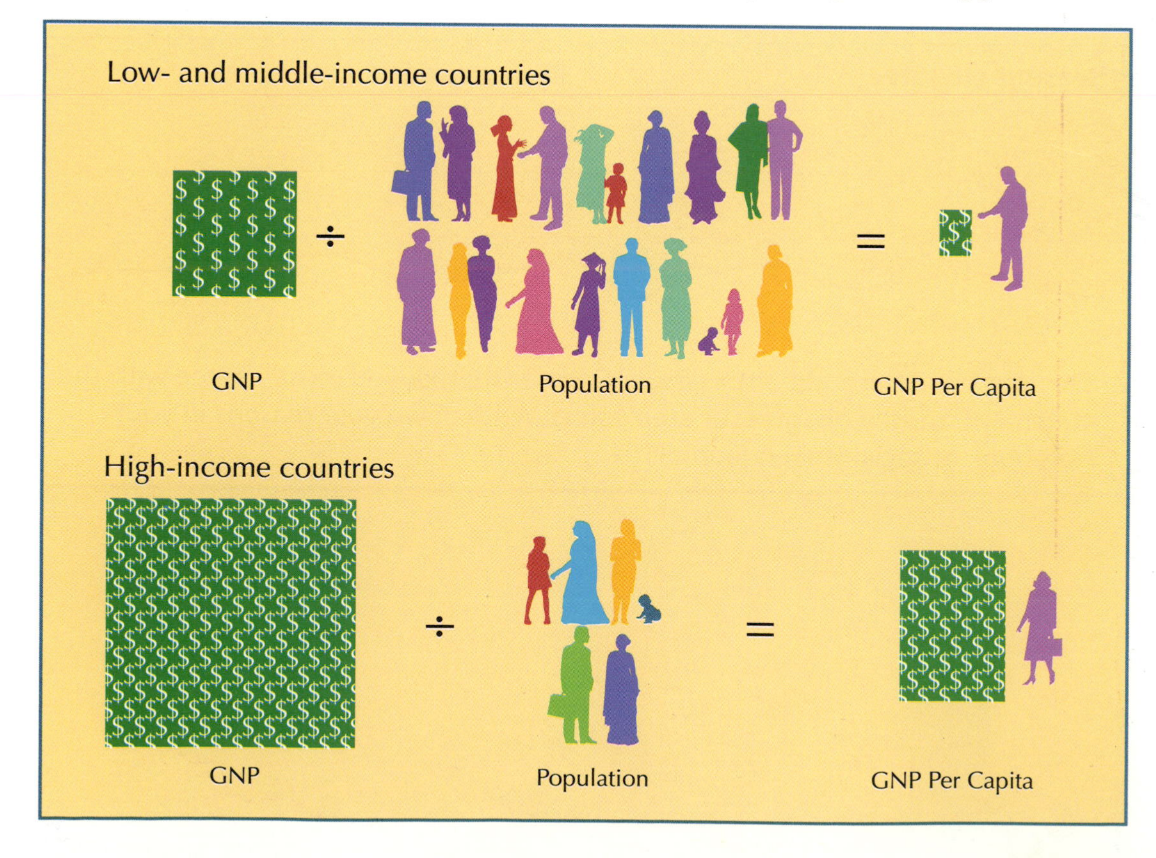

GNP Per Capita

Medical care improved in many countries. This meant that fewer people died from disease at a young age. New technology created better farm equipment and improved crop species, which made farming more efficient and produced more food. This meant that fewer people died at an early age from starvation. Now even more people were living longer and having more children.

Now the world's population began to increase by millions of people each year. This pattern continued year after year. Today, the world's population is over 6 billion and still growing quickly.

World Population Increase Since 1750

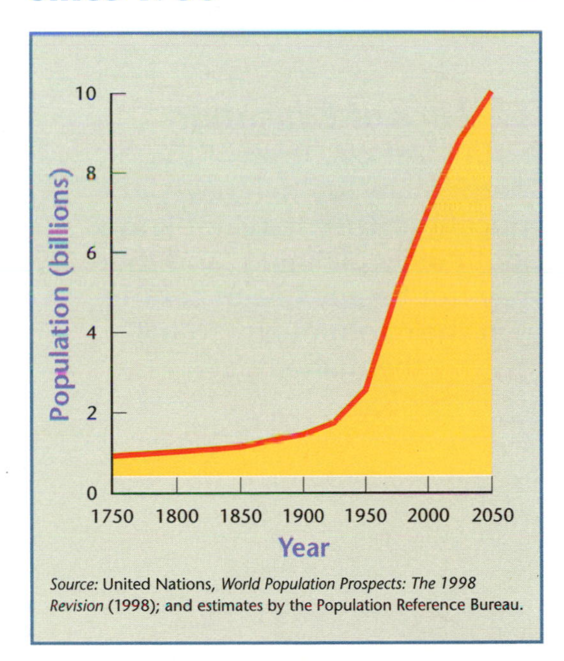

Source: United Nations, *World Population Prospects: The 1998 Revision* (1998); and estimates by the Population Reference Bureau.

This graph shows how the world's population has increased since 1750. It also estimates what the population will be in 2050 if it continues to grow at the current rate. Can you imagine how much 10 billion is? What effect do you think this many people will have on the earth's resources?

All of the people living on the planet today need resources to meet their basic needs. They also need land to live on and to store their waste. It's a challenge to meet everyone's needs and still protect the environment by not overusing the earth's natural resources.

Patterns Today

Many people believe that rapid population growth is the biggest challenge facing the global village today. There are ways in which population growth can be controlled, though. **Family planning** allows parents to decide how many children they will have. In the North, most people choose to have smaller families—just one or two children. For this reason, the population in these countries is growing slowly, and population growth is mainly the result of people moving to an area.

In the South, many people have larger families. For this reason, the population is growing at a faster rate in these countries.

Why do many people of the South have larger families? One reason is that many cultures welcome large families and people choose to follow this cultural tradition.

Often, though, there are other reasons for large families. People at UNICEF have concluded that there are four main reasons why families in the South have many children. The web on page 80 explains these reasons.

Populations increase when more people are added to an area than are dying. This happens when people move to a place or when people have many children.

Experts disagree about the challenge of population growth. At one end, some people believe that the world's population will grow until there's no more room on the planet. Others believe that population growth isn't a serious problem. What do you think?

Each day the world's population increases by about 260 000 people. That's about the number of people who live in the city of Victoria and its surrounding communities.

If you were 10 billion seconds old, how old do you think you would be? (*The answer? 317 years old!*)

Population Growth in the North and South, 1950 to 2050

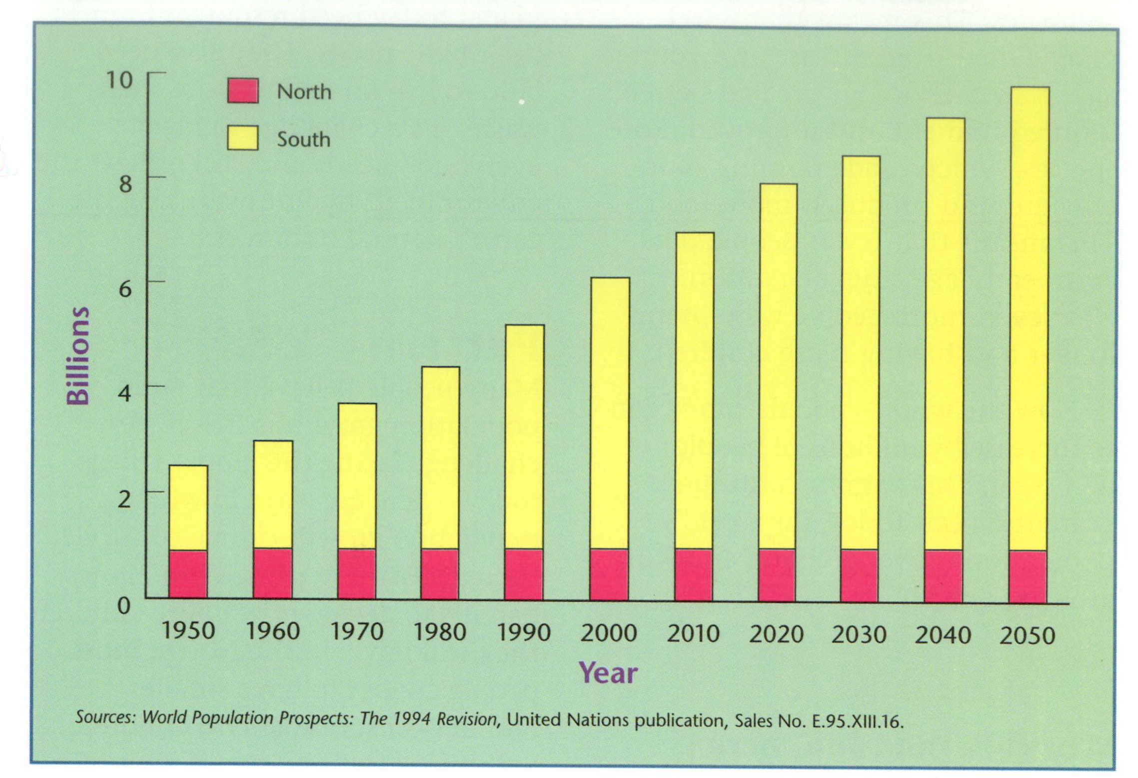

Sources: World Population Prospects: The 1994 Revision, United Nations publication, Sales No. E.95.XIII.16.

This bar graph compares the population growth of countries in the North with countries in the South between 1950 and 2050. How would you describe the pattern?

REASONS FOR LARGER FAMILIES

Care

In the South, people often rely on their children to take care of them when they are older or sick. Having a large family means there are many children to share this responsibility.

Lack of Education

In most countries of the South, many women have little education. They may not know about family planning, and there may not be any health centres in their community to tell them about it.

Helpers Are Needed

Because wages are low, children often work to help the family meet its basic needs. Sometimes children are needed to help on the family farm as well.

Many Children Die

In places where health care is poor, many babies and young children die from diseases. Parents have many children because they expect that some of them will die.

India is a multicultural country, so there are many different family traditions. This Hindu family is enjoying a day at the park. What do you enjoy doing with your family?

Think For Yourself

Statistics gathered by UNICEF show that population growth slows down when certain changes take place. This chart lists three important changes. In a group, complete a chart like this one by explaining why each change might cause a family to choose to have fewer children.

If . . .	Then . . .
• girls and women receive a better education	
• health care is improved	
• people are able to get well-paid work	

Investigate

Research and report on a project in which Canadians are providing aid in the area of health care or education. If you want some ideas, you could start with the Canadian branches of UNICEF, Oxfam, or World Vision. All of these organizations have Web sites. Find out how people your age can help.

Meanwhile, Back in Canada

Countries of the North make up 17 per cent of the world's population but consume more than half of the world's energy. On average, a person in the North uses nine times more energy than a person in the South.

You've seen that rapid population growth in the countries of the South is one reason we're overusing the earth's natural resources. There's another important reason why the earth's environment is in danger, though. Can you think what the North might be doing? Read on!

Consuming Resources

In what ways do the things many Canadians use everyday consume the earth's resources?

Canada doesn't have rapid population growth. Yet Canada and other countries of the North are the biggest consumers of the earth's resources.

Resource Consumption Per Person

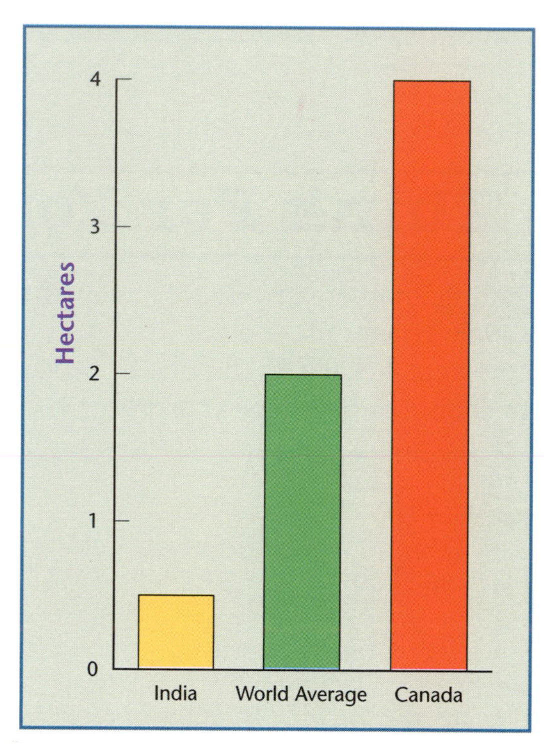

Per person, Canadians use up the world's resources at least *four times faster* than people in the countries of the South.

Think of it this way. Imagine how much space on the planet it takes to produce the resources to support one person. This would include farmland to grow food, forests to produce wood, and places to hold the water, oil, and gas we use. The world average is about 2 hectares per person. A person in India uses about 0.5 hectares. The average Canadian, though, uses more than 4 hectares. So if everyone in the world used resources the way we do, we'd need two more planets like earth to produce enough!

Producing Waste

So you can see that the people of the North consume more than their fair share of the earth's resources. All of this resource consumption means that the countries of the North also produce more waste per person than the countries of the South. This waste is causing even more damage to the environment.

Table 2: Waste Production in the North and the South

	Carbon Dioxide Per Capita (tonnes)	Garbage Per Capita (kilograms)
The North		
United States	19.7	720
Norway	15.4	590
Canada	13.8	630
Belgium	10.5	480
Japan	9.3	400
The South		
Burundi	less than 0.1	—
Ethiopia	less than 0.1	—
Burkina Faso	0.1	—
Niger	0.1	—
Sierra Leone	0.1	—

Carbon dioxide per capita: Carbon dioxide is one of the most serious forms of air pollution. It is produced in the burning of fuels such as gas.

Garbage per capita: This is the number of kilograms of garbage produced by each person in a country.

Source: United Nations Development Program, *UN Human Development Report, 1999* (New York: Oxford University Press, 1999). The figures used are from 1995 and 1996.

How does Canada rate as a "waste producer"? The symbol — means that there is no information on garbage for the South. Based on the other information in this section, do you think the per capita figure would be higher or lower than for the North?

Doing Something Today

The statistics show us that many people of the North, including Canadians, are consuming too many of the earth's resources and are producing too much waste.

One reason we do this is because we live in a **consumer society**. Our economy depends on people buying things all the time. When people buy things, other people have jobs making these things and providing services. People who have jobs then have money to spend, so they can go out and buy more things!

Buying is also an important part of our culture in other ways. Going to the mall is a popular form of recreation. Many people also place a high value on owning many things and having new things, such as the latest fashions and the coolest computer games.

How can we reduce the damage a consumer society like ours causes to the environment? If each of us cut back just a little on the resources we consume, it could make a big difference.

Buy Nothing Day

One thing a lot of people around the world do each year is take part in **Buy Nothing Day**. The idea is to try to go for one whole day without spending any money. It wouldn't be possible to do this every day, but having a day like this gets people thinking about the issue. That's a good start towards getting us to change the way we consume the world's resources.

Eighty per cent of the things we buy are thrown away after being used only once!

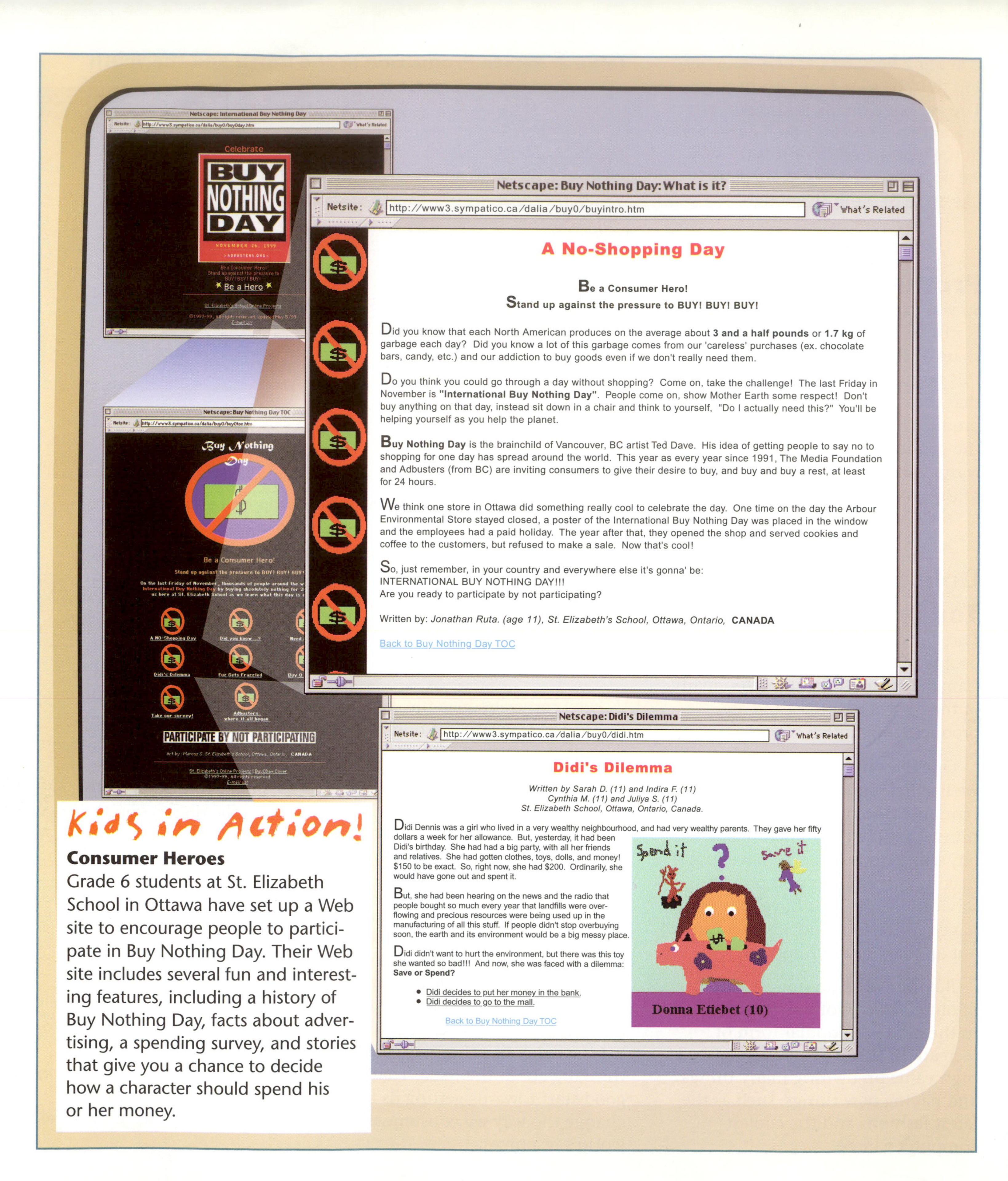

Kids in Action!

Consumer Heroes

Grade 6 students at St. Elizabeth School in Ottawa have set up a Web site to encourage people to participate in Buy Nothing Day. Their Web site includes several fun and interesting features, including a history of Buy Nothing Day, facts about advertising, a spending survey, and stories that give you a chance to decide how a character should spend his or her money.

How Can *You* Make a Difference?

- Don't buy things you don't need.
- Repair broken items. Don't buy new ones.
- Reduce, reuse, and recycle.
- Walk, cycle, or take public transit.
- Choose products that come in returnable containers.
- Plant a tree. (They take carbon dioxide out of the air.)

Think For Yourself

Many people depend on making and selling goods to earn a living. If we solve one problem by consuming less, we could create another problem by putting people out of work!

So be creative and think of jobs people can do that use few resources. For example, one job could be making dog leashes out of woven strips of old bicycle inner tubes. In a group or with a partner, brainstorm as many job ideas as you can think of. Display your ideas in a Jobs for the Global Village web.

Try This

Get your school participating in a Buy Nothing Challenge. You might plan it for International Buy Nothing day (the last Friday in November) or for any date that works for your school. Instead of just one day, though, challenge students to see how many days they can last without buying something.

This is a big project, so your class will probably have to work in groups to get everything organized and done. Consider putting on a multimedia presentation to get your message across. Use the Action Organizer at the back of your text to help you plan your project.

Looking Back

This chapter showed why all countries in the world have to work together to find solutions to sharing resources.

How can countries of the South contribute? How can countries of the North contribute? How can *you* contribute?

Chapter 6

Planning for the Future

What's going to happen to the earth's natural resources in the future? Will the people of the North *and* the South be able to get what they need?

If we use our resources carefully now and plan for what we will need in the years to come, the future looks good. This way of managing resources is called **sustainable management**. (*Sustain* means something can continue for a long time.) In order to manage a resource in a sustainable way, we need to understand it—how it is formed, how we use it, and how we can keep it in good condition.

This is true for all resources, such as trees, soils, minerals, oil, and oceans. All of these are important resources in various parts of the world. Fresh water, though, is a resource everyone in every part of the world needs. In this chapter, you can find out what it takes to manage water in a sustainable way and decide for yourself how well Canadians are doing.

Fresh Water

Water is one of our basic needs. The United Nations estimates that each person needs approximately 100 litres of fresh water a day for drinking, cooking, and bathing. What other uses of water do you see here? What other uses can you think of?

Lots of Water?

If you look at a map of the world, you'll see that about two-thirds of the earth's surface is covered in water. Ninety-seven per cent of this is salt water. Although salt water is a great habitat for sea life, and the oceans are important transportation routes, we can't drink salt water or use it to irrigate crops.

So only 3 per cent of the earth's water is fresh water. Of this fresh water, at any point about 2 per cent of it is frozen in **glaciers**. That leaves us with only 1 per cent of the earth's water to meet all our needs.

Water on Earth

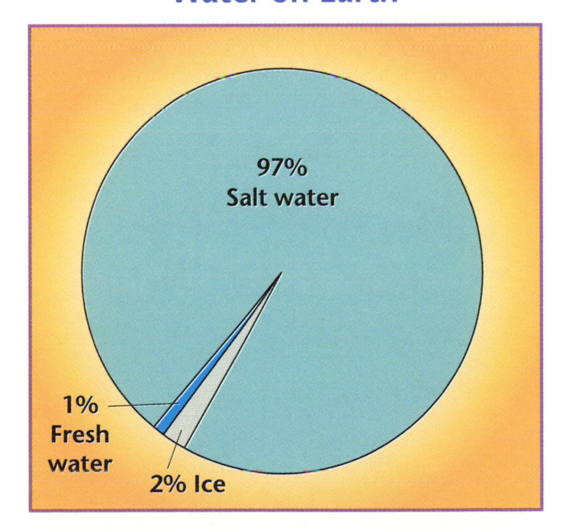

In order to manage this water in a sustainable way, we first have to understand the **water cycle**.

Why is a circle graph a good way to show this information? How else could you show it?

A glacier is a large area of water frozen into ice. Glaciers form in high mountain regions and in the Arctic and Antarctic. In Canada's far north, some glaciers contain water frozen 100 000 years ago.

Oil and gas and minerals such as copper are examples of **non-renewable resources**. The natural cycles that produce these resources take place over millions of years, so once the resources are gone, it will be millions of years before there are any more.

A resource that keeps reproducing itself is called a **renewable resource**.

Trees and other plants also take water in through their roots and release clean water vapour into the air.

The Water Cycle

For millions of years the amount of water on earth has remained pretty much the same. While a lake might dry up in one place and a flood might occur in another, the earth's water is really just changing places.

The reason we have been able to use the same water for so long is because of the water cycle. Here's how the cycle works.

The heat of the sun causes the water from the earth's oceans, lakes, and rivers to **evaporate**—that is, to change from a liquid into a vapour. When it does this, the salt and most **pollutants**, such as dirt and chemicals, that were in the water are left behind. This means the water vapour is clean.

This water vapour forms clouds, then falls to earth as **precipitation**—rain, hail, or snow. Some of the precipitation flows directly back into the rivers, lakes, and oceans. Some of it seeps into the ground, where it is stored in **aquifers** (rocks with small holes) beneath the earth's surface. This **groundwater** eventually flows into rivers and lakes, but much more slowly. The underground area where the water collects is called the **water table**.

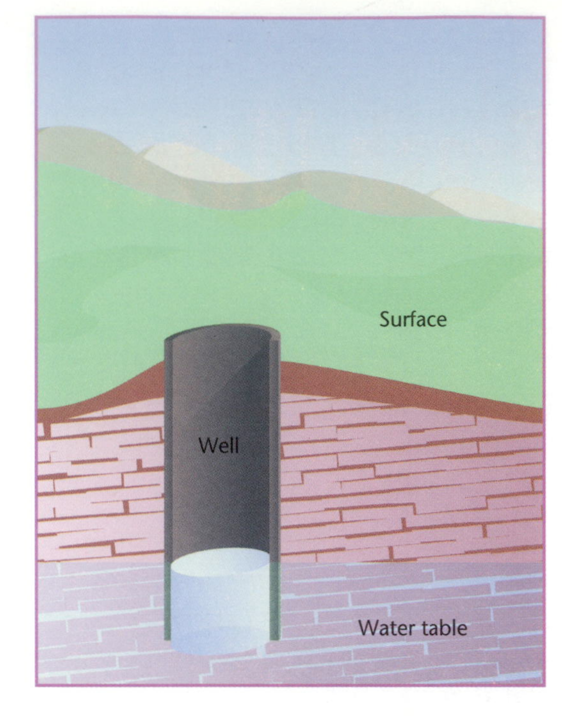

People get the water they need from lakes or rivers, or by drilling **wells** down to the groundwater.

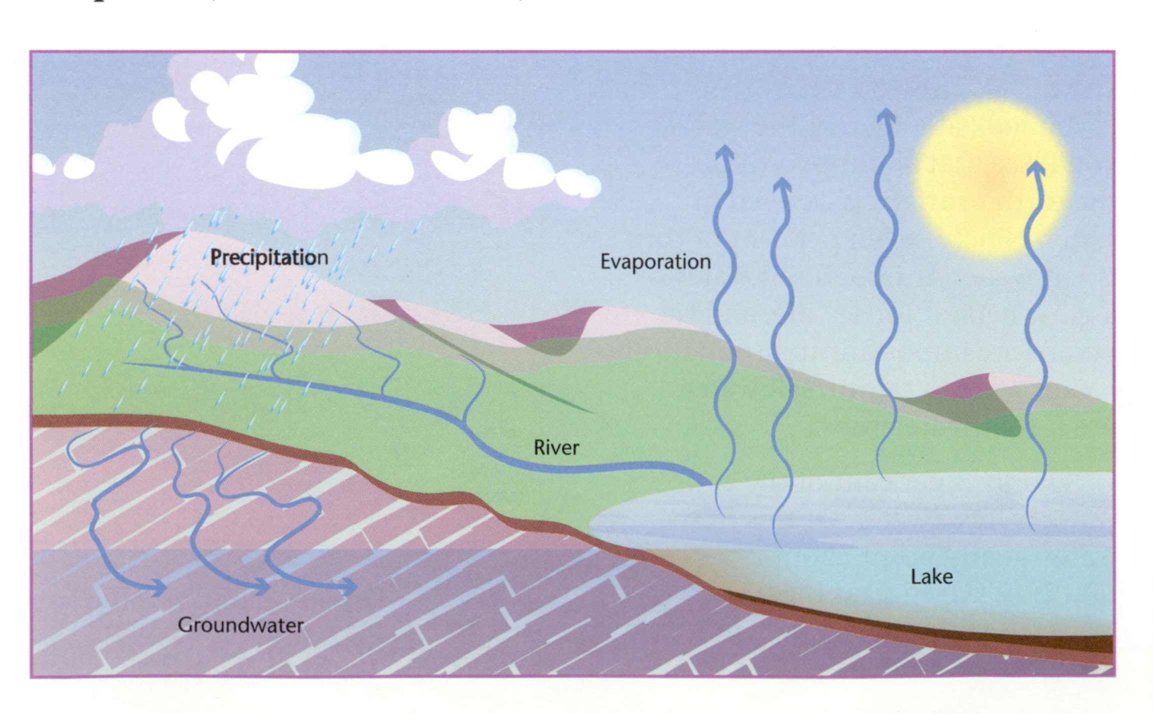

Take your time with this diagram. Read the labels and follow the arrows. Check back to what you've read to make sure you understand the process. How could understanding the water cycle help you manage water in a sustainable way?

Watersheds

You've probably noticed that water always runs downhill. A **watershed** is an area of high land from which precipitation and groundwater flow down on both sides. The flow of water begins as small streams, but as these streams meet up with other streams they form rivers and lakes. The watershed is an important part of a water system.

The Path of a River

One way to understand water and watersheds is to follow the path of a large river. The path described here is the same for all the great rivers of the world, such as the Amazon, the Nile, the Ganges, and Canada's own Fraser River in British Columbia.

The **headwaters** are where a river begins, usually high in a mountain region. A river might begin from a small spring of water bubbling out of the ground or from a melting glacier. This water gathers and runs downhill into a valley, then follows along the valley. As the river flows downhill from one valley to the next, other streams and rivers flow into it. These streams and rivers are called **tributaries**.

As the river flows downhill, it grows bigger and more powerful. As it does, it begins to take some soil from the riverbank along with it. As the river flows out of the mountains and onto a flatter area, it starts to flow more slowly. When this happens, the river **deposits**, or drops, some of the soil it is carrying. This creates a fertile area called a **delta**. Finally, the fresh river water meets the salty ocean water in an area called the **estuary**.

Look back at the diagram of the water cycle to see how the small streams flow into the river.

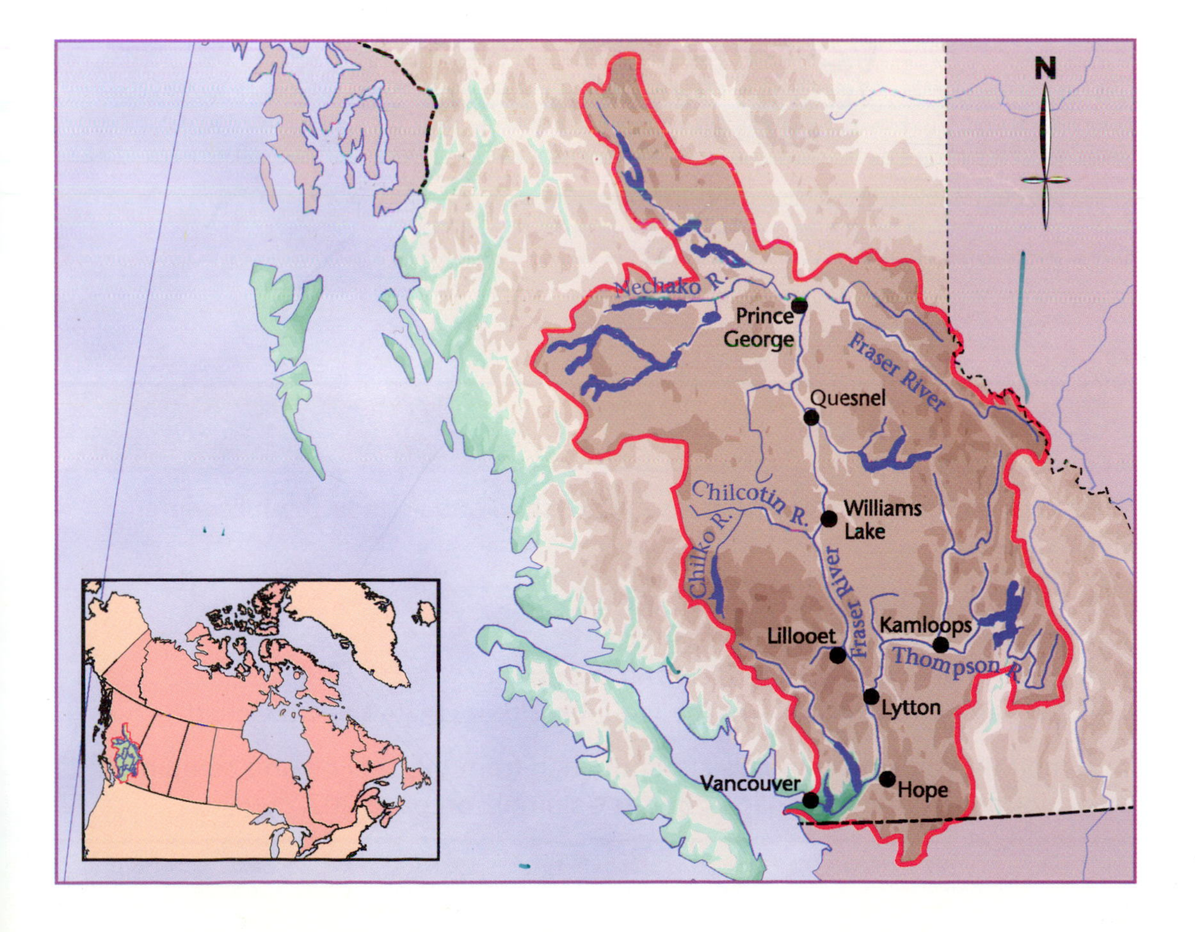

This map shows the Fraser River watershed. Where is the estuary of the Fraser River? Where are the headwaters? How could pollution in the water in Prince George affect the people of Quesnel?

GLOBAL VISIONS GLOBAL VOICES

Water is also valued for its beauty. Many people have said that an appreciation for water is part of the Canadian identity.

This print is by the Inuit artist Pitseolak Ashoona. Here's what she says about it: "We would often camp at Natsilik, a place about a week from Cape Dorset, near many lakes. It has the most beautiful drinking water, the most beautiful water I have found."

From *The Inuit Print*, Ottawa: Canadian Museum of Civilization.

Try This

Make your own map of the Fraser River watershed and include the following information:

- the path of the river and its tributaries
- the area covered by the watershed
- the location of the headwaters and the estuary
- the names and locations of the mountains that create the watershed

To do this, you'll need to collect information from this section and combine it with information from the map of British Columbia on page 207.

Think For Yourself

In the rest of this chapter you'll find out how Canada and other countries of the world manage their water resources. Before you read more, write down your **hypothesis** about the answer to this powerful question:

- *How well do Canadians do when it comes to sustainable water management?*

Give your hypothesis and your reasons for it. Keep it to check from time to time as you read this chapter.

HOW TO... Develop a Hypothesis

A hypothesis is your best answer to a question based on what you know so far. Having a hypothesis can help you organize your research because it makes you think about what you already know and about what you need to find out.

Once you have a hypothesis, you have to check your idea by finding facts and examples to support it. As you find new information, you sometimes find out your hypothesis was correct. Sometimes, though, you need to change your hypothesis to include what you have learned. Checking your ideas and making changes if you need to is called **developing a hypothesis**.

Water Management

In 1997, the United Nations Environment Program predicted that 3 billion people could face water shortages within the next 50 years.

The water cycle is an efficient system, but it does have limits. If we take out too much water from one part of the system or pollute too much water at once, then the cycle can't keep up. Because all the water in the world is connected in some way, poor water management in one area could eventually affect everyone.

To manage our water use in a sustainable way, we have to think about **water flow** and **water quality**. We must also take especially good care of our watersheds.

Water Flow

Water flow is about getting water where it needs to be. Water systems pipe water from where it is to where people need it. Sewage systems take waste water away.

Water shortages happen when there isn't enough water. They can happen because of climate change, such as less precipitation than usual for a long period. Shortages can also happen if people in one part of the system use more than their share of the water and therefore leave less for others.

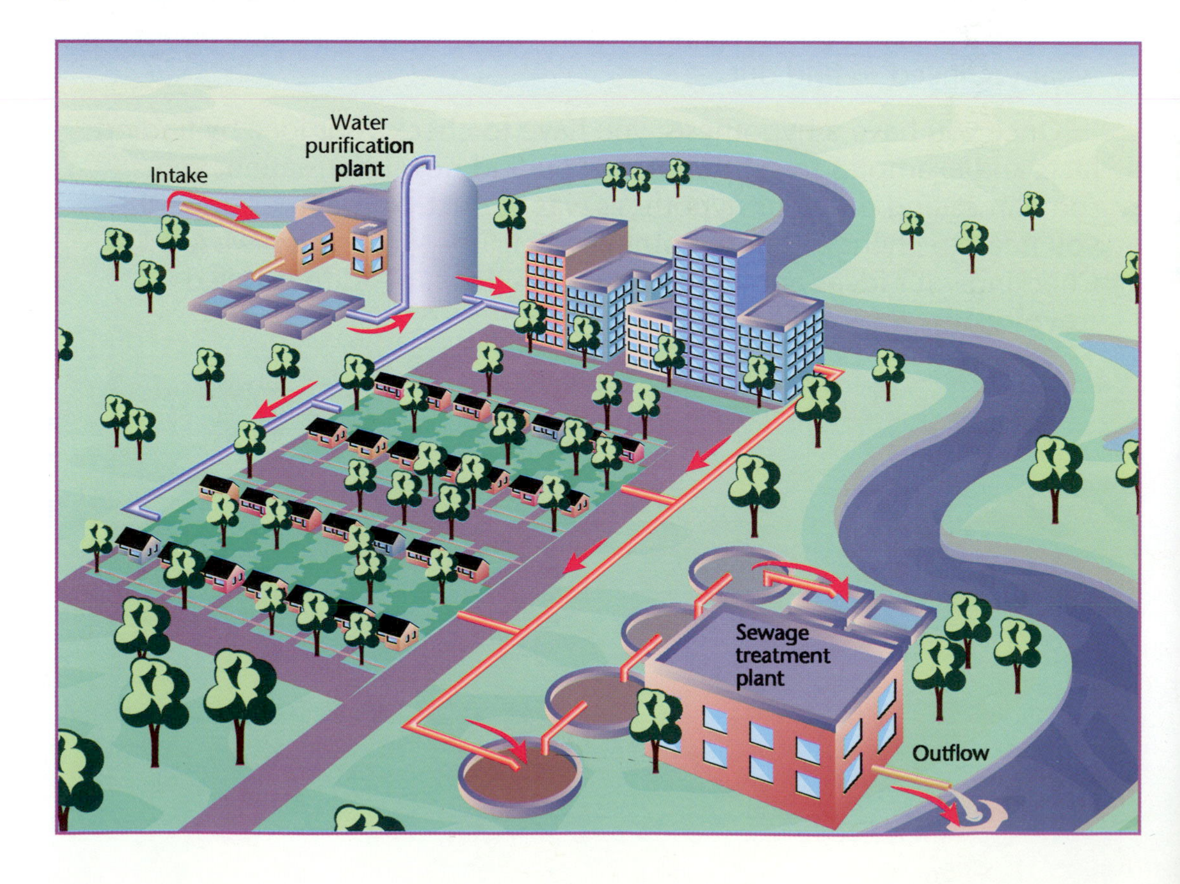

This diagram shows the way many communities in Canada manage their water flow. What are two ways this system helps keep water quality high? What would be different if the water came from groundwater?

Water Quality

Water quality refers to how clean the water is. We use different qualities of water for different purposes. For example, you might think the water in a lake is clean enough to swim in—but you wouldn't want to drink it!

As long as people live and work near sources of water we will always have some pollution. Sustainable water management means figuring out how to pollute as little as possible. There are two ways to do this: by not putting harmful things into the water in the first place, and by cleaning the water after we've used it.

Watersheds

Good water flow and water quality depend a lot on how well we take care of our watersheds. Forested areas with few or no people living in them make the best watersheds. The branches of the trees catch the rain and the roots hold the soil in place so that water filters slowly into the rivers.

If trees and other plants are removed, though, the rain hits the ground hard and the water rushes too quickly downhill. This can cause sudden floods. Rushing water also removes soil from the hillsides, which in turn clogs up the rivers and makes the water muddy and undrinkable. The more people who live, work, and travel in a watershed, the greater the chance of polluting the water system.

There are three main types of water pollution: animal and human waste, chemical poisons, and soil.

A Closer Look

Types of Water Pollution

Human and Animal Waste

Human and animal waste get into the water system from sewage and run-off from farms. One of the dangers of this type of pollution is that it can spread disease. Another danger is that it can destroy fish and other aquatic life by providing too much food for plants that grow on the water's surface. These plants use up oxygen while they are alive. Then the bacteria that eat the plants after they die use up even more oxygen. Eventually, there is not enough oxygen for other plants and fish, and so they die.

This shows a pond where the surface plants are growing too quickly because of pollution. How could this problem have been avoided? What could be done to help the water now?

Chemical Poisons

Poisons are the chemicals that people dispose of in the water. They cause harm or death to plant and animal life. Many of the everyday things we use, such as paper and plastic bottles, are made using such chemicals. These poisons get into the water system in the form of waste from factories, farms, and homes. Sometimes large amounts of chemical poisons are spilled into the water during an accident, such as an oil spill.

Sewage treatment plants remove some of these chemicals from the water, but a solid waste called **sludge** is left behind. The sludge must be disposed of someplace. Often this is in landfill sites where the poisons can seep back into the groundwater. So the most sustainable way to handle chemical poisons is to not let them into the water in the first place.

Soil

Soil is a natural part of the water system—rivers always carry small amounts of soil along with them. If the banks of a river are disturbed by human activity, such as ranching, cutting down trees, or building roads, then too much soil can get into the water. When this happens, fish and other aquatic life can suffocate and the water is unfit for people to drink.

Which of these two methods of planting rows of crops would be a better way to stop water from carrying soil into the river? Why?

Many people use **pesticides** in their gardens to kill the bugs that eat their plants. Pesticides are one source of poisons in our water system. How might pesticides get from a person's garden into a nearby river?

Try This

1. Read "A Closer Look: Types of Water Pollution" on pages 93 to 94 with a partner. Make point-form answers to the questions with each picture. Then meet with another pair of students and share your ideas.
2. On your own, make a drawing that shows water being managed in a sustainable way. Include the watershed and the people who live there or nearby.

Investigate

A **survey** is one way to find out what people think and how they act.

1. Conducting the Survey

Create a form like the one below to survey your class to find out how often their families try to use water in sustainable ways. This is called **conservation**. You might think of other questions to add to the survey.

Water Survey Please circle the answer that applies most often in your family.				
• Do you try to reduce the amount of water you use?	Don't Know	Always	Sometimes	Never
• Do you use cleansers that are biodegradable (don't pollute)?	Don't Know	Always	Sometimes	Never
• Are you careful not to pour pollutants such as paint or paint thinner down the drain?	Don't Know	Always	Sometimes	Never

2. Sorting the Results

To sort the results of your survey, calculate each question separately. Add up the number of answers in each category. Show the results for each question in a bar graph.

3. Drawing Conclusions

Answer these questions to help you analyse your survey results.

- *Compare the answers to the questions. Is there one way of conserving water that people practice more than the others?*
- *In general, how would you rate conservation practices in the families you surveyed: poor, average, or good?*

4. Checking Your Hypothesis

Check back to your hypothesis about how well Canadians do when it comes to sustainable water management. Does the information in your survey support your hypothesis, or do you need to change your ideas?

How Are We Doing?

What pattern do you see in this map? Are problems with water quality more common in the countries of the North or the South? Why do you think this might be?

In the past, the global village hasn't done well in global water management. In many places in the world people cannot get safe drinking water. Many countries are already short of water all year round, and the United Nations predicts that more and more countries will run short of water in the future.

The good news is that we can do better. Because of the work of the United Nations and other groups, the number of people in the countries of the South who have access to clean water increased from 40 per cent in 1975 to 70 per cent in 1995. This big change was brought about by many small changes, such

Percentage of Population with Access to Safe Water

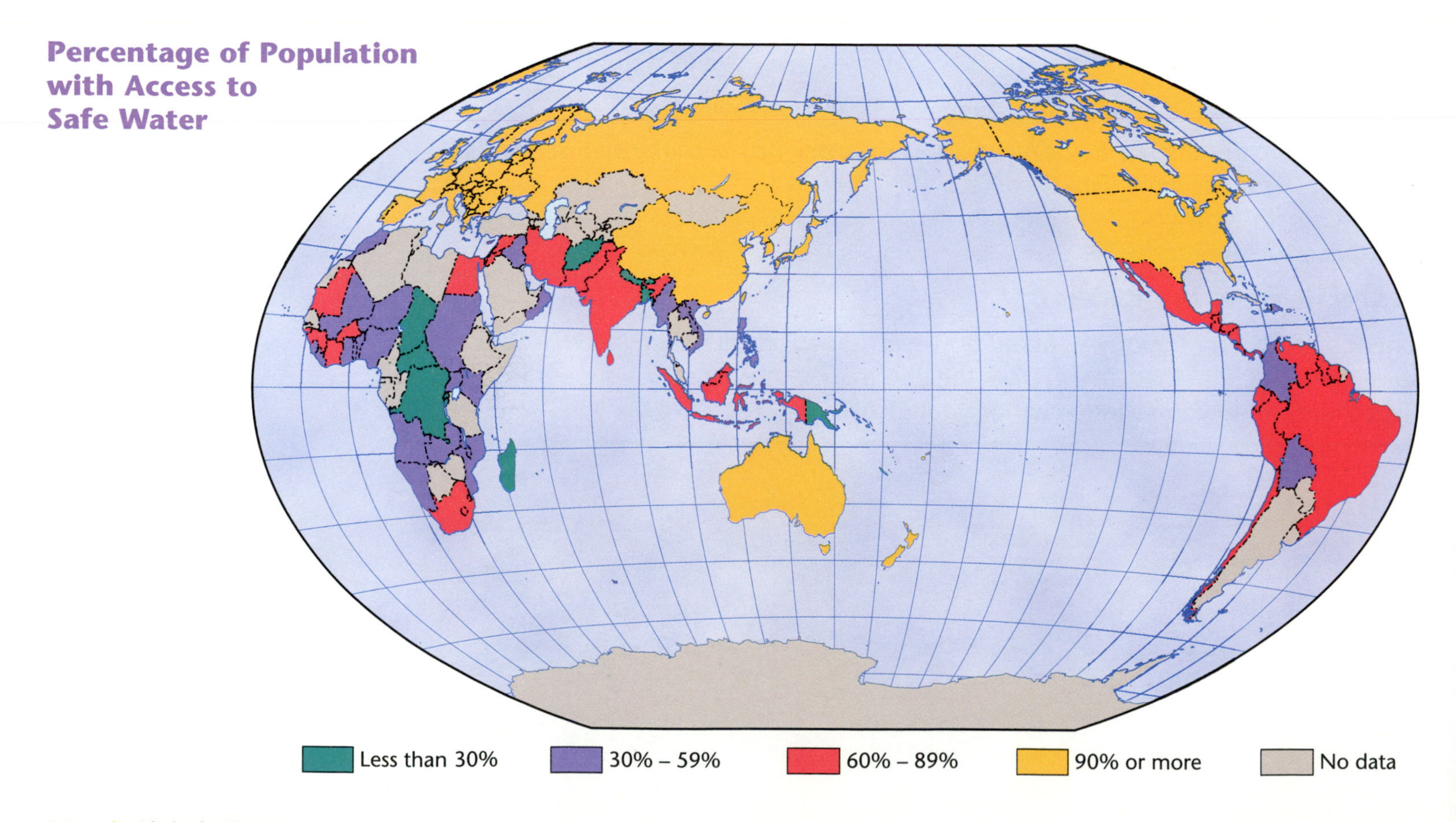

as digging deeper wells to reach more groundwater and building better toilet facilities so that human waste isn't returned to the water system.

To manage this global resource, we all have to work together: countries, communities, and individuals. In this section, you can find out what we need to do and you can read about a group of students in Uganda who are making a big difference in their community.

Countries

The governments of countries have to pass laws to prevent water resources from being used in unsustainable ways. These might include laws against polluting water and laws requiring communities to reduce the amount of water they use.

It's not enough to have laws alone, though. There must also be ways to make sure people follow the laws, and fines for people who do not.

Water flows across international boundaries—it's a resource that the whole world shares. So it's also important for countries to sign agreements to make sure that all sides take care of the water resources they share. Countries also have to co-operate to make sure that one country doesn't stop the flow of water to another country. This could happen if people in one country used up all the water in a river.

Communities of the North

All communities have to find the best ways to manage their water. How they do this depends on the needs of the community, what the climate is like, and whether the community is in a high- or low-income part of the world.

Most communities in the high-income countries of the North can afford to get the water they need.

Most of England receives as much rain each year as British Columbia. Yet the UN predicts England will have water shortages by the year 2050 because of population growth and the way people use water.

The Great Lakes are a shared water resource between Canada and the United States. Why is it important for both countries to have the same laws about pollution?

This aerial photograph of Laval, Quebec, gives some clues about how much water some people use. What are the clues? Do you think people in this community worry about how much water they use?

In May 2000, the water supply in the town of Walkerton in Ontario was contaminated with a deadly bacteria called e-coli. Over 2000 people became ill and at least seven people were known to have died.

In many countries of the South, 80 per cent of all diseases result from people coming into contact with water polluted by human waste. This causes up to 35 000 deaths worldwide each day.

They can usually set up systems to deliver clean water to people, even in communities in drier climates that may be hundreds of kilometres away from a clean water source. In addition, they can also afford sewage treatment plants to make sure they return clean water to the system.

Still, deadly bacteria can slip past these systems. When they do, they can cause widespread illness in a community. Another problem is that many people rely on groundwater for their water supply. But these water sources can be contaminated by bacteria from human and animal waste and poisons from fertilizers.

Communities in the North also need to make sure they use water wisely. Just because a community can afford to use lots of water doesn't mean it should! As populations in towns and cities increase, there is a real danger that even communities in wet climates will run out of usable water. So people must also understand the importance of treating sewage and be willing to see their tax money spent that way.

Communities of the South

Communities of the South face different challenges than those in the North when it comes to managing water. Their challenges are mainly the result of climate, poverty, and population growth.

Many communities of the South have drier climates where there is not a lot of water to start with. Other communities are in places where sudden heavy rains cause sewers to overflow and pollute drinking water.

Smaller communities can rarely afford modern water systems and sewage treatment plants. Drinking water must be collected by hand from wells that are shared by people in the community or from nearby rivers and lakes. Toilets are often simple pits dug into the ground. If the pits are in the wrong place, human waste can get into the groundwater that flows into wells.

Often, growing populations mean that people cut down more and more trees in their watersheds for fuel. They also need the land for farming. This leads to floods, loss of soil, and muddy water.

So the most important things for communities of the South to do are to keep their wells clean and make sure that human waste doesn't find its way into drinking and bathing water. They must also plant their crops in ways that hold as much soil as possible in their watersheds.

Individuals

You're probably not surprised to find out that individuals can make a big difference in water management. For people in the North, this means cutting back on waste and pollution to make sure there is water for the future. For people in the South, there is often a more immediate reason to practice water management. "A Closer Look" on page 101 tells what the children of Bbira in Uganda did to protect the water supply in their community.

In many communities of the South, girls and women collect water for the household. How would collecting water this way affect the way you think about water and the way you use it?

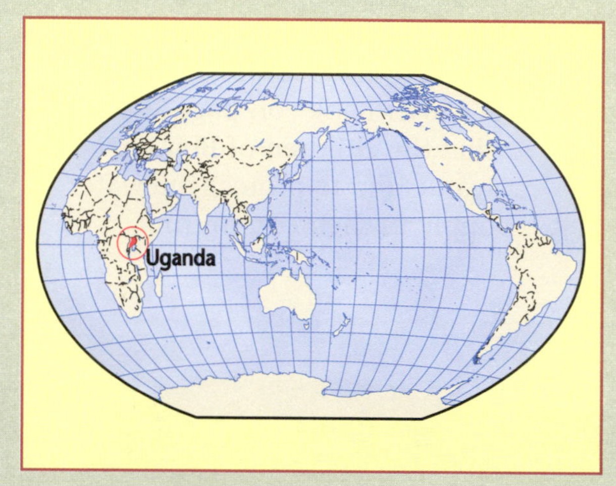

In the centre of the flag is the red-crested crane, the official bird of Uganda. The colours symbolize black for Africa, yellow for sunshine, and red for people working together.

CAPITAL CITY
Kampala

LARGEST CITY
Kampala, population 954 000

LOCATION
Central Africa, 0°29′N/32°46′E (based on the largest city)

MAIN LANGUAGE
English

HEAD OF GOVERNMENT
Elected president (with an honorary king)

CURRENCY
Shilling (USh)

CLIMATES
Tropical, high mountain

Uganda's most famous physical feature is Lake Victoria, which it shares with Tanzania and Kenya. Lake Victoria is Africa's largest fresh water lake—69 490 square kilometres—and it is the main source for the Nile River. No rivers feed into the lake—it is created entirely from rainwater.

Clean Water for the Village

This section describes a water management project in Uganda. It is adapted from a book published by UNICEF called It's Only Right: A Practical Guide to Learning About the Convention on the Rights of the Child. *When you see [square brackets] this tells you that the author of this textbook has changed the original words to make it easier for you to read. When you see three periods . . . this tells you that a section from the original book has been left out here.*

Kids in Action!

In the village of Bbira, north-west of Kampala, the main source of drinking water is a well fed by rainwater. After the rains, water runs off the nearby hillsides and accumulates in a low-lying area. Each day, people from the village bring containers to this well to collect water for cooking, drinking, and washing. Until recently, [animals such as cattle and chickens would also come and stand in and drink this water.] But then the children of Bbira Primary School decided to do something about this water management problem.

The children were involved in a Child-to-Child health education project. In their school, they learned about health issues such as community hygiene [keeping clean], nutrition, road safety, and the use of traditional medicine. With their teachers, they identified the need for clean, safe water as a priority for their village. Then they began making a plan of action.

First, they met with the community leader and discussed the risk of . . . diseases that can result from drinking **contaminated** [polluted] water. The leader then called a village meeting. At this meeting, the children made presentations—poems and dramas that carried messages about the importance of clean water:

Little creatures and plants, hunting for hours and hours—
Water, where are you?
Water, water, water,
When clouds and moisture dance with gusts in the air:
Water, water, water!

The whole community talked about what the children's presentations meant for them. As a result, adults and children set aside time to work together on clearing the well of plant growth and litter. They then built a secure fence to keep out animals. When the entire project was finished, adults and children celebrated together with music and songs. . . .

[The children didn't stop there, though. They decided they must keep up the work of making sure everyone understands how to use the well in a way that keeps the water clean.] By identifying a local health priority and taking practical action, the children are making a life-saving contribution to their community.

'Clean Water for the Village' from *It's Only Right!* by Susan Fountain (UNICEF New York, 1993), page 15. Reprinted by permission of UNICEF.

Try This

With a partner, answer these questions to help you check that you understand what the children in Bbira did in their project.

- *What type of water problem did the village have? (Was it a water shortage problem or a water quality problem?)*
- *Why did the children decide to take action?*
- *Why do you think they talked to the community leader first?*
- *What ways did they use to communicate their ideas at the community meeting?*
- *What was the result of their work?*
- *What are their plans for the future?*
- *What could you learn from their work that would help you make a difference in your school or community?*

Water in Canada

Does Canada have any big water worries? The answer is, yes—and no!

Let's start with what we have. Compared to other countries, Canada has a lot of water. We only have 0.5 per cent of the world's population, but 9 per cent of the world's fresh water.

This water isn't spread evenly around the country, though. A lot of it is in the North, in the Mackenzie River area. This water flows into the Arctic Ocean. Few people live in this part of Canada. In Ontario, Québec, and the Atlantic provinces, there are many people but far less water. In some of the most populated areas in Ontario, most of the water comes from groundwater left from long ago when glaciers covered many parts of the earth. These groundwater deposits are not part of the water cycle, so they're not renewable. Once they're gone, they're gone for good.

Water Use

In our homes, each Canadian uses an average of 340 litres of water a day.

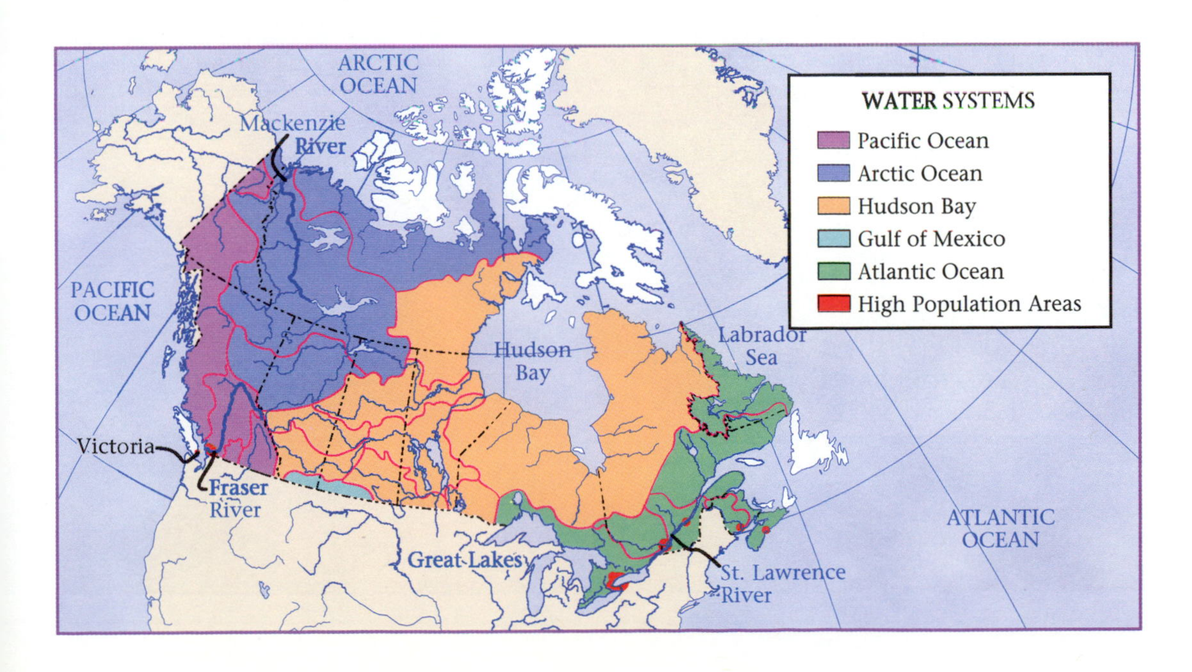

This map shows the water systems and areas of high population discussed in this section. What does the text tell you is the connection between the two?

Water Use in Canadian Homes

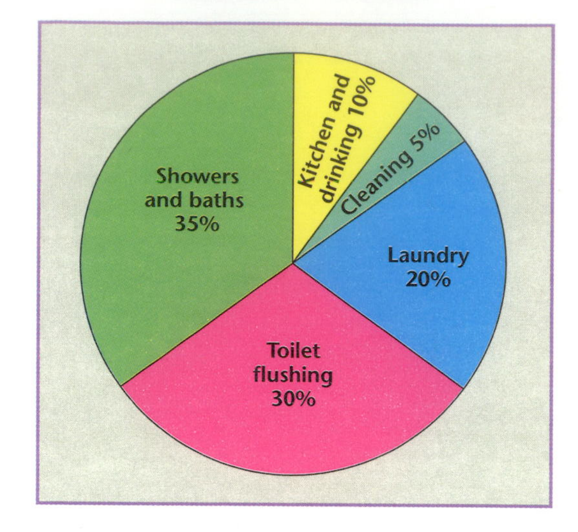

If you had only 6 litres of water a day, what would you use it for?

Americans are the only people in the world who use more water than we do—each American uses 500 litres a day! Some people in other parts of the world, such as Madagascar in Africa, use only 6 litres a day.

Water Quality

In the past, we Canadians haven't taken very good care of our water. Pollution is the worst in areas with the highest population because that's where the most sewage and poisonous chemicals get dumped into the water. These are also the areas where there is the most urban development and farming, both of which can damage watersheds.

In Canada, the Great Lakes, the Fraser River, and the St. Lawrence River have the most serious pollution problems. In the Great Lakes, tests have shown evidence of 360 different chemicals in the water. Many of these chemicals are harmful to people and aquatic life, such as fish, waterfowl, and plants. Many fish species in the Great Lakes suffer from tumours and can no longer reproduce. So the birds and mammals that depend on these fish as a food source are also dying out.

Solutions: Laws

When it comes to passing laws against pollution, Canada is a little better than average. Some countries have more laws and stricter laws. But many countries have fewer laws or

This photograph shows pollution in Lake Ontario. What types and sources of pollution can you identify?

the laws are not followed. Most of Canada's laws and **regulations** (rules made from laws) are to make sure industries don't pollute.

As the harmful effects of pollution are becoming clearer, though, regulations are becoming tougher. Environment Canada has introduced Action Plans to make sure that regulations are followed in areas with the worst pollution problems. There have been some positive results. In the St. Lawrence River, for example, pollution from 50 industries has been reduced by 96 per cent since 1988. In the Fraser River, chemicals used by mills to preserve wood were once a big problem. Today, the dumping of these chemicals has been reduced by 90 per cent. These improvements are just a start. We still have serious pollution problems to solve.

Not everyone agrees that strict laws are the best way to reduce water pollution, though. Some industries say that if the laws become too strict, they won't be able to afford the cost of pollution controls. They say they'll have to shut down and move their businesses to other countries that don't have such strict laws. This would hurt Canada's economy and put people out of work. So the solutions to our pollution problems are not so simple.

Solutions: Technology and Planning

Many Canadian communities need to plan for the future of their water systems. This means thinking of ways to use less water, to pollute less, to treat waste water, and to replace old treatment systems with newer, better ones.

Only 57 per cent of Canadian communities treat their waste water. The others simply return waste water directly to the water system. Canada's record on this issue isn't good compared to other high-income countries. In the United States, 74 per cent of communities treat their sewage, while in Germany the figure is 85.5 per cent and in Sweden it is 99 per cent.

Victoria, the capital of British Columbia, is one example of a Canadian city that has chosen not to treat its waste water. Victoria is located on the tip of Vancouver Island, which means it is surrounded by the Pacific Ocean on three sides. Victoria's water comes from the watershed formed by the mountains to the west of the city. It does not have a sewage treatment plant. Solid waste (such as paper) is filtered out of the water, but everything else flows right into the ocean.

It costs less money to stop pollution from getting into the water than it does to clean it up once it is there. How could this information help communities plan their water management system?

This shows one of the beaches in Victoria. Considering that Victoria gets water from the nearby watershed, and that you can't drink ocean water, do you think that the city manages its water in a sustainable way?

Solutions: Individuals

As individuals, Canadians need to stop thinking about water in the short term and start thinking about how the amount of water we use will add up in the long term. A report prepared for the British Columbia government in 1999 showed that pollution and wasteful water use by individuals is actually a bigger problem in the province than pollution from industries. Inspectors don't go around checking what people do with water in their own homes, so it's up to individuals to regulate themselves.

Water Use	Short-term Thinking = Unsustainable Use	Long-term Thinking = Sustainable Use
Washing hands	Running tap: 9 litres	Filling sink: 4 litres
Brushing teeth	Running tap: 44 litres	Rinsing brush at beginning and end: 2 litres
Bathing in tub	Filling tub: 264 litres	Using just what you need: 110 litres
Having shower	Running water for 10 minutes: 200 litres	Running water for 5 minutes: 100 litres Running water to get wet, soaping up, rinsing off: 18 litres
Flushing toilet	Old-style toilet: 18 litres	New "low-volume" toilet: 6 litres

Subtract the "Sustainable" water amount from the "Short-term Thinking" amount to see how much water would be saved. How could you use this information to make a difference in your community?

Try This

Make a chart like the one below that compares Canada's use and management of water with other countries in the world. You'll have to skim this section to find the information you need.

Water Issue	Canada	Rest of the World
Amount used per person		
Sewage treatment		*(compared to other high-income countries)*
Laws protecting water		

After you have completed your chart, check back to your hypothesis about how well Canadians manage our water. Does this information support your hypothesis, or do you need to change your ideas?

Think For Yourself

In a **debate**, people give oral presentations agreeing or disagreeing with a perspective on an issue. Here's a topic for debate in your class.

The Issue

Many parts of the United States have water shortages. Canada has extra water that could be transported to the United States in various ways. Some people think that selling water to people who can afford it is a good use of this valuable resource. Other people say that we should keep our water for ourselves in case we need it one day.

One Perspective

- Canadians should sell water to the United States.

In a debate, you or your team will be asked to give the main points either *for* or *against* this statement.

Making a Strong Case

Even though you might only have to talk about one perspective, you should write down points for both sides. For each point, think of an argument against it. This will help you decide which are the strongest points you can present for your side. It also means you can have some answers ready when the other team tries to prove you're wrong!

Looking Back

In this chapter, you've learned how the water cycle works and some things we need to do to manage water in a sustainable way.

Why do we have to think of our community, our country, and the global village when we make decisions about water management? What would happen if we only thought of one of these perspectives?

Chapter 7

Cities

Would you rather live in a city or the country?

One hundred years ago, most Canadians lived in the country. Now most Canadians live in cities. This movement of people from the country to the city is happening all over the world. It's called **urban migration**.

As people move from the country to the city, the result is bigger and bigger cities. We're finding out that big cities often mean big problems for people and for the environment. One way to learn about cities and their problems is to investigate one in detail. So we're going to look at Mexico City, the biggest city in the Western Hemisphere.

In this chapter, you can read the story of Mexico City from earliest times until now. You can find out why people first came to live in the area, and why 1700 people a day keep moving there!

What Is a City?

You probably have an idea of what a city is, but how would you define it? What makes a city different from the country?

Population

Geographers usually define cities by population and **population density**.

Each country has its own definition of how many people it takes to make a place a city instead of a town, village, or rural area. For example, in Canada a city is any place with a population of 1000 people or more and a population density of 400 people or more per square kilometre. In Uganda, where there are few cities, a city is a few hundred people or more. In the United States, where there are many cities, the minimum population to make a city is 2500.

The Urban Environment

We can't rely only on statistics to tell us what makes a city a city, though. We also have to know what an **urban environment** is like. You probably know about different natural environments such as forests and deserts. Well, a city is an environment created by people. The comparison chart on page 110 shows you some of the qualities of life that are different in urban and rural environments.

Rural is another term for "country." *Urban* is another term for "city."

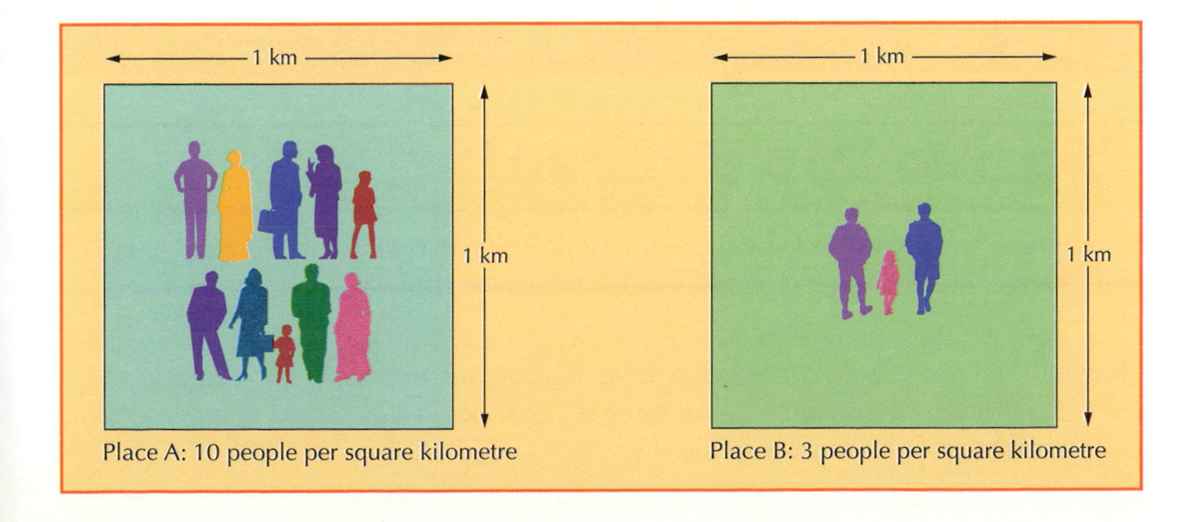

Place A: 10 people per square kilometre

Place B: 3 people per square kilometre

Population density refers to how many people live in a certain area. The usual way to show this is in "people per square kilometre." Which of these places has the highest population density?

Urban and Rural Life

Urban	Quality of Life	Rural
high	Population Density	low
very little—roads and buildings occupy most of the land	Open Space	lots of open space in natural areas or on farms and ranches
offices, shops, factories, and services	Types of Jobs	farming, ranching, forestry, fishing, mining
great variety: basic needs and luxury goods	Shopping	little variety: mostly basic needs
many general doctors and specialists	Health Care	few general doctors, no specialists

Vancouver is the largest city in British Columbia. What can you see that tells you this is an urban environment?

Think For Yourself

Lifestyle refers to how we live our lives, such as what we do for fun and work, our relationships with friends and family, and the things we own.

In a group, brainstorm all the things you can think of that would be part of an urban lifestyle. Then sort your ideas into categories: plus, minus, and interesting. Repeat this for "rural lifestyle." Summarize two or three big changes in lifestyle that happen when people move from the country to the city.

Infrastructure

You might know that **ecosystems** keep the earth's natural environments running. An ecosystem is a community of natural resources that are linked together to make sure every part gets what it needs.

A city environment also needs systems to keep it running. In cities, this is called an **infrastructure**. An infrastructure includes all the services people living in a city need, such as electricity, roads, and water. The people pay for these services through their tax money or by paying directly for some services, such as public transportation. Being able to get these services is one reason people like to live in cities.

Look back to Chapter 6 for more detailed information on water and sewage systems.

Services in a Canadian City

Service	Infrastructure
• drinking water	• plumbing
• sewage disposal	• sewers, sewage treatment centres
• garbage disposal	• garbage pick-up, garbage dumps
• electricity	• above-ground or underground electrical wires
• Internet access	• cable or telephone lines
• telephone	• telephone lines
• public transportation	• roads, buses, trains, subways
• health care	• hospitals, clinics

In many countries of the North some of these services, such as roads, telephones, and electricity, are also available in rural areas. What other services can you think of that you might find only in a city?

Investigate

What do you know about the infrastructure in your community? Pick one of the services that you get in your home and do some research to find out how the technology works, who provides the service, where it comes from, and how it gets to you.

You might want to use a Know Wonder Learn chart like the one below to focus your research. Write down what you know in the first column, what you wonder in the second column, and the information you learn in the final column. Don't forget to check that the facts in your "Know" column are correct!

Know	Wonder	Learn

Once you've gathered your information, make a drawing that illustrates how the service is provided. Use labels, and be colourful and creative!

Tenochtitlán

One of the questions we often ask about cities is, "Why did people first settle here?"

Tenochtitlán [teh-no-shteet-LAN] is the name of the first city built at the site that is now Mexico City. It was built by the Mexica [me-SHEE-ka] around 1300. The Mexica were one of the peoples who made up the great Aztec Empire. Tenochtitlán had beautiful homes, gardens, and canals and great pyramids. In this section, you can find out what made this location a good spot for settlement.

Mexico is a middle-income country in North America. The capital is Mexico City, the official language is Spanish, and the currency is the peso. Mexico has a variety of environments: high mountain, desert, tropical, and equatorial. Mexican culture is a mix of the traditions of the first people who lived in the region and the later Spanish settlers.

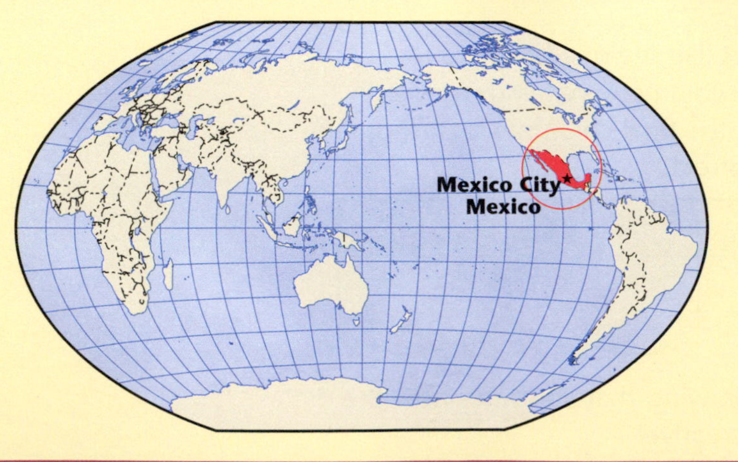

Looking for a Home

According to a traditional story, the Mexica wandered in the deserts of northern Mexico for 100 years before they came to the thick forests and swamps of the place we now call the Valley of Mexico.

Here they found good farmland—the ash from the nearby volcanoes made the soil rich. In the past, farmland was valuable because people could not easily bring in food from other places. There were also lakes and rivers to supply lots of water. Because the valley is high in the mountains it also has a pleasant climate—cooler than the tropical coastal areas.

Other people had already lived in the area for many centuries and had built cities that had large stone buildings. This was something the Mexica had not seen before. They chose a place near the southern end of the valley and started to build their own city.

Based on the records kept by the Mexica and Spanish soldiers, it seems that 200 000 to 250 000 people lived in Tenochtitlán. This is a drawing of what archaeologists think the main square of the city looked like. The pyramids were built to honour their gods.

A City in a Lake

The Mexica built their city on an island in Lake Texcoco [tehs-KOH-koh]. There are several reasons why this was a good site for a city.

- An island was easier to defend because attackers would be slowed down trying to cross the water.
- The lake provided lots of food in the form of fish. Fish could also be traded for resources that weren't available on the island.
- There was plenty of fresh drinking water in the hills nearby, as well as timber and stones for building.

Lake Texcoco was very shallow, so the Mexica easily built **causeways** (bridges of earth) to the shore. There was a wooden bridge on each one that could be pulled up to prevent enemies from crossing. They also used mud and **reeds** (a type of large grass) to fill in the lake and build up areas for growing vegetables and flowers—flowers were an important part of the Mexica's special ceremonies.

The water in Lake Texcoco was slightly salty from all the soil washed into it. So the Mexica built **aqueducts** to bring fresh water from nearby springs. Aqueducts are water pipes that run above the ground. The Mexica also had a garbage collection service and a sewer system that recycled human waste to use to fertilize crops.

Gradually, the city grew bigger and bigger. Canals connected the different areas of land that they had built in the lake. When Spanish soldiers arrived in Tenochtitlán in 1519, they told of the many canoes that crowded the canals—the first Mexican traffic jams!

Tradition says that the Mexica chose their new home because of a sign from one of their gods. They saw an eagle perched on a cactus eating a snake. This was their sign to build their own city. They called it *Tenochtitlán*—Place of the Cactus.

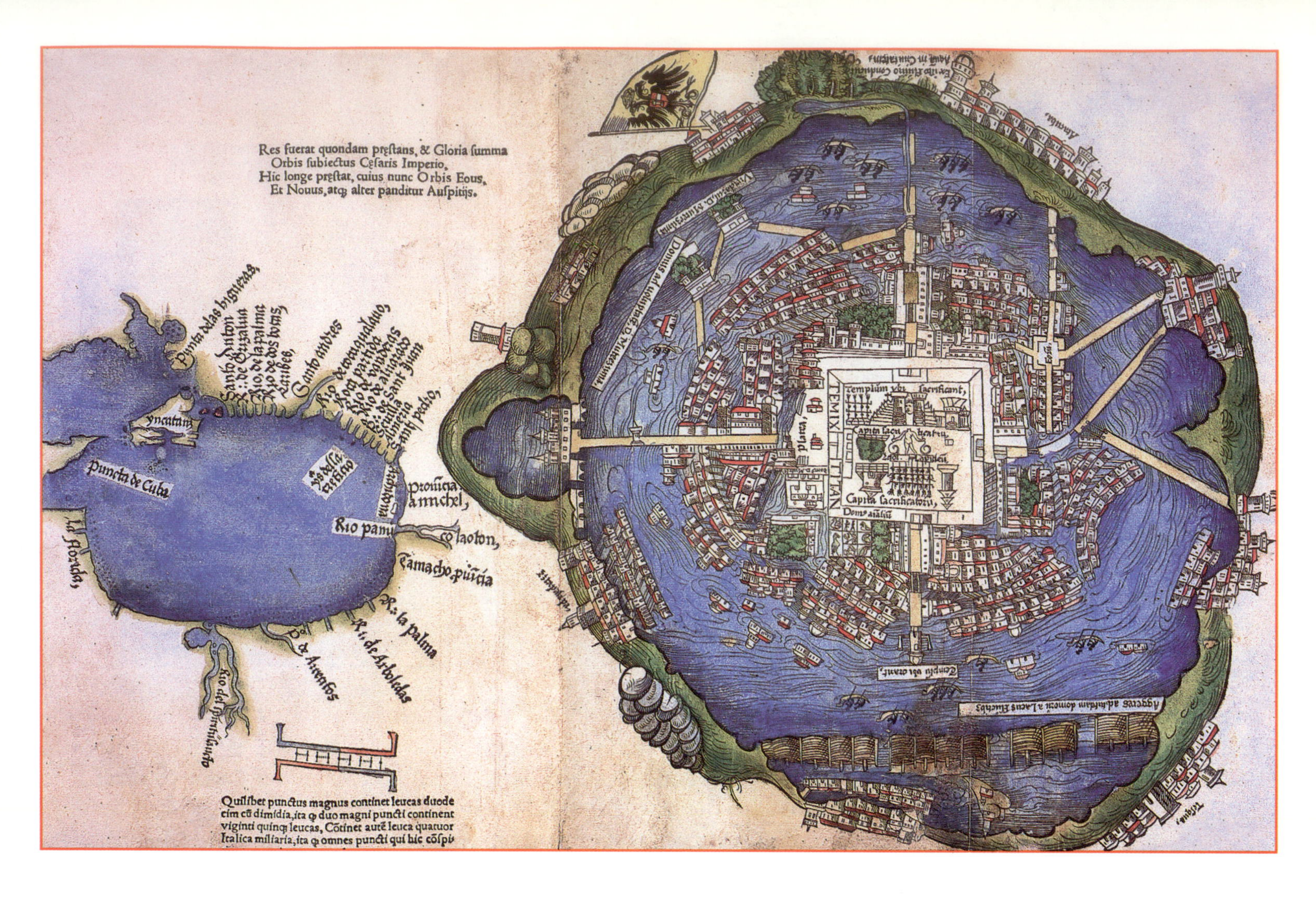

This is a Spanish map of Tenochtitlán. Notice the canals and causeways. In what ways is it like a map you might see of a city today? In what ways is it different?

The Spanish

In 1519, a group of Spanish soldiers, led by Hernán Cortés [er-NAHN kor-TASE], arrived in Tenochtitlán. They were searching for gold and land to claim as colonies for Spain. Battles between the Mexica and the Spaniards soon broke out. In the end, the Aztec Empire surrendered to the Spanish forces and the land became a colony of Spain.

To take control of the area, Cortés had his men build a new city in the same place. Although the buildings were in the Spanish style, Cortés followed much of the plan of Tenochtitlán. The central square of Tenochtitlán, for example, became the central square in Cortés's new city, and the site of the largest Aztec pyramid became the site of a church.

GLOBAL VISIONS GLOBAL VOICES

Diego Rivera [dee-YAY-goh ree-VER-uh] (1886–1957) was a Mexican artist who was famous for the **murals** he painted showing the history and life of the Mexican people. (Murals are large paintings done on walls or buildings.)

Rivera's work reflected traditions from Mexican folklore and Aztec art. He used large, simple shapes and bold colours to tell stories about Mexico's social and political history. Rivera's work can still be seen today on public buildings in Mexico City and in a museum named after him.

This painting is called *Le Grand Tenochtitlán*. What does it tell you about life in this beautiful city?

Try This

Work with a partner or in a small group to create a multimedia display that tells the story of Tenochtitlán. In your display, think of ways to help the viewer understand:

- what resources the environment offered
- other reasons why the island was a good site for a city
- how the Mexica altered the environment to build their city

Do some research to find some information about Tenochtitlán that isn't included in your text. Start by thinking about what you know and what questions you have.

Mexico City

The Zocalo is the central square in Mexico City.

Mexico remained a colony of Spain for 300 years. Then in 1810, the Mexican people rebelled, and Mexico became an independent country in 1821. There were many civil wars as the new country sorted out its problems. More than a million Mexicans died in the worst civil war, which took place between 1910 and 1920. Through it all, Mexico City survived and grew into the place it is today.

In this section, we'll ask some simple questions about Mexico City, such as *How big is it?* and *How many people live there?* But you'll find out the answers aren't so simple!

How big is Mexico City?

In the past, it was easy to say where an urban environment ended and a rural environment began. Cities often had walls around them, and there were large areas of rural land between cities. In those days, you could say "This city is 100 square kilometres." Today, it's not so easy.

Today, cities do not have walls and they spread in many directions, creating large areas that are not quite urban and not quite rural. In areas of dense population, one city can spread into another. So now we usually talk about the size of the **city centre** and the size of the **metropolitan region**. The city centre is the main part of the city where most of the businesses are located. The metropolitan region is the area that surrounds the city centre. It includes many of the homes of people who work in the city.

Over the years, most of the lakes in the Valley of Mexico were filled in to make land to build on as the city grew. Today in Mexico City, the city centre is approximately 1500 square kilometres. The metropolitan region is 2300 square kilometres.

How many people live in Mexico City?

In 1996, the population of Mexico City was almost 17 million people, and the population continues to grow by more than 3 per cent each year. By comparison, the population of Vancouver in 1996 was just under 2 million.

In reality, though, it is hard to get an exact count of the population of

Mexico City. Approximately 1700 new people arrive every day. Many of these people end up living in small, simple shelters built of tin and cardboard around the edge of the city. These communities are called *ciudades perdidas* [see-ooh-DAH-dehs per-DEE dahs]—"lost cities"—by the Mexicans. These areas do not receive services from the city, and nobody knows exactly how many people live in them.

HOW TO... Interpret Aerial Photographs and Satellite Images

Aerial photographs are pictures taken above the earth by someone in a plane. The higher the plane, the more area you see, but the smaller the objects are below. An aerial photograph shows you what things look like from above, usually in the same colours as you would see if you were flying in a plane yourself.

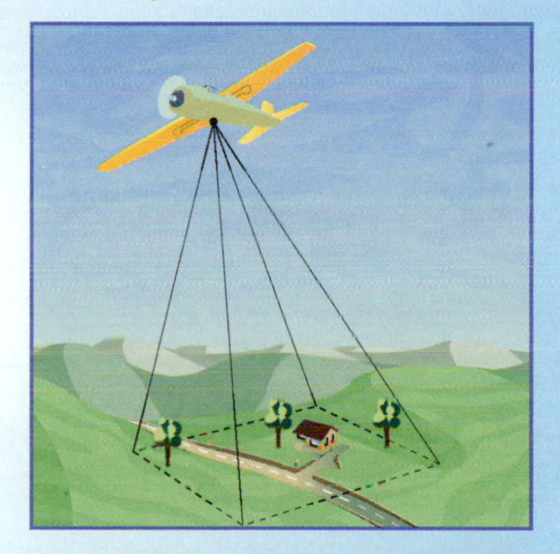

Satellites orbit the earth at a far greater height than airplanes. **Satellite images** are created using a technology called **remote sensing**. Remote sensing may create maps of the earth in unusual colours, depending on the type of equipment and the way the computer is programmed to make the image. For example, warmer areas on earth may be shown in green.

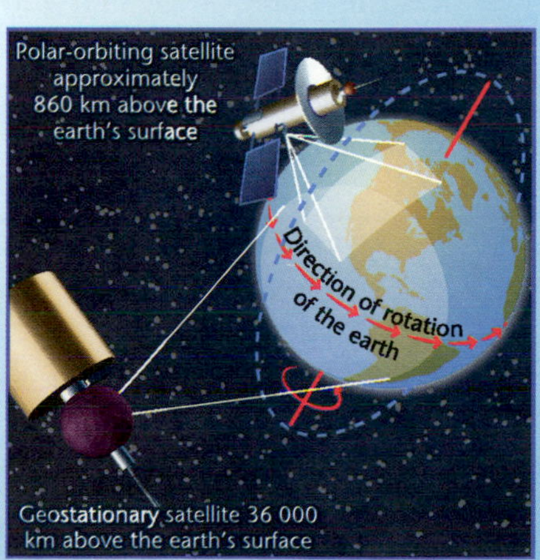

By putting together several photographs or several images, aerial photographs and satellite images can have a **3-D** look. This means that an image can look more like a model of the place than a map. One clue is that you can see the "shadows" of shapes.

There is a satellite image of Mexico City on the next page. There is an aerial photograph on page 98.

This is a satellite image of Mexico City. It shows the Valley of Mexico and the surrounding mountains. This is a view looking towards the southeast. That is, this is almost how you would see it if you could stand really tall in Vancouver and look down towards Mexico City.

Try This

Use the map and satellite image on pages 118 and 119 together to answer the following questions:

- *Is the satellite image a 3-D image or a flat image? Why do you think that?*
- *What colour does Mexico City show up as on the satellite image?*
- *What are the names of the two large volcanoes shown in the satellite image? In what direction are they from the city?*

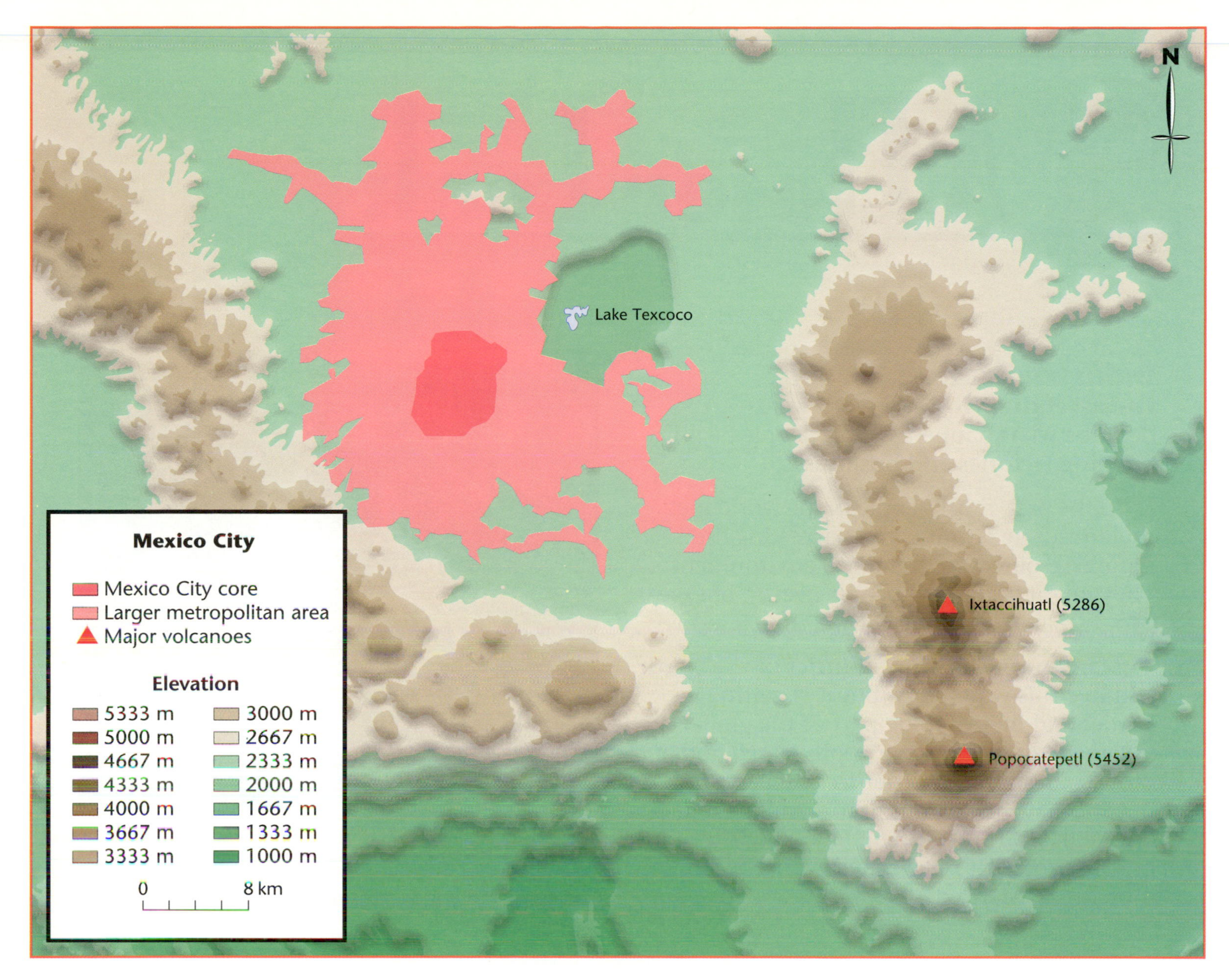

This is a map showing the area in the satellite image on page 118.

What's the big attraction?

Twenty-five per cent of all Mexicans live in Mexico City—that's a very high percentage of the population to live in one place. This wasn't always the case, though. The big movement to the cities started around 1950 when the country began to **industrialize**. Mexico City was already important because it was the centre of government, but now there were more businesses and factories there, too. People started moving to the city hoping to get jobs.

The population density of most of Mexico is 45 people per square kilometre. The population density of Mexico City is 13 925 people per square kilometre. How could you show this on a map?

Industrialization

Industrialization is a word we use to describe what happens when people begin building factories and businesses.

In the past, most people in the world met their needs by farming and harvesting the natural resources in their local environment. They might trade with people nearby, but most people managed to live without much money.

Many people in the countries of the South still live this way today, but it is getting harder and harder to be part of the global village if you don't have goods to sell and money to spend. In order to take part, you need to have industries employing people and making things to sell. So one of the goals of some countries like Mexico is to become more industrialized.

Industrialization requires modern technologies. What changes do you think occur in people's lifestyle and environment as a result of industrialization?

Today, over 30 per cent of all of Mexico's factories are in Mexico City.

At the same time, life in rural areas was becoming more difficult. Growing populations meant that there were more people to support on the same area of land. New farming equipment meant that fewer people were needed to farm the land. So now there were many more people but fewer and fewer jobs.

Think For Yourself

Before learning more about Mexico City, hypothesize possible problems the city might be facing as a result of rapid population growth. Then hypothesize what effects you think industrialization has had on the environment in the Valley of Mexico.

¡Qué Problema!

¡Qué problema!—What a problem!—is what many Mexicans say about their huge capital city. Many of Mexico City's problems are because the infrastructure can't keep up with the fast pace of population growth. This same problem faces all large cities, including cities in Canada.

Every city has a **municipal government** to make decisions and a **planning department** to figure out the best way to provide people with services. In this section, you can look at some of the challenges facing the planning department in Mexico City.

Water

"You never know if you will have water or not," says Paula. "Last year our taps were dry from May to August. Then when there is water, it is dark brown and sometimes it even has worms in it."

Paula lives in the eastern part of Mexico City. This is a fast-growing neighbourhood of middle-income people. People who live in the western part of the city are closer to water sources, so they have a better water supply than people in Paula's neighbourhood—but it's still not safe to drink. The people in the *ciudades perdidas* have no water service at all. The problem is not only a lack of water for drinking and washing, but also a lack of water to carry away sewage.

This family in Mexico has gathered to celebrate a special event. In what ways does your family celebrate special events?

The main sources of water for Mexico City are the same aquifers the Aztecs used. Because of the high population, though, this is not enough, and the valley is drying up. Water has to be brought in from further and further away and piped to more and more homes. This is very expensive, and the planning department can't keep up with people's needs.

The second problem is that the many miles of water pipes are hard to keep in good repair. Mexico City is built on land that was once marsh and lakes. This means the land is very soft, so buildings and pipes can sink and break. The area is also in an earthquake zone, so small tremors frequently shake the ground and add to the damage. When there is a big earthquake, it is a real disaster.

Building to withstand earthquakes is important in Mexico City. Sometimes people living in tin and cardboard dwellings are better off than those people living in poorly built brick buildings. In earthquakes, poorly built brick buildings tumble, causing a lot of damage and injuries.

Housing

"Yesterday we found a large piece of tin roofing. I'm really happy because it will be better in the rain than the cardboard wall we have now."

Miguel lives in one of the *cuidades perdidas*. He and his family of two sisters, one brother, mother and father, and an aunt share a small, simple shelter that is about the size of a living room in the average Canadian home. They are glad to have this place to live in. Many of the poorest people in Mexico City have no homes at all and must live on the streets.

There are, of course, many nice homes and apartment buildings in Mexico City. The problem is that there is such a demand for housing, it can't be built fast enough. This means the housing that is available is too expensive for many people, and so they create their own shelter in the *cuidades perdidas*.

Transportation

"It is always faster to walk in Mexico City than to drive!"

Imagine rush-hour traffic in a big city. Mexico City is like that pretty much all the time! When there are a lot of people living in a small space, there needs to be a way to

The people who live in the *ciudades perdidas* take pride in their communities. In many areas, people have worked together to provide services such as garbage collection for themselves.

get them to where they want to go. As Mexico's economy improves, more and more people own their own cars. But there aren't enough roads to handle all of the traffic, so there are many traffic jams.

A faster way to move people is on a **subway** system. These are trains that travel mostly underground. Mexico City has one of the cheapest and best-maintained subway systems in the world. The system carries almost 5 million people each day. This is one way to help the city's pollution problem and traffic jams.

Many students in Mexico City take the *Metro* to school. How does this compare with how you get to school? If you lived in Mexico City, would you prefer to ride on the subway (shown at the bottom of the photo) or use a car? Why?

Air

"One year the air was so polluted we all got to stay home from school for two months!" explains Maria. "The bad part is that it's not much fun playing outside when the air is hard to breathe."

The many industries and cars in Mexico City have created serious air pollution problems. High carbon dioxide levels are one problem. Another problem is that Mexico doesn't have strict laws about fuels and car engines, so the exhaust from vehicles puts out a high amount of lead into the air. Lead is especially dangerous to children.

Because Mexico City is in a valley, the air pollution doesn't blow away. Instead, it settles over the city. All the trees that grew in the valley when the Mexica first arrived have long been cut down to make farms or space for the city to grow. So there are no natural filters to take the pollution out of the air.

The pollution is so thick that you can no longer see the volcanoes of Popocatepetl [pah-puh-KAT-uh-pe-tul] and Ixtaccihuatl [iks-TAK-ee-wah-tul] from the city. They were once Mexico City's most famous sites.

Work and Conflict

In Mexico City, at least 30 per cent of people cannot find work—that's a very high number.

"My father thought he would be able to get a job in a factory, but it's not so easy," explains Elvira. "My mother makes party hats for children to wear at festivals and I sell them on the street. Sometimes I have to move on, though, when another person wants my spot."

Although there are more opportunities for work in the city than in the country, there are also more people looking for work. This means wages are often quite low and jobs are hard to find. Of course, people who are unemployed have trouble meeting their basic needs. Sometimes this leads to other problems, such as crime. People who already work in the city may feel their jobs are threatened when newcomers arrive. Sometimes this causes conflict between different groups of people.

A **street vendor** is a person who sells things on the sidewalk. This is an inexpensive way to do business because you don't need to own or rent a store. Many children work as street vendors by themselves or with their parents.

Try This

1. In a group, make a point-form summary of the challenges facing Mexico City described in this section. You might want to use an organizer like the one below to record your notes.

Problem	Reasons

2. Check the hypotheses you made about the challenges facing Mexico City. Is there anything you'd like to change or add? This book doesn't describe *all* the challenges facing Mexico City. You might have some hypotheses that you still think are good, but haven't been proven or disproven by this new information.

Think For Yourself

Here's your chance to do some city planning.

In a group, brainstorm possible solutions to two or three of Mexico City's problems. Pick a solution that you all agree seems like a good idea. Use an organizer like this one to think about it in more detail.

The Proposed Solution

Who would benefit and how?	
Who else would be affected and how?	
How would it affect the environment?	
How could this be paid for?	

What additional information do you need to make a complete plan?

Looking Back

The reasons for urban migration that you learned about in this chapter are similar in all parts of the world. The challenges for cities are also similar. Canadian cities such as Vancouver are also working to find solutions to poverty, homelessness, traffic jams, air pollution, and poor water quality or water shortages.

How can studying one city give us ideas about how to improve all cities? What is your vision of the "city of the future"?

Chapter 8

Sharing the Knowledge

For as long as anyone can remember, the Chukchi have herded reindeer in the far north of Asia. The Haisla of British Columbia have hunted and fished in the forests of the Kitlope Valley. The Yanomami have farmed in the tropical rainforests of the Amazon River in South America. What do these people have in common?

These are all examples of **indigenous** [in-DIJ-uh-nus] **peoples**. They are the first people to have lived on their lands. People of indigenous cultures have generations of knowledge about how to live in a sustainable way in their environments. This is valuable information for the global village.

Today, indigenous peoples around the world say that their rights are not respected in the countries where they live. Some cultures are actually **endangered**—their traditions, knowledge, and sometimes even the people themselves are at risk of disappearing forever from the planet.

In this chapter, you can learn some basic information about this issue that can help you learn more on your own.

Land and Culture

There are about 5000 different indigenous peoples in 70 different countries in the world. Each group has its own culture, with different ways of meeting basic needs, expressing thoughts and feelings, and keeping organized.

Some indigenous people live in traditional ways on the same lands where their ancestors lived for as long as people can remember. Some live in towns and cities where they work at a variety of jobs. Wherever they live, their cultural identities as indigenous peoples are important to them. In this section, you can learn about three big threats to indigenous cultures: loss of land, assimilation, and resource development.

Loss of Land

One thing that people of indigenous cultures have in common is a strong feeling that they are part of the land where they live. They feel that the land takes care of them, and that they must also take care of the land. Many parts of their cultures, from daily life to beliefs, are based on this important idea. To be separated from their land is the same as being separated from their culture.

Assimilation

Assimilation means to become part of something else. When people are assimilated, they become part of another culture and lose their own traditions. If this happens to everyone in a culture, then the culture dies out.

Language is one of the most import ways in which people pass on their culture. Assimilation can happen in many ways, but people are always in danger of being assimilated if they cannot easily use their own language. For example, if children must speak another language at school they might forget their first language.

"Travelling the Sahara is our life. It's who we are. If we are held back, our life is ripped from us." *A Tuareg [TWAH-reg] man*

The Tuareg

The Tuareg's home is the Sahara Desert of North Africa. They live in small groups that spend most of their time travelling to find pasture for their herds of goats, sheep, and camels. In the past, the Tuareg were also important and rich traders.

Since the 1960s, countries in the Sahara have made it hard for the Tuareg to cross their borders when they travel. Growing populations in these countries also mean that there is less food for their animals to eat. Life is changing for the Tuareg now, and many are afraid their culture will not survive.

In the past, the Canadian government thought Aboriginal peoples would have better lives if they were assimilated—that is, became more like Europeans. Traditional ceremonies were illegal and children were forced to live at schools where they had to speak French or English. This made it difficult for the Elders to pass on their traditions. Even with this great challenge, though, many Aboriginal peoples kept their cultures strong.

"I am the only one left now. The only full-blooded Eyak [EE-yak]. . . . The only one who speaks the language. I tell you, it hurts. It really hurts." *Marie Smith, Eyak peoples of Alaska*

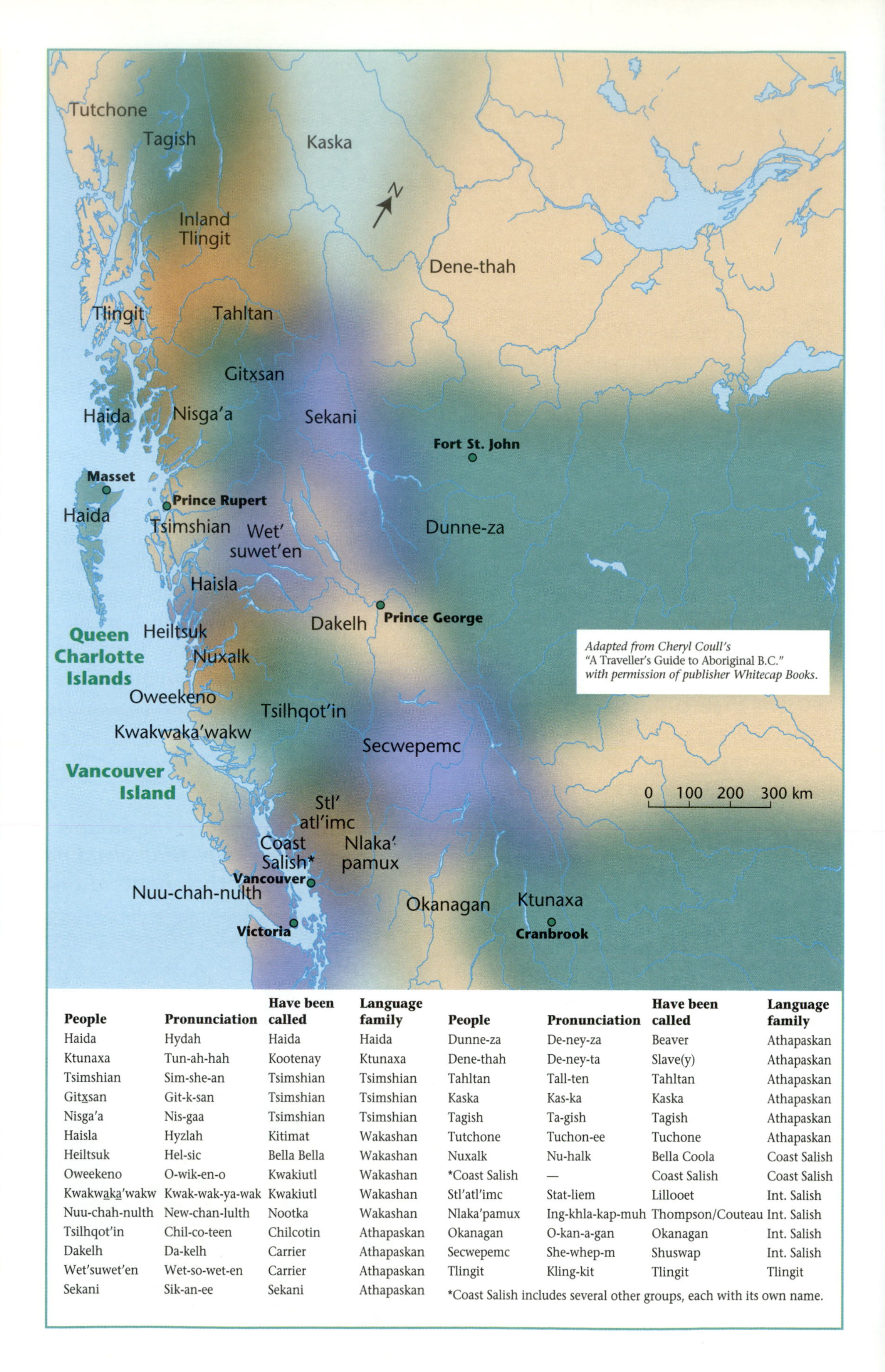

People	Pronunciation	Have been called	Language family
Haida	Hydah	Haida	Haida
Ktunaxa	Tun-ah-hah	Kootenay	Ktunaxa
Tsimshian	Sim-she-an	Tsimshian	Tsimshian
Gitxsan	Git-k-san	Tsimshian	Tsimshian
Nisga'a	Nis-gaa	Tsimshian	Tsimshian
Haisla	Hyzlah	Kitimat	Wakashan
Heiltsuk	Hel-sic	Bella Bella	Wakashan
Oweekeno	O-wik-en-o	Kwakiutl	Wakashan
Kwakwaka'wakw	Kwak-wak-ya-wak	Kwakiutl	Wakashan
Nuu-chah-nulth	New-chan-lulth	Nootka	Wakashan
Tsilhqot'in	Chil-co-teen	Chilcotin	Athapaskan
Dakelh	Da-kelh	Carrier	Athapaskan
Wet'suwet'en	Wet-so-wet-en	Carrier	Athapaskan
Sekani	Sik-an-ee	Sekani	Athapaskan
Dunne-za	De-ney-za	Beaver	Athapaskan
Dene-thah	De-ney-ta	Slave(y)	Athapaskan
Tahltan	Tall-ten	Tahltan	Athapaskan
Kaska	Kas-ka	Kaska	Athapaskan
Tagish	Ta-gish	Tagish	Athapaskan
Tutchone	Tuchon-ee	Tuchone	Athapaskan
Nuxalk	Nu-halk	Bella Coola	Coast Salish
*Coast Salish	—	Coast Salish	Coast Salish
Stl'atl'imc	Stat-liem	Lillooet	Int. Salish
Nlaka'pamux	Ing-khla-kap-muh	Thompson/Couteau	Int. Salish
Okanagan	O-kan-a-gan	Okanagan	Int. Salish
Secwepemc	She-whep-m	Shuswap	Int. Salish
Tlingit	Kling-kit	Tlingit	Tlingit

*Coast Salish includes several other groups, each with its own name.

In Canada, indigenous peoples include Aboriginal groups in every province and territory. This map shows the traditional territories of Aboriginal groups in British Columbia. In which territory do you live?

The Haisla

The Haisla's traditional lands include the Kitlope Valley in British Columbia. This area is rich in natural resources, especially salmon. In the past, the Haisla spent winters in their villages and travelled during the summer to gather resources. Today, most Haisla live in communities in the area, such as Kitamaat Village.

It is not always easy for Haisla youth. There are few jobs in their communities, but if they move away then they will leave behind their families and their culture. This means some hard choices. But the Haisla will always have their land. When companies wanted to log the Kitlope Valley, the Elders organized a protest. Because of this, the Kitlope Valley is now a protected area—it can never be used for industrial development.

Resource Development

As the world's population increases and more countries become industrialized, there are greater and greater demands for the world's resources.

Many indigenous peoples live in lands that were once considered unimportant, such as the far north and deep within tropical forests. Today, though, these areas are valued for the natural resources they contain. Businesses and governments want to develop these areas—that is, to go in and harvest the resources. The problem is that such development often doesn't benefit indigenous peoples and may even go against their way of life and their ideas about caring for the land.

The Yanomami

These photos show a Yanomami [yah-noh-MAH-mee] village and a girl getting ready for a party. The Yanomami live in villages in the Amazon jungle in Brazil and Venezuela. They gather jungle plants, and hunt and fish with bows and arrows. They also plant gardens with almost 60 different kinds of crops.

Until about 1975, the Yanomami had very little contact with other cultures. Then gold miners came to the area. They brought diseases that killed hundreds of Yanomami. They cut down trees and their mining operations poisoned the rivers with mercury. When the Yanomami tried to protest, many of them were shot by the miners.

With the help of people from other countries, a Yanomami man called Davi travelled around the world to tell others about what was happening to his people. He brought attention to their problem, and because of this a large area was set aside for the Yanomami. The gold miners don't always respect the Yanomami's right to this land, though, and so the problems continue.

The Chukchi

The Chukchi [CHOOK-chee] live in the Arctic region of Russia. This is a very cold climate, with few plant or animal resources. Reindeer have traditionally provided the Chukchi with food, shelter, and clothing. Chukchi communities keep large herds of reindeer. They travel with the reindeer, moving constantly to find enough food for the animals to eat.

The first big change to Chukchi life came in the 1930s when people from the southern part of the country came to the area and built a tin mine. The people from the south introduced manufactured goods and the Russian language. Soon, Chukchi children were attending Russian schools, and everyone was learning new ways of doing things.

Recently, though, the tin mine closed down, and things are changing for the Chukchi again. The people from the south are leaving and many of the Russian schools are closing. Now many Chukchi wonder what's best for their future. Should they go back to their traditional ways, or try to become more Russian?

Think For Yourself

With a partner, look at each of the photos in this section. Discuss the facts about the culture you can gather from the photos and the descriptions. Look for information on traditions, threats to the culture, and how things are today. For each photo, also write down one question that you have.

On your own, pick the photo that you find most interesting. In your social studies journal or notebook, explain why this culture or this particular photo interests you.

The Challenge of Change

A minority is a small group of people that is outnumbered by others. When a group is in the minority, it doesn't have much power to affect government decisions.

Wherever they are in the world, indigenous peoples are concerned about protecting their cultures. For some peoples, the damage to their cultures started one or two hundred years ago, and now they want to make their cultures strong again. This is the case for many Aboriginal groups in Canada. For some peoples, the threats are more recent. This is the case for people such as the Yanomami.

Indigenous peoples know the world is changing and that their cultures may also need to change in some ways—all cultures change over time. But they want to make sure that *they* are the ones to decide which traditions to keep and which ones to change. They don't want change forced upon them by others. Because they are **minorities** in the countries where they live, their rights are often ignored.

Grand Chief George Manuel was a Secwepemc [she-whep-m] Elder who helped get the World Council of Indigenous Peoples started. He was its president from 1975 to 1981. Manuel, who died in 1989, is remembered for helping others to see that the rights of indigenous peoples were not being respected and for helping indigenous peoples to feel strong enough to speak out about their concerns.

Taking Action

In recent years, indigenous peoples from around the world have decided to form groups to work together to make sure others respect their rights. One such organization, the World Council of Indigenous Peoples, was started in Port Alberni, British Columbia, in 1975. One important thing they did at the first meeting was to write a **declaration** setting out their views on the rights of indigenous peoples. Today this is one of the groups that speak for indigenous peoples at the United Nations.

Think For Yourself

In your own words, **summarize** the four main ideas in the section of the World Council of Indigenous Peoples' declaration shown on page 133.

The Solemn Declaration of the World Council of Indigenous Peoples

We glory in our proud past:
when the earth was our nurturing mother,
when the night sky formed our common roof....
when our great civilizations grew under the sun....

Then other peoples arrived:
thirsting for blood, for gold, for land and all its wealth,
carrying the cross and the sword, one in each hand
without knowing or waiting to learn the ways of our worlds,
they considered us to be lower than the animals,
they stole our land from us and took us from our lands....

However, they have never been able to eliminate us,
nor to erase our memories of what we were....

Now, we come from the four corners of the earth,
we protest before the concert of nations....

And rising up after centuries of oppression,
evoking the greatness of our ancestors....

We vow to control again our own destiny and
recover our complete humanity and
pride in being Indigenous People.

HOW TO... Summarize Main Ideas

Here are some tips on how to summarize main ideas. In addition to words, you might also want to draw pictures.

1. Read the selection once to get the big picture.
2. Read the selection again to find the main ideas. Headings are often clues to main ideas.
3. Write down the ideas in point form.
4. Summarize the ideas in a few sentences or a paragraph *written in your own words.*

Learning from Each Other

We don't know for sure if the answers to the world's problems can be found in the traditions of the past, but if we don't listen while we still can, we will never know!

In recent years, many people in the global village have started to wonder if industrialization and urbanization are the best ways to live on the earth—chapters 6 and 7 told you about some of the challenges we face. Today, people are looking for better ways to do things.

Sometimes people are finding that some of the oldest ideas may be the best. In their **traditional knowledge**, indigenous peoples have a wealth of information to share. This section tells you about three important ways traditional knowledge is helping solve problems in the world today.

The Inuit Circumpolar [sur-kum-POLE-ur] Conference is an organization of Inuit in Greenland, Canada, Alaska, and Russia who work together to watch over the environment and to protect the way of life of the Inuit. Inuit know a great deal about the environment, and they want to share their knowledge with others.

Development and Conservation

In recent years, many projects to extract resources, such as mining and logging, have badly damaged local environments. Now some people think that we should gather information and predict what the results might be *before* we do something that might harm the environment.

This type of study takes a lot of time and money, though. Now scientists are learning that they can save time *and* do a better job if they work with local indigenous peoples. Indigenous people already have gathered traditional knowledge, and it is reliable because it is based on centuries of careful observation.

Sustainable Resource Management

Traditional knowledge includes many ideas about sustainable ways to farm, fish, use forests, and herd animals. Many farms in industrialized countries rely on chemical fertilizers to keep the soil rich and pesticides to kill harmful insects. But these chemicals are expensive and they harm the environment. Here are three sustainable solutions from indigenous cultures:

- Farmers in Zacchilla [sahk-CHEE-yah], Mexico, use the waste left in anthills to fertilize tomatoes, chillies, and onions.
- Several different peoples in East Asia and Oceania use fishing and farming systems that work together. Waste from the farms feed fish that are kept in ponds, and waste from the fish is used to fertilize the soil.
- In Niger [NY-jer] in Africa, insects called *locusts* are a problem. A swarm of locusts can completely destroy an entire field of crops. People use the leaves and seeds of the neem tree to keep locusts away.

Keeping Healthy

In the past, all people relied on the plants in their environment to help them when they got sick. People learned from their Elders such things as which roots might cure a stomach ache and which leaves would help heal a wound.

Today many people use medicines manufactured by drug companies. But even these may come from traditional knowledge. Approximately 120 modern medicines are based on plants. For example, the chemical in aspirin was first found in willow trees. Seventy-five per cent of these plant-based medicines came from knowledge shared by **shamans**—the healers in indigenous communities. Some researchers believe that plants in tropical forests are our best hope for finding new treatments and cures for diseases.

Traditional medicines are still an important part of health care, especially in the countries of the South. The World Health Organization estimates that 80 per cent of the people in the world rely on traditional medicines.

Preserving Traditional Knowledge

When you preserve something, you keep it safe for the future. Because of the threats of loss of land, assimilation, and development of resources, it is becoming more and more difficult for indigenous peoples to preserve their knowledge of their environment and the useful plants in it. For example, researchers estimate that about 90 indigenous groups in the Amazon River area have become extinct since 1900. Their knowledge of their parts of the tropical rainforest is gone forever.

To preserve this kind of knowledge, people need two main things: their land and the freedom to practice their culture. The Amazon Action Team (ACT) is one group that is working to make a difference. In Colombia, Costa Rica, Mexico, and Suriname, people from ACT are working with people in indigenous communities to find ways to keep cultures strong and protect people's rights to their land.

This kind of work isn't only going on in the tropical regions, however. In Canada, many Aboriginal groups have projects to record the knowledge of their Elders, and they are active in protecting their lands from over-development. They are also sharing their knowledge with medical researchers.

The whole global village benefits from these kinds of projects. Indigenous peoples benefit because their rights to their way of life are protected. People from other cultures benefit from the knowledge indigenous peoples have to share and from the environments they protect.

The Ojibway people of the Serpent River First Nation are one group who are teaching researchers what they know about the plants in their traditional lands.

Think For Yourself

Imagine that you are a member of the World Council of Indigenous Peoples. You have been asked to speak at a meeting of the Commission on Human Rights at the United Nations. Prepare a short oral presentation that will help others understand the challenges facing indigenous peoples and why others should listen to what they have to say. Think about human rights as well as the benefits to the global village. (Check "How To. . . Speak Out" on page 172 for tips on making a strong oral presentation.)

Aboriginal Peoples of Australia

With 5000 cultures to chose from, it's hard to pick just one indigenous culture to study in depth! In this section, you can find out about the Aboriginal peoples of Australia. This may give you ideas on how you could research and report on an indigenous culture that interests you.

The First Peoples of Australia

The country known as Australia today was started by colonists from England. When the colonists arrived, there were about 300 000 Aboriginal people living in the land. There were about 650 separate groups, who spoke about 250 languages. The people lived well in the many different environments in Australia, including the great central desert. Their culture included a tradition of beautiful rock paintings, storytelling, and music. The Aboriginal peoples of Australia are the descendants of these peoples. Here is their story.

Cultural Traditions

In the past, Aboriginal peoples of Australia lived in family groups that spent most of their time travelling.

Cathy Freeman was the first Aboriginal athlete to represent Australia at the Olympics. In 1996, she won a silver medal for the 400 metre dash.

Each group moved across its territory to hunt, fish, and gather plants. They made their tools, shelter, and clothing out of natural materials, such as sticks, bones, and hides.

Use of Resources

Australia has a variety of environments, so people relied on different resources depending on where they lived. For example, people who lived near rivers and oceans would spear fish. People who lived in the drier

Think what you know about Canadian history. What things does Canada have in common with Australia?

regions became skilful at finding water—one way was to dig up a type of frog that stores water in its belly! Some groups had small farms.

Today, Aboriginal methods of finding food and water are taught to Australian soldiers so that they can survive in the desert.

To survive, Aboriginal groups had to study the land and animals carefully. They knew when to move on before they took too much and when to come back to an area when the hunting, fishing, or gathering would be good again.

Values and Beliefs

According to Aboriginal beliefs, the land and its people were created by their ancestors during a long ago Dreamtime. Every person is connected to a particular place in the land by stories called *Dreamings*. Dreamings also tell about why the land and animals are the way they are.

Because Aboriginal culture was so unfamiliar to the English, they didn't consider Aboriginal peoples to be "people." They declared the land "empty" and ready for settlement.

The Elders teach that the ancestors gave them the responsibility to care for the land by using resources with respect. They have many sacred sites and special ceremonies to honour these responsibilities.

The English Arrive

Aboriginal culture was almost destroyed when the English took over Australia. This began in 1770, when the explorer Captain James Cook claimed the land he called *Australia* for England.

Conflicts Over Land and Resources

From the beginning, the newcomers and Aboriginal peoples did not understand each other. Aboriginal peoples did not understand the idea that people could own land, crops, and animals. When settlers set up farms and ranches on Aboriginal lands, Aboriginal peoples thought it was their right to take whatever crops and animals they wanted. Besides, the settlers had made it impossible for them to hunt in their traditional ways. The settlers saw this as stealing and they shot many Aboriginal people. Aboriginal people also killed settlers.

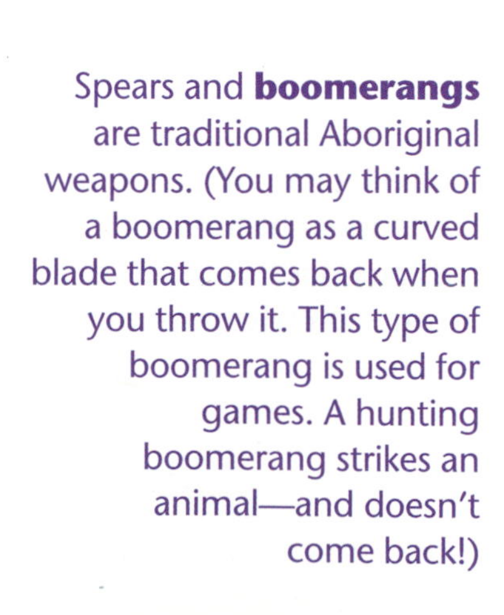

Spears and **boomerangs** are traditional Aboriginal weapons. (You may think of a boomerang as a curved blade that comes back when you throw it. This type of boomerang is used for games. A hunting boomerang strikes an animal—and doesn't come back!)

GLOBAL VISIONS GLOBAL VOICES

The Wiradjuri [wee-ruh-JOO-ree] Aboriginal people tell this Dreaming to explain why the platypus is a special animal that is not to be hunted.

Very early in the Dreamtime the ancestor spirits were deciding on the animal shapes they would take. The animals, the water creatures, and birds were all trying to prove they were the best.

All the birds decided to hold a special meeting to prove they were the most important of all the creatures. Birds of all species came along, and it was an impressive gathering. The birds decided to invite the platypus [PLAT-ah-pus]. "He and his mate certainly belong among us," they said. "She lays eggs and they each have a bill like a duck."

The platypus went to the meeting and listened as the birds all declared they were the most important of all the creatures. Once they had said many speeches and convinced themselves they were important, they invited the platypus to join them.

"I'll think about it," promised the platypus as he scampered back to his mate in their waterside hole, the birds all screeching and squawking or chirping a 'goodbye.'

Soon after this, all the land animals had their own special meeting. They also wanted to prove that they were the most important of all the creatures. Every animal, large and small, was invited, and many speeches were made. They also decided to invite the platypus to join them. "After all," said the kangaroo, "he runs on land and is covered in fur as we are."

The platypus was surprised and happy to be receiving so much attention, but he gave them

the same answer as he had given the birds—he would have to think about it.

Not long after, a big fish called a meeting of the water creatures to prove their importance. They too decided to honour the platypus by asking him to join them. "After all," said the big fish, "his home is by the water's edge, and he has webbed feet and swims well."

The platypus was very polite, but he gave the same answer—"I will think about it." And he did think about it—he didn't know which group to join. He discussed it with his family, who weren't sure what to do. Then his friend the echidna [ih-KID-nuh] gave him some advice that he decided to follow.

He invited all the creatures to come to a meeting near his home. You can imagine the noises and chatter and fuss as so many creatures gathered together! Each group thought the platypus would join them and was pleased the other groups would hear the decision. But here is what the platypus said.

"You are all my friends. I am grateful that Byamee, the father-of-all, has seen fit to make me a little bit like each of you." Platypus paused and everyone listened eagerly for his decision.

"After much thought, my family and I have decided not to join any one group." The other creatures murmured in disbelief. "It is my hope that each time one of you sees a member of my family, you will be reminded that Byamee made each one of us differently for a reason. We may not understand the reason, but we must learn to respect each other much more than we do." Platypus bowed his head to show he had no more to say.

For a moment, there was complete silence, but gradually the creatures began to clap. They realized that what the platypus said was important and true. Slowly, in a quiet way, they all left the gathering—wiser than they had been before.

"Why the Platypus is Special" from *From the Dreamtime*, by Jean A. Ellis (North Blackburn, Victoria: Collins Dove, 1991). Reprinted by permission of Harper Collins Publishers, Australia.

In fights between Aboriginal peoples and settlers, historians estimate 20 000 Aboriginal people and 2000 settlers were killed. In the end, the settlers won because they had rapid-fire rifles and organized themselves to fight.

Although Australia is a high-income country, many Aboriginal people live in very poor conditions. They live an average of 20 years less than other Australians. Their average income is approximately half the income of non-Aboriginal Australians.

Disease

Aboriginal peoples also had no resistance to European diseases such as smallpox and tuberculosis. Death from disease and from the conflicts with Europeans meant that 100 years after Europeans arrived there were only about 80 000 Aboriginal people left in Australia. They became the minority in their own land.

Discrimination and Assimilation

Aboriginal peoples were not given any of the benefits that settlers in Australia received. They had to move onto reservations, which prevented them from hunting and gathering resources in a sustainable way. Their children were taken from them to be taught European culture. Aboriginal people were not allowed to vote. There seemed to be no place for Aboriginal culture in the new country of Australia.

Taking Action

Aboriginal peoples were scattered in small groups across the country, so it was hard for them to have one strong voice to demand their rights. In the 1960s, though, it looked like some of the lands that they still had were about to be developed by mining companies. Aboriginal peoples in Australia had heard about action taken by Aboriginal groups in North America. They decided to fight for their rights.

Over the next few years, Aboriginal people made speeches and wrote letters to the government demanding the rights to their lands. As a result of their protests, they got the right to vote. Soon some Aboriginal people were elected to the government. They also got back the rights to care for some of their most sacred sites, such as Uluru. Now there are many different land rights issues being discussed in Australia.

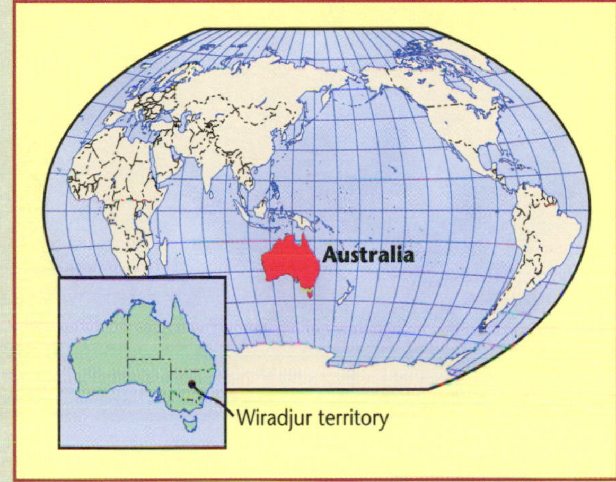

The British flag in the corner shows Australia's connection to England. The large star represents the joining of the Australian states. The pattern of small stars represents the Southern Cross—a **constellation** you can see from Australia.

CAPITAL CITY
Canberra

LARGEST CITY
Sydney, population 3 770 100

LOCATION
Oceania, 33°55′S/151°10′E (based on the largest city)

MAIN LANGUAGE
English

HEAD OF GOVERNMENT
Elected prime minister (with a constitutional monarchy headed by the British monarch)

CURRENCY
Australian dollar ($A)

CLIMATES
Tropical, desert, coastal, Mediterranean

Uluru is a large rock located in the desert of central Australia. It is approximately 2.5 kilometres long and 300 metres high. Uluru is a sacred site for Aboriginal peoples—the name means "Earth Mother." In the past, Europeans called it Ayers Rock.

In a court case called the Mabo judgment, the highest court in Australia decided that Aboriginal peoples have the right to their traditional lands. Because miners and farmers are already on those lands, though, it will take some time to figure out the fairest solutions.

A Better Future

As well as fighting in court, Aboriginal peoples are working to help themselves in their communities. Community centres teach young people about their culture and the skills they need in today's world.

Residents of some communities have formed groups to improve housing and health care. There is also a new interest in Aboriginal art and music, which is becoming famous around the world.

These Aboriginal children are taking part in a traditional ceremony that includes body painting. Why is it especially important for children to take part in cultural events in the community?

Try This

Work with a partner to make an outline that shows the topics, subtopics, and main ideas in this section on Aboriginal peoples of Australia. Look over the outline. What other topics or subtopics would you include in a report on an indigenous people? What ways besides writing could you use to present information?

Investigate

Prepare a report on an indigenous people that interests you. Once you have sorted your evidence, make an outline to help make sure your report has a strong introduction, body, and conclusion. To begin, write down one powerful question you have about each of these topics:

- the environment
- the culture
- traditional knowledge
- challenges facing people today

When you do your research, challenge yourself to find *reliable* information from three different sources. For example, you might choose a book, the Internet, and a magazine. Use **key words** to help you find information.

HOW TO... Use Key Words in Research

1. Look over the work you are doing to focus your research. This might be your questions or a list of topics. Circle the words that seem like they are most important. These are your *key words*.

   What sort of beliefs do the Yanomami have?

2. In the library, use your key words to look up subjects in the catalogue of books.

   Author: Rudel, Christina
   Title: Children of the Moon
   Subject: Yanomami folktales
   Call Number: 398.2 RUD

3. On the Internet, use key words in your searches.

Looking Back

In this section, you found out some of the concerns of indigenous peoples. You also thought about why people from different cultures should work together to share what they know.

What did you learn in this chapter that might help you investigate other cultures in the global village? What did you learn that might help you understand your own culture?

Chapter 9

Good Government

All groups have some form of government—it's the way people organize getting things done and making decisions.

Think about it. How do you make decisions when you're with friends? How are decisions made in your family? What about when you play ball? In all these situations, people have to agree on the rules and on who has the final say when it comes to making decisions.

For governments of countries, it is more complicated, but the basic ideas are the same. The laws of the country are the rules that people follow, and the political leaders are the people who get the final say when it comes to making decisions. Fair governments get things done and protect people's human rights at the same time. Ensuring that everyone in the world lives under a fair government is one of the challenges facing the global village.

In this chapter, you can find out what jobs all governments do, and you can learn about some different systems of government. You can also take a close look at the governments of Canada and China. Once you know a little more about governments, you can invent one of your own!

Who Has the Power?

All governments have three main jobs:

- to make and enforce laws
- to help people meet their needs and wants
- to deal with other governments

The governments of countries all work in slightly different ways—no two are exactly the same. There are some ideas about governments, though, that we can use to help classify different systems of government. Two important things to look at are, "Who has the power to make decisions?" and "How do they get power?" In this section, you can find out about power in four systems of government: direct democracies, representative democracies, undemocratic governments, and hereditary leaderships.

These are some of the ways in which governments are a part of our lives in Canada. What other ways can you think of?

Voting is the main way decisions are made in a direct democracy. Can you think of a time when you voted for something?

In a representative democracy, people vote for their representatives, then their representatives vote on issues. Can you think of a time when you represented someone else's point of view?

Direct Democracy

In a **direct democracy**, everyone in the group shares the power. There is usually a leader to keep things organized, but everybody has an equal say in what goes on. Here's how this system might work in a club.

The Kids for Peace club at Marigold Elementary School is holding a meeting to decide the best way to raise money for their anti-landmine project in Kosovo. After talking about it for awhile, they have two good ideas to choose from: a bake sale and a car wash. They vote, and the decision is five in favour of the bake sale, ten in favour of a car wash. So everyone gets to work making plans for a car wash.

Representative Democracy

One problem with direct democracy is that it isn't a practical way to get things done in a large group. Ten or twenty people might be able to discuss an issue and then vote. But if you have a few thousand people, you can imagine it would take a long time to discuss an issue and then count the votes. This might be worthwhile for big issues, but if everyone in a large group has to be involved all the time, then it would take a long time to get anything done.

Representative democracy solves this problem by having people **elect** (vote for) **representatives**—people who will go to meetings and make decisions for them. Here's how this system might work in school.

Marigold Elementary has a student council. The student council is responsible for making plans for special events such as fun fairs. There are 498 students in the school. Council members are chosen by voting—two members for each grade for grades 4 to 7. Each ***candidate****— a person who wants to be a council member—gives oral presentations to tell people what she or he would do if elected. Students then vote for the candidates they think will do the best job of representing their grades.*

No Democracy

There are several different systems of government in which ordinary people don't have much say in the decisions made in the country or in who gets to be the leader. You might have heard of **dictatorships**. A dictatorship is where one person mostly controls the government. Other times it is a small group of people who control the country.

Leaders in these governments sometimes first get power through an election, but then they don't want to give up the power in another election. Either there are no elections or the elections are unfair, so nobody else has a chance to win. Other times people take power through force. Leaders in undemocratic governments often stay in power by imprisoning or even killing people who don't agree with their ideas.

Hereditary Leadership

A **hereditary leader** is a person who becomes leader by being the son, daughter, or close relative of leaders in the past. For example, a chief or a queen is a hereditary leader. In many cultures, people believe that the right to be a hereditary leader comes from a spiritual connection in the past.

At one time, most countries and cultural groups in the world were ruled by hereditary leaders. These leaders had a lot of power, in the same way that dictators have power. Some used this power wisely; some did not. Over time, most hereditary leaders have been replaced by other forms of government, often democracies. Many countries still have hereditary leaders who are respected and are an important part of their culture, but these leaders do not hold the power. These are called **honorary** positions.

There is no reason why **undemocratic** systems of government *have* to be unfair. If there are laws protecting human rights and the leaders follow these laws, then having a strong leadership can be an efficient way to get things done.

Many Aboriginal groups in Canada have hereditary chiefs who are greatly respected in their communities. Although these leaders may not hold all the power today, their opinions are valued when decisions are made.

If somebody takes control of a situation by force at your school, you might call that person a bully. What can you do if you face a bully?

Canada was once a colony of England, so the king or queen (the **monarch**) of England is still the honorary head of the government. Although the current monarch, Queen Elizabeth II, doesn't have any power to make decisions for Canadians, many people respect her as part of our heritage.

Try This

1. In a chart like this one, summarize the information on systems of government you've read about in this section.

Type	Who has the power?	How do they get power?
Direct Democracy		
Representative Democracy		
Dictatorship		
Hereditary Leadership		

2. In your own words, explain what a government has to do to protect people's individual rights.

The Government of Canada

The first governments in the land that became Canada were the governments of the many different Aboriginal groups who lived here.

Starting around 1600, England and France both claimed lands in North America. For about 150 years, France and England fought over the land until England won in 1759.

At first there was more than one British colony. The leaders of these colonies were chosen by the government in England. In 1867, the colonies joined together in **Confederation**. In the new country of Canada, each province voted to send representatives to the **federal government**. This is the government that makes decisions for all of Canada.

John A. Macdonald was Canada's first prime minister.

Although there have been some changes and many other provinces and territories added since 1867, we still have the same basic system of government we decided on at Confederation. This section describes how it works.

How the Federal Government Works

The government of Canada is made up of representatives elected to their jobs by the people of Canada. There must be an election for a new government at least every five years.

For the purpose of elections, the country is divided into **ridings**. A riding is a geographic area that elects one **member of Parliament** [PAR-luh-munt] **(MP)** to represent it in the **House of Commons** in Ottawa.

Reading Hint

When you start to read a new section, it helps to think about what you already know about the topic. For example, think about what you already know about the government of Canada before you read this section.

In Canada, we also have community and provincial governments with special areas of responsibility. For example, your community decides whether dogs must be on leashes and the provincial government makes decisions about what Grade 6 students in BC should learn.

A political party is a group of people with the same ideas about what makes a good government. It's like a large club. To be strong, a political party needs members in all parts of the country.

There are approximately 300 ridings in Canada—the exact number and the boundaries change from time to time as the population changes in different areas.

Each **political party nominates** (chooses) one candidate to run in each riding. The people living in a riding listen to the views of the different candidates and their political parties, then vote for the candidate whose views they like best. On election day, the candidate who gets the most votes wins the right to represent her or his riding in Ottawa.

This happens in all the ridings across the country. When the election is over, all of the newly elected MPs go to Ottawa to take up their jobs in the House of Commons. The political party that gets the most MPs elected forms the government and their leader becomes the **prime minister**. The other MPs have an important job to do, too—they ask questions, debate issues, and try to make sure that the government makes fair decisions.

Every Canadian citizen over the age of 18 can vote in federal elections.

Investigate

One of the responsibilities of being a member of a democracy is to understand how the government works so that you can make your voice heard.

Work in a group to design and conduct a survey to find out what people your age know about the federal government of Canada. Here are some questions you could ask:

- *Who is the prime minister?*
- *What political party does the prime minister belong to?*
- *What other political parties are represented in Ottawa right now?*
- *Who is the MP representing our community?*

Of course, you'll have to start by making sure you know the answers yourself!

Who Has the Power?

The Governor General

When you look at a diagram showing how the federal government of Canada is organized, you'll notice that the monarch is shown at the top. Even though Canada is now an independent country, we still have traditional ties to England. The **Governor General** is a person suggested by the prime minister to be the king or queen's representative in Canada. This is an honorary position —the Governor General can't make decisions for the people of Canada.

The Cabinet

In the government, the prime minister has the most power to make day-to-day decisions, but he or she usually takes the advice of the people in the **Cabinet**. These are MPs from the prime minister's party that advise him or her on important issues that come up, such as whether or not we should send peacekeeping troops to another part of the world or how much money should be spent on health care.

The House of Commons

When it comes to important decisions or making new laws, issues must be debated in the House of Commons. Representatives from the other political parties in the House can question the government. If enough of them agree, they can sometimes win the vote against a decision the government wants to make. Everything they do, though, must follow the rules set out in the **Constitution** [kon-stuh-TOO-shun]. The Constitution describes how our system of government works and what powers the government has.

The Senate

The **Senate** also has a say in our laws. Senators are not elected. Instead, they are selected by the prime minister, then they keep their jobs until they are 75 years old. Usually senators are people who have made important contributions to Canada in business or politics.

The Senate's main job is to review all laws passed in the House of Commons to make sure they make

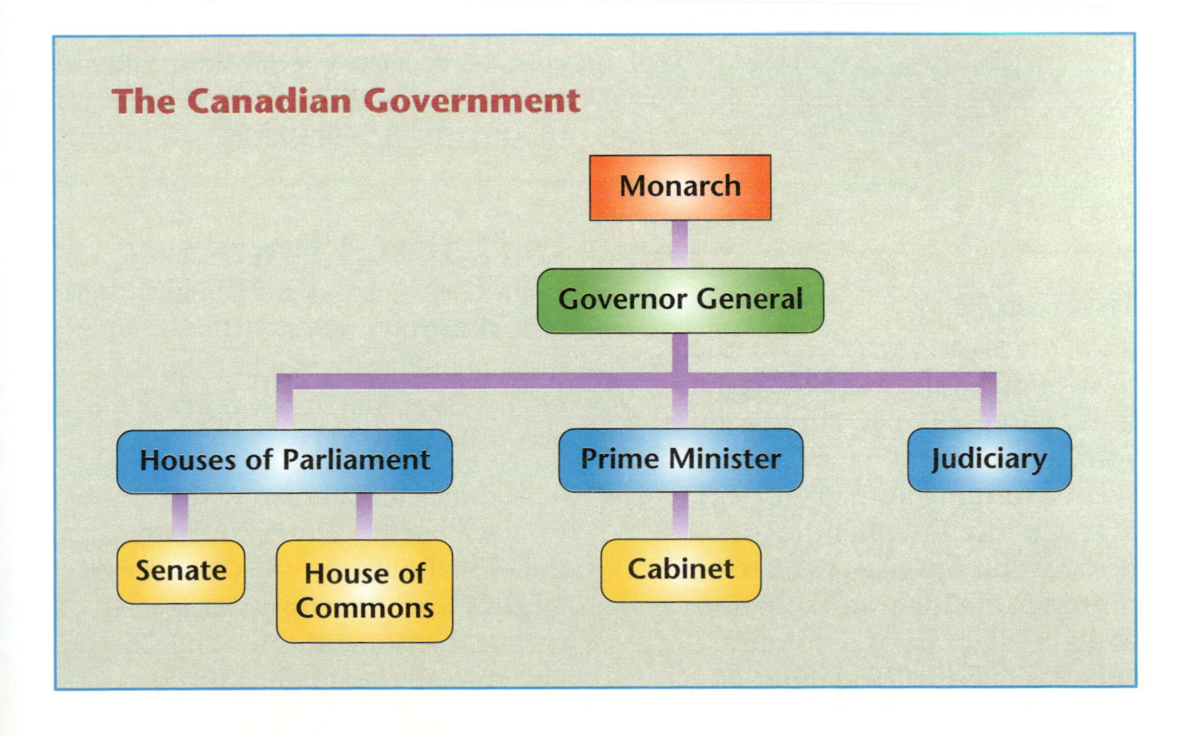

In the Canadian system of government, the power is spread among many different people and many different parts of the government. This diagram shows you the main parts of the government. Read about each part to find out who has the power.

The House of Commons meets in the Parliament Buildings in Ottawa. People are welcome to listen while the government and the opposition debate issues.

sense and are good for the country. Although the Senate has the power to stop laws that have been approved by the government, this almost never happens.

Seats in the Senate

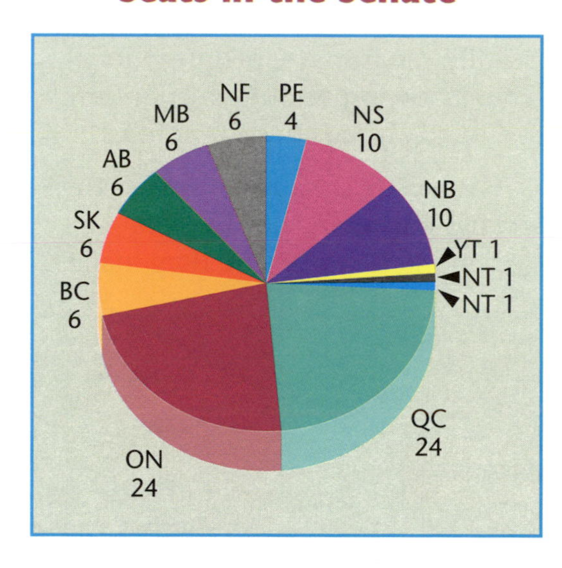

There are 105 senators, some from every region of the country.

The **Supreme Court of Canada** is at the head of Canada's judiciary. If a person isn't happy with a decision made by another court, he or she can sometimes take the case to the Supreme Court for its opinion.

The Judiciary

It's a lot easier to create a law than to **interpret** and **enforce** it! Just think of school rules. For example, your school might have a rule against running in the halls. The first step is to interpret the rule. How fast do you have to go to be running? Are there any situations when it might be okay to run? Once you decide these questions, you have to decide how to enforce the rule. Who will watch to see if someone is running? Will there be penalties for people who are caught running?

You can see that making decisions about laws can be complicated. The **judiciary** [joo-DISH-uh-ree] is the branch of the federal government that takes care of these legal matters. In Canada, the judiciary is separate from the elected government. It bases its decisions on laws, not on what a particular political party wants. The elected government has to follow any decisions made by the judiciary.

The People

The people of Canada don't show up on the diagram of the government, but they have a lot of power. Their power comes through voting. If people don't like the decisions a government makes, they only have to wait a few years until the next election. Then they can vote for a different government. Between elections, people can write or talk to their MPs about their concerns and form groups to protest government actions. Because governments like to stay in power, they try to do what most of the people want!

Individual Rights

Democracy is based on the idea that "the **majority** rules"—that is, what most people want is what should happen. So what about everyone else—the **minority**?

You may already know that we have laws to protect people's individual rights in the **Charter of Rights and Freedoms**, a special part of the Constitution. The Charter says that all Canadians must be treated fairly and equally, even if they are in the minority. The Charter also protects peoples' rights to speak out if they don't agree with the government (for example, in newspaper articles or in speeches).

In Canada, the Supreme Court interprets the laws set out in the Charter of Rights and Freedoms and makes sure they are followed by all levels of government, as well as by individuals.

What Makes a Democracy a Democracy?

Political scientists (people who study politics) say there are four important signs of democracy:

- There are open elections in which anyone can run and people are free to choose from different political parties.

- There is **freedom of the press**. This means that newspapers and other media can say what they want, even if they don't agree with the government. This helps people get true information about what the government is doing.

- There is **freedom of speech**. This means that people are free to speak out or protest when they don't agree with government decisions.

- The judicial system is independent of the government. This makes sure that everyone gets a fair trial, even if they don't agree with the government.

Try This

Give the Canadian government a "democracy test." In the information in this section, look for evidence that Canada has the "four signs of a democracy" described in "What Makes a Democracy a Democracy?"

Think For Yourself

Here's a problem that could come up in your class:

Your class is planning an end-of-year celebration. After several ideas are suggested, the class votes to go on a camping trip. It turns out that one student can't go for medical reasons and two other students aren't permitted to go by their parents.

In a group, discuss why this is an issue of "minority rights" and what you think would be a fair way to solve the problem.

The Government of China

The land that is now China has a long cultural tradition. The first Chinese government that we have evidence of was the Shang dynasty. Records carved on bone, tortoise shells, and bronze tell us that the Shang ruled a large area of southeastern China from about 1766 BCE to 1123 BCE.

Over the next 2000 years, China went through 22 different dynasties. Each dynasty was controlled by a family that claimed the right to rule through inheritance. A new dynasty would take over by force, but then rule through inheritance until it lost power to another family.

Making Modern China

The last Chinese dynasty, the Qing [ching], lost power in 1911. This was followed by many years of civil war as different political parties battled for control of China.

Two-thirds of China's population live in rural areas, and many people still farm in traditional ways. In contrast, life in the city can mean an office job and all the latest technologies. How does this compare with other countries you know about?

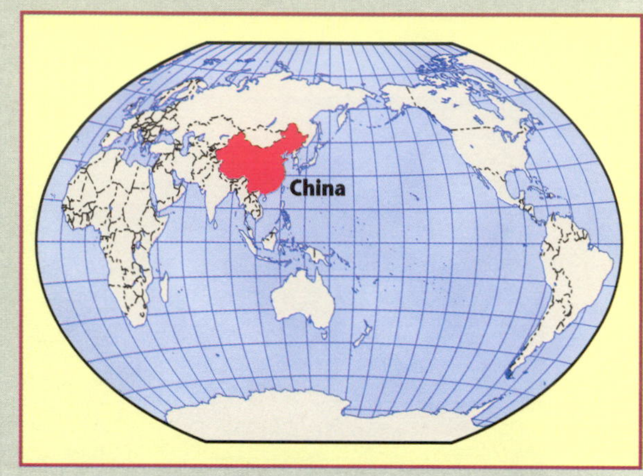

The red background in the flag symbolizes the revolution—when the Communist Party came into power. The large star represents communism, and the four smaller stars represent the workers.

CAPITAL CITY
Beijing

LARGEST CITY
Shanghai, population 18 082 000

LOCATION
Asia, 31°23′N/121°36′E (based on the largest city)

HEAD OF GOVERNMENT
Elected president (must be a member of the Communist Party)

MAIN LANGUAGE
Mandarin Chinese

CURRENCY
Yuan (¥)

CLIMATES
Continental, desert, high mountain, coastal

Tourists from around the world come to see the rock formations near the city of Guilan [kway-LIN] in southwest China. Can you see why this area has also been a favourite subject for Chinese painters for centuries?

On 1 October 1949, the Chinese Communist Party won the fight, and the People's Republic of China was formed. Three big challenges faced the new nation: poverty, high population in the few areas of good farmland, and a poor infrastructure—few roads or other methods of communication.

Since 1949, the country has gone through many changes, including a time where there was very little contact with other countries and, lately, a big push towards industrialization and trade with other nations. For most people, life is now much better than it was. All this time, the Chinese Communist Party has stayed in power. In this section, you can find out how China's government works.

How the Government Works

The official government of China is the National People's Congress (NPC), which is made up of representatives elected by the people.

There are about 3000 members of the NPC. It meets for two or three weeks once a year to make decisions about the national economy and pass laws. It also elects the **president** of the People's Republic and appoints a **State Council**, headed by a **premier**. The State Council consists of about 60 members. This group handles the day-to-day running of the country.

Two other important parts of the government are the Central Military Commission (the army) and the judiciary (the legal system).

Who Has the Power?

If you look at the official government system in China, it looks like the people have the power through their elected representatives. Actually, it doesn't work that way. This is because China is a **one-party state**—anyone who runs in an election must be a member of the Chinese Communist Party (CCP) and be approved by the CCP.

The CCP has a big influence at every level of government in China. For example, there are CCP representatives where people work, in city and town governments, and on provincial committees. But the real power is in the hands of a few people at the top of the organization, in the **Politburo** [POL-it-byur-oh]. The Politburo has about 22 members and is led by a general secretary. A person gets to be in the Politburo by making good connections and being friends with people who are already in power. Once people get into these powerful positions, they don't give them up!

China is the third-largest country in the world. Its population is the highest of any country—a little over 1 billion. That means that 1 out of every 6 people on earth is Chinese.

The CCP has the final say about who holds all of the important positions in the Chinese government, including the military, the judiciary, and even schools. How does this compare to political parties in Canada?

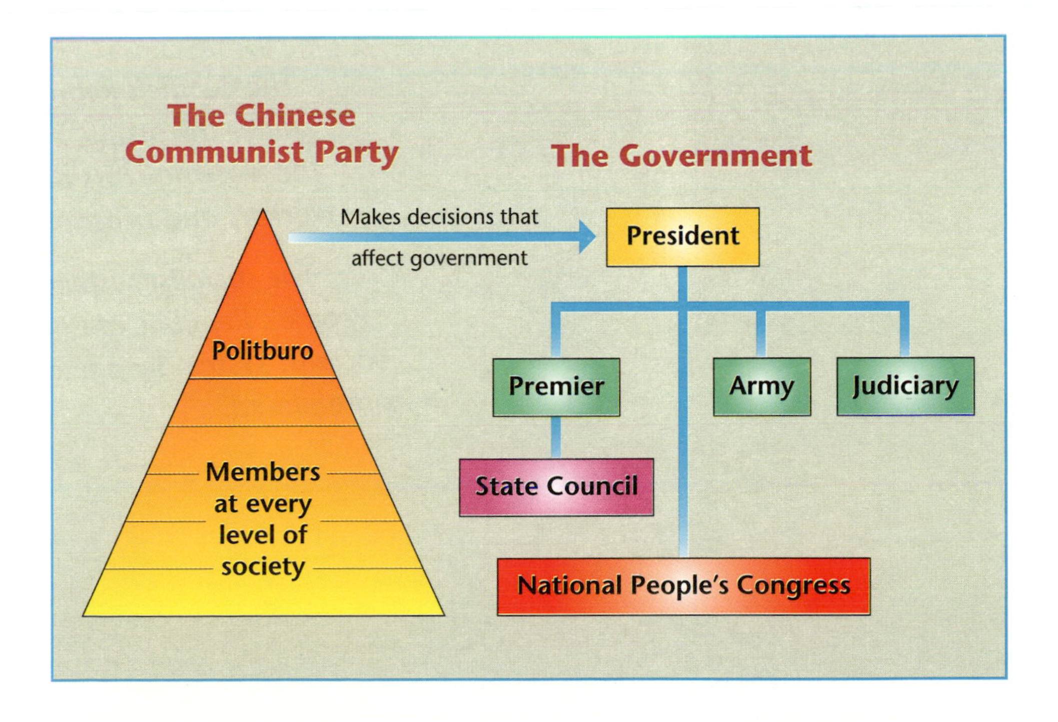

There are 22 provinces in China, 5 other regions, and 3 cities that are counted as separate areas. People in each part of the country elect representatives to the NPC. Elections are held every five years.

If people don't like the decisions the government is making, there is no opportunity to elect a different government in the next election. The government will always be made up of people approved by the CCP.

Individual Rights

The Chinese Constitution guarantees people basic rights, such as freedom of speech, the right to vote and run for elections, and the right to employment and education.

In fact, though, these rights are often not respected in China. You may recall that you can't run in an election unless you are approved by the CCP—that isn't really being free. Here are some other examples of government control:

- Although many people now have access to the Internet and get international news, the newspapers and radio and television broadcasts in China are strictly controlled by the government. People only hear the government's view of events.
- The police have a lot of power. If a person is arrested, the trial may be very quick, with no opportunity for the person to get legal help.

Article 1

The People's Republic of China is a socialist state under the people's democratic dictatorship led by the working class and based on the alliance of workers and peasants.

The socialist system is the basic system of the People's Republic of China. Disruption of the socialist system by any organization or person is prohibited.

- People are often arrested if they speak out against government policies.
- Parents lose work benefits and have to pay fines if they have more than one child.

One reason for the great amount of government control is that the Chinese Constitution begins with an important part that says having a **socialist** [SOH-shul-ist] system of government is the most important thing to the Chinese people. This guarantees that the Chinese Communist Party will always have the power.

Changing Times, Changing Perspectives

The people in power believe they have good reasons for doing what they do. For example, the one-child policy is a way to try to control the problem of China's rapid population growth. Chinese leaders think strong central control is the only way to make sure the country does not end up in civil war and poverty again. They point out how much progress China has made with this type of government.

In the early days of the People's Republic, most Chinese people agreed with these ideas. Today, though, some people think it would be better to have more say in their government.

This group of young people has come to see the Great Hall of the People in Tiananmen [TYE-nun-men] Square in Beijing. This is where the NCP meets and many government departments are located. The red scarves the students are wearing show they support the Chinese Communist Party.

Socialism is both a government system and an economic system. Communism is one type of socialism. The main idea of communism is that people contribute whatever work they can to the country and are guaranteed to get whatever they need.

In 1989, protestors filled Tiananmen Square demanding that the government of China allow freer elections. After several weeks, the government sent in soldiers and tanks to break up the demonstration. Many people were killed. From the government's perspective, they had to do this to avoid a civil war. What do you think?

Try This

1. Give China the "democracy test." Look back at the "What Makes a Democracy a Democracy?" on pages 153 to 154 and use the information in this section to decide whether or not China is a democracy. Give examples for each point.
2. Make a chart to compare the systems of government in China and Canada. Make sure you look for similarities and differences. Hypothesize some reasons you think there might be for the differences.

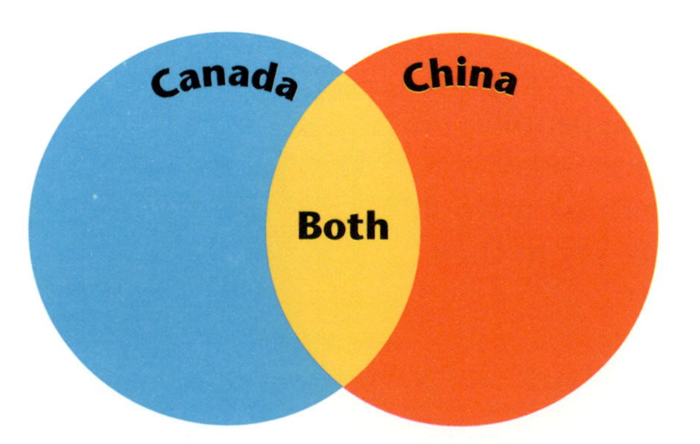

Think For Yourself

Here's a fun way to show what you know about how governments work. In a group, invent your own government for the imaginary country of Keewara.

Keewara is a middle-income country on a 600 square kilometre island in the subtropical region of the world. The centre of the island is mountainous, with one active volcano. There is farmland along the coast, though, and many beautiful beaches. There is some poverty, but most people have a good quality of life. Keewara's main source of income is tourism and selling fish to countries on the mainland. The population is about 125 000.

You can make any type of government you want. Here are the things you'll need to decide:

- *Who has the power?*
- *How do they get the power?*
- *What is the leader called? (Be creative—you don't have to use common words like* king *or* prime minister.*)*
- *How are laws made?*
- *How are laws enforced?*
- *How important are individual rights?*
- *What are the three most important services the government provides for people?*

Think of a creative way to present your ideas to others. You might want to include some of the following: a map; a drawing of Keewara; a national flag; a diagram showing how the government is organized; a pamphlet describing government services; a short summary of the main points of the constitution.

Looking Back

In this chapter, you read about different types of government and the rights and responsibilities of people in different political systems.

The United Nations thinks representative democracy should be a goal for all countries in the world. Do you agree? Why or why not?

Chapter **10**

Countries and Economies

Have you ever listened to the news or heard people talk about the economy? It seems the economy affects just about everything!

- Few jobs for people—a sign of a weak economy!
- More houses being built—a sign of a strong economy!
- A new factory opens up—a boost for the local economy!

Many important decisions made by governments are strongly influenced by one question: *Is this good for the economy?* In a strong economy, most people have the ability to get the things they need as well as many of the things they want. In a country like Canada, a strong economy also means lots of jobs and good wages.

What are some of the ways in which governments manage their economies? What happens to people when economies are weak? These are some of the questions you can investigate in this chapter.

I'll Buy That!

An **economic system** is the way we get the goods and services we need. Today, most people in the world get what they need by paying for it with money. This is the consumer culture we talked about in Chapter 5.

In this type of economic system most people are both **producers** and **consumers** of goods and services. When you produce something, you sell it in exchange for money. Producers include the businesses that make things or provide services, plus the people who work in these businesses. When you consume, you pay money to get something. Keeping money moving from one person to the next is the most important part of an economic system.

What Is Money?

What makes a loonie worth more than a quarter? Why can't you print legal 50 dollar bills in your basement? One way to understand money is to think about how it came to be.

In the past, if you wanted a chicken, you might trade some carrots and wool to get it. This is called **bartering**. The problem with bartering is that each person has to have goods or services another person needs.

After awhile, governments started making coins out of **precious metals**—metals that people wanted but were hard to find. Gold was the most precious metal, so gold coins were worth the most. Other coins

Goods are the things we want and need, such as food and computers. **Services** are the jobs we want or need to be done, such as medical care and car repairs.

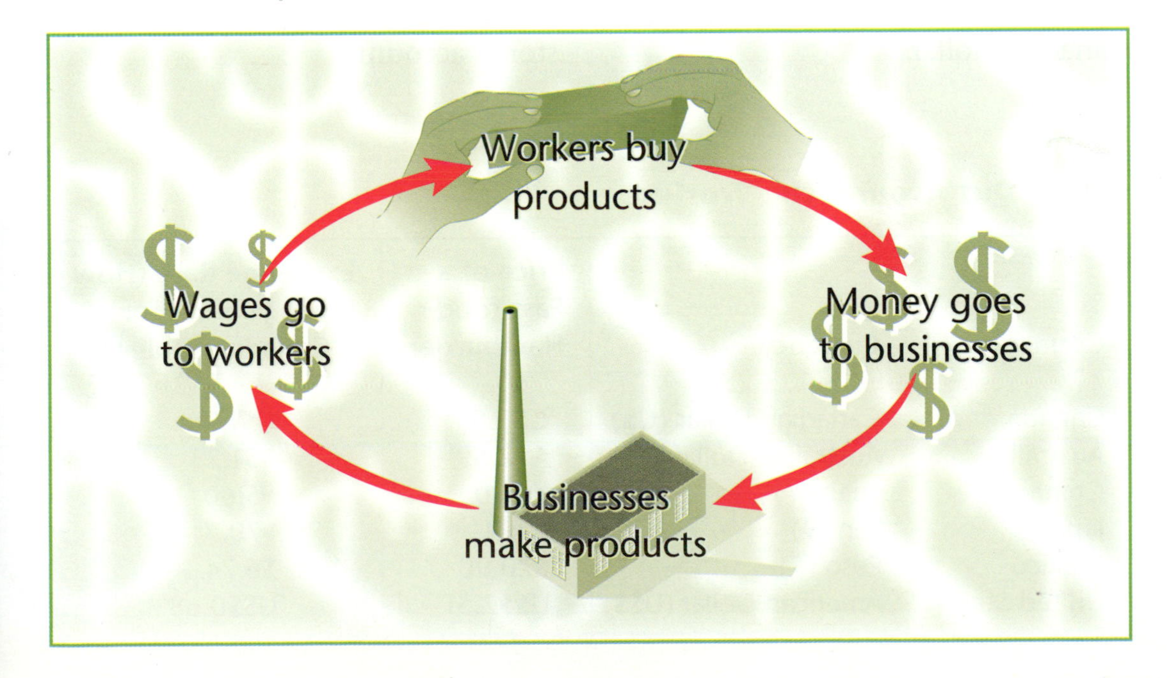

This **flow chart** shows how money moves through an economic system. How do *you* fit into this system?

In Europe, many countries have joined together to share one currency—the Euro. How do you think this affects buying and selling between the countries?

were made of silver, copper, and brass. You could then sell your carrots and wool for a few copper coins to one person, then use those coins to buy a chicken from another person.

Coins could be heavy and difficult to carry. This was especially true for traders who often had to send large sums of money long distances to buy their goods. Also, sometimes there wasn't enough precious metal to make all the coins needed. The first government to use paper money was the government of China. It began to use paper money around 600 CE. Europeans heard about this paper money from travellers around 1295, but most people didn't trust something written on paper as much as they trusted coins. In 1661, the government of Sweden made the first paper money in Europe. Soon, everyone could see how convenient this form of money was.

Currencies

Today, each country has its own system of money, called its **currency**. Canada's currency is the Canadian dollar.

Countries can't just print as much money as they want, though. They must have something to "back up" the value of the money. This could be gold, other goods the country owns, or even money the country has in other parts of the world. It's different from country to country.

One thing countries are interested in is how much their currency is worth compared to other countries. If your currency has a high value, then it is easy for you to buy things from another country. If your currency has a low value, then it is more difficult. The amount of another country's currency you get for your own currency is called the **exchange rate**.

The Future of Money

Today, more and more people around the world are starting to use **electronic banking** when they shop. In electronic banking, you use a **debit card** to pay for the things you buy. Your debit card tells the bank that it should take $15.95 for the CD you're buying out of your bank account and put it into the store's account.

Exchange rates and the price of hamburgers both change from time to time. These figures are from June 2000. To find out how much a hamburger in another country cost in Canadian dollars at that time, divide the cost of the hamburger by the exchange rate.

Eating Out Around the World

Country	Currency	Price of a Fast-food Hamburger	Exchange Rate (How much you get for 1 Canadian Dollar)
Canada	Canadian Dollar (C$)	C$2.85	C$1.00
Australia	Australian Dollar (A$)	A$2.59	A$1.23
China	Yuan (¥)	¥9.90	¥5.60
Japan	Yen (¥)	¥294	¥70.71
Mexico	Peso ($)	$20.90	$6.74
United States	American Dollar (US$)	US$2.51	US$0.68

How We Pay Our Way

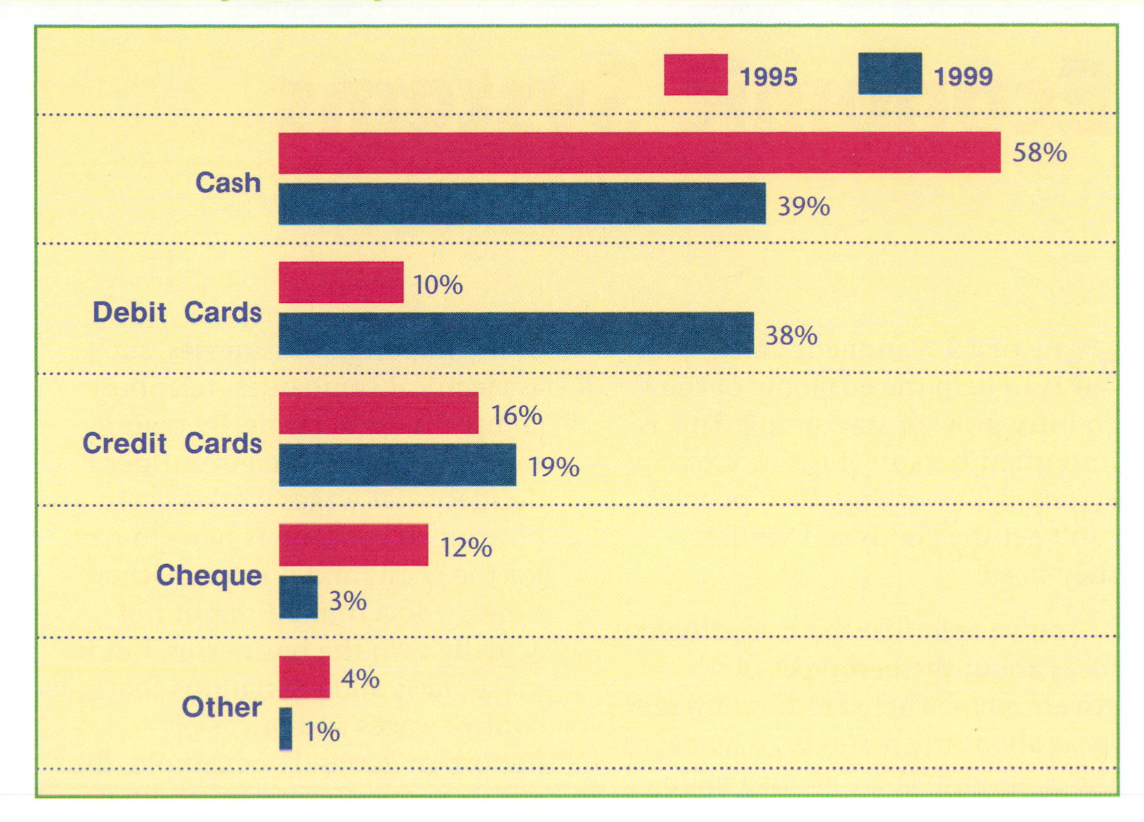

Source: Interac Association Tracking Research. *The Globe and Mail*, 3 May 2000.

These statistics show changes in the way Canadians pay for things they buy. What form of payment became more popular between 1995 and 1999?

Think For Yourself

Discuss these questions with a partner or in a group:

- *Will there come a time when we don't have "real" money at all?*
- *What might replace money? Might there be something else besides debit cards?*
- *How will this affect how we get the goods and services we need?*

Economic Systems

One of a government's main jobs is to help the economy of the country grow or stay strong. This is important because if the economic system isn't working, then people can't get the goods and services they need.

You've seen that there are different ideas about the best types of government. There are also different ideas about the best way to manage the economy. There are two main economic systems. One is called a **centrally planned** system. The other is a **market-oriented** system. No country in the world is entirely one system or the other.

There are many different parts to an economic system. In this section, we'll focus on understanding how goods and services are produced and sold in a country.

Profit is the amount of money a business earns after it subtracts what it costs to make the product. Costs include workers' wages and buying the goods needed to make the product.

Centrally Planned Economies

In a centrally planned economic system, the government keeps a close watch on all the businesses in the country. In other words, all the economic planning comes from the "centre" of the country—the government.

How does a centrally planned economy work? One thing a government might do is actually own many of the important businesses, such as electrical companies, telephone companies, and farms. By owning these businesses, the government decides what wages workers earn and how much consumers have to pay for the goods and services. Other times, a government might not actually own the businesses, but it makes laws and regulations that control wages and prices of important goods. For example, the government might control the price of basic foods, such as rice or bread.

Benefits and Drawbacks

The benefits to producers in a centrally planned economy are that the government makes sure that businesses keep going and people get their wages. This happens even when there might not be any profit in selling the goods they produce. The benefit to consumers is that the government makes sure that the prices for their basic needs are not so high that they can't afford them.

One drawback to producers in centrally planned economies is that individuals can't make their own decisions about the best way to make money. No matter how hard people work or what great ideas they have, they will get the same wages and make the same profits. From the consumer's point of view, the main drawback is that there is usually less

At the Allbridge Elementary Fun Fair the prices for each product or service were decided in advance.

choice in the type and quality of goods and services that are available. For example, if auto manufacturing were controlled by the government, there might be only one or two types of cars available to buy.

Market-oriented Economies

Oriented means to be directed towards. *Market* is a general word for the world of business, in which goods and services are bought and sold. So a market-oriented economic system is one that is directed towards making things good for business.

In this type of system, there is little or no government interference in business. Instead, each business does whatever it thinks will work best to make a profit. The government usually has some basic regulations to protect workers and the environment. But it is up to the business to decide what products to make, how much to charge for them, and what to pay the workers. Businesses compete with each other to get the consumer's money.

Benefits and Drawbacks

The main benefit to businesses in a market-oriented system is that if people have a good idea and the business is managed well, they can make higher profits than if the system is controlled by the government. Higher profits can also mean higher wages for the workers. The benefits to consumers are that there is usually a greater selection of goods and services, and sometimes

Inflation is when the costs of goods go up. If the cost of goods and people's wages increase at the same rate, then people might not notice inflation.

At the Westside Elementary Fun Fair students in each class decided what products they wanted to sell and the price they would charge.

there is the opportunity to buy things on "sale" as businesses compete with each.

One drawback to producers in a market-oriented system is that there is little protection for a company during poor economic times. If the company can't make a profit for awhile, then it may have to shut down and the workers will lose their jobs. A drawback for workers is that a company may choose to keep their wages low in order to increase its profits. The main drawback for consumers is that goods and services that are in high demand can become very expensive. If people's wages don't increase by the same amount that the cost of basic goods increases, then some people might find they can't afford food, clothing, and shelter.

Try This

This section includes illustrations of two different school fun fairs. One shows a centrally planned economic system. The other shows a market-oriented economic system. In your notebook or social studies journal, briefly explain the main idea about the system shown in each picture and one important benefit of the system to producers and consumers.

Balancing the Budget

A **budget** is a way of keeping track of **income** and **expenses**. Income is the money you receive. Expenses are the monies you have to pay out. Most families have to think about their budgets when they decide what to spend their money on. Governments have to do the same thing. In this section, you can learn a little about how government budgets work.

Government Income

Governments get their incomes in a variety of ways. The main way, though, is through **taxes**. A tax is an amount of money that businesses and individuals pay to the government.

There are many different types of taxes. In Canada, different taxes are collected by all levels of government. For example, people who own houses pay taxes in their local communities, and most provincial governments collect sales taxes on the goods we buy.

The two main federal taxes in Canada are the **goods and services tax (GST)** and **income tax**. GST is extra money you pay each time you buy something. The more expensive the item is, the more tax you pay. Income tax is paid by people and businesses who earn money. Each year, they must pay some tax to the government, based on how much

You may have heard or read about a **balanced budget** in the news. A balanced budget is when the amount of money being spent is not greater than the amount of money coming in. Today, many governments are trying to balance their budgets. Why do you think they would want to do this?

My Budget for May

Income	Expenses
Birthday money: $15	Entertainment (movies, tennis): $20
Babysitting: $35	Sweater: $20
	Savings: $10
TOTAL: $50	TOTAL: $50

Young people often budget their allowance or money they earn from part-time work to make sure they get the things they want. Is the budget you see here balanced?

People report their income on **tax returns** each year. Government workers have to check all the forms to make sure each person has paid the right amount of tax. Why do you think it is set up so that people who make more money pay more taxes?

money they made that year. The more money a person or business makes, the more tax they pay.

Government Expenses

Governments use tax money to provide the goods and services people and businesses need. For example, the federal government uses tax money to pay for many different services, including:

- defence (the soldiers and equipment we keep in case of war)
- health care (so that you don't have to pay to see a doctor)
- social programs (such as help for low-income people)
- airports
- environmental protection
- the Royal Canadian Mounted Police (RCMP) and federal prisons
- aid to other countries.

Balancing Budgets

In order to balance a budget, the government has to make important decisions about what things to spend money on. Different groups in society want money to be spent in different ways. For example, the military may think it is important to buy new helicopters, while doctors may think that more money should be spent on health care. In a democracy like Canada, it's the government's job to try to figure out what things most people in the country consider to be the most important.

Governments also have to decide what to do when there is a budget **deficit**—that's when a government's income isn't enough to meet its expenses. When this happens, the government has to decide whether to provide fewer services or to raise taxes or borrow money in order to keep providing services. Raising taxes

Generally speaking, the more market oriented an economy is, the lower the taxes. This makes it easier for businesses to make more money because they have lower costs.

usually makes people angry. Higher taxes can also result in people having less money to spend, which can weaken the economy.

Governments can borrow money from banks or other countries. Eventually, though, this money has to be paid back, with **interest**. Interest is an amount of money that has to be paid back in addition to the amount of money borrowed.

The total amount of money a country owes is called its **debt**. If a country keeps borrowing more and more money, it gets further and further into debt.

You might be surprised to know that most countries, including high-income countries, carry some kind of debt. Part of their budget each year goes to paying off this debt.

First balanced budget in eight years

Tax breaks announced

National debt at all-time high

Newspapers regularly report on how the government is managing the budget. Why do you think they do this?

Try This

Draw a flow chart that shows all the parts of the Canadian federal government budget discussed in this section. Include sources of income and types of expenses. Explain your diagram in a brief oral presentation.

HOW TO... Speak Out

Speaking out in an oral presentation is a good way to express your opinion and make a difference. Here are some things you can do to clearly communicate your ideas.

Preparing

- Write a well-organized presentation with a strong introduction and conclusion. Make sure your topics and subtopics are supported by facts and ideas.
- Practice making your presentation in front of a friend. Ask him or her to identify one thing you are doing well and one thing you could improve upon.

Speaking

- Before you begin to speak, breathe deeply in and out. Then look at your audience and wait for the room to be quiet before you speak.
- Don't rush. When you make an important point, pause and look at the audience. Use your voice to express your meaning.
- Make your conclusion especially strong and be sure to look at your audience. When you've finished, thank them for listening.

How To...
Make a Strong Impression

How To...
Lose Your Audience

Social Safety Nets

In most of the world today, it takes money to be part of an economic system. But what if you don't have enough money? How do you get the things you need?

Many countries have a **social safety net** as part of their economic system. A social safety net is a collection of programs and government services that helps make sure the country's wealth is shared more evenly. One part of a social safety net might be lower taxes for families and inexpensive daycare for children whose parents have lower incomes.

Another part might be programs that provide food, shelter, and clothing for people who are having trouble meeting their basic needs. This can also help the economy. When people are doing well, they are better able to take part in the economy as producers and consumers.

When high-wire performers walk a tightrope, there is a *safety net* below to catch them if they fall. Of course, tightrope walkers hope they never need the net, but it's there just in case.

When a country has a social safety net, it helps all people at some time in their lives.

Making Choices

How strong a country's social safety net is depends on two things: **cultural values** and **economic strength**.

In some cultures, people believe it is important that the government take care of those who need help. In these cultures, people usually think a social safety net is important. In other cultures, though, people believe that individuals should be responsible for their own success. These cultures usually have few government-supported programs for people in need.

In earlier chapters, we talked about the GNP—the total amount of money a country makes. One sign of a strong economy is a high GNP. When there is a high GNP, then there is more money available to pay for the services needed in a strong social safety net. If a country's economy is weak, there might not be enough money to create a strong social safety net, no matter *what* people believe.

Social Safety Nets and Children

Many people believe one of the most important things in a social safety net is to make sure children's basic needs are met. You may recall that the Convention on the Rights of the

Percentage of Children Under 18 Living in Poverty

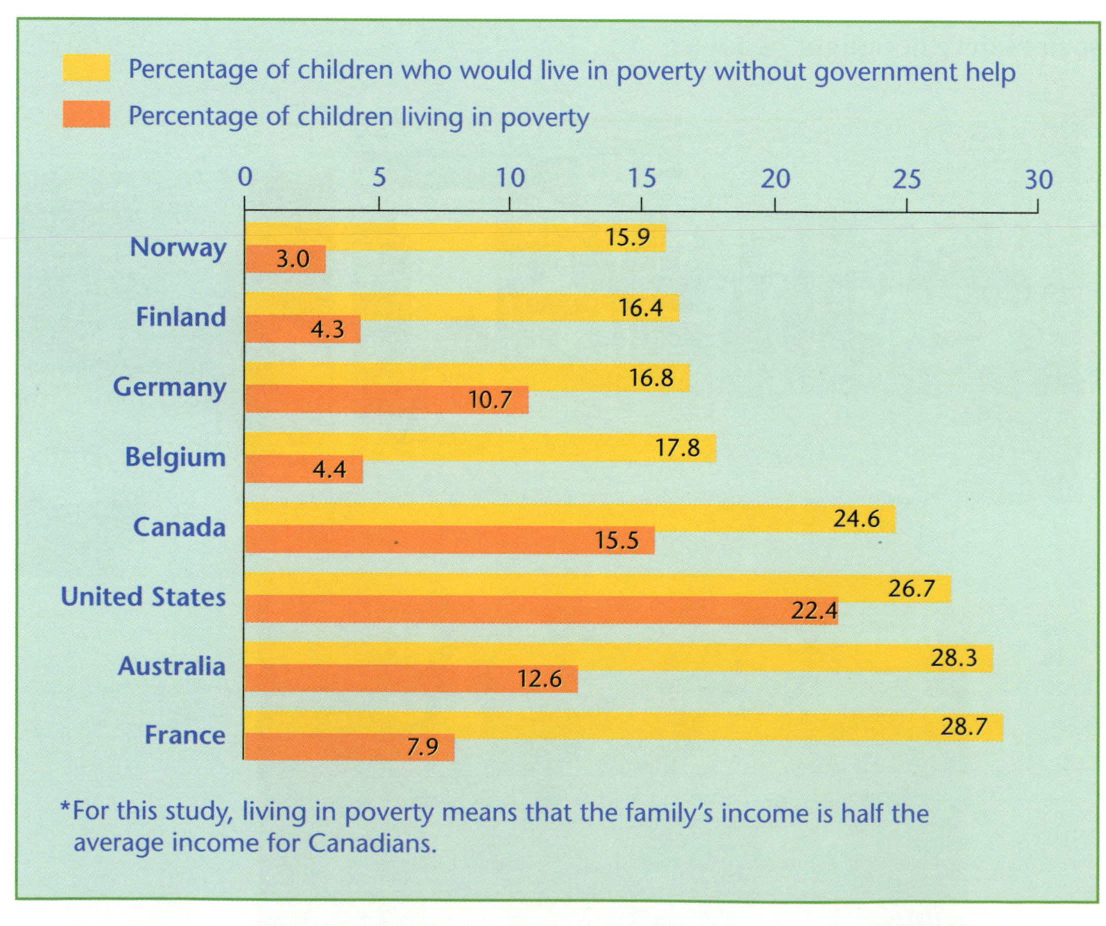

Source: UNICEF Innocenti Research Centre, Florence, Italy. *Innocenti Report Card* No. 1, June 2000. "A league table of child poverty in rich nations."

To tell how strong the social safety net is in a country, look at how much of a difference government help makes in the percentage of children living in poverty. How does Canada compare to these other high-income countries?

Child says that every person under 18 years of age has the right to have his or her basic needs met. If the family cannot do this, then the government should help.

UNICEF compared how well different high-income countries do at this job. This study showed that, although the countries all have strong economies compared to many other countries in the world, they make different decisions about how much to put into the social safety net.

Many communities have food banks. This is one way communities can provide for their own social safety nets. People who can afford to share make contributions of food or money so that others can get food when they need it.

Think For Yourself

Write a letter to your MP expressing your opinion about whether or not Canada's social safety net is strong enough. In your letter, make it clear that you know what a social safety net is and why it is important to children. Also be sure to support your opinion with facts and examples.

Before you write your letter, you might want to do some research to see if the information in this section is still up to date.

Economic Trends

A **trend** is a general way things seem to be going.

Now that you know a bit about economic systems, let's look at the economies of three countries: the United States, China, and Canada. These summaries tell you about the economic trends in each country. Although there are only three countries here, they represent the most common trends in all countries in the world. See if you can figure out what these trends are.

The United States

Trend: *Remain a market-oriented economy*

Challenges for the future: *Trying to reduce the big differences between the very rich and the very poor*

The United States has always had a strong market-oriented economic system. Businesses make most of the decisions that affect the economy. The government provides goods and services by buying them from businesses. Taxes are low to encourage businesses to operate there, and success in business is highly valued in American culture.

In a market-oriented economy, one sign of a strong economy is low **unemployment**. If people can get jobs, then they can spend money and contribute to the economy as both producers and consumers.

Because many Americans believe that anyone who works hard can meet her or his basic needs, the United States does not have a strong social safety net. For example, the government does not pay for health care, and there is little social assistance for the poor. Companies often make large donations to private charities, though, and these organizations help people in need.

The United States has the strongest economy in the world today. The GNP in 1998 was approximately $12.5 trillion (in Canadian dollars). By comparison, Canada's GNP for the same year was approximately $1 trillion. Since 1975, however, most of the benefits of this strong economy have gone to the wealthiest 20 per cent of the population—those who already have high incomes in the first place. Although companies are doing well and there are plenty of jobs, the workers are not receiving higher wages or more benefits, such as health insurance.

China

Trend: *To quickly become more market oriented*

Challenges for the future: *Making sure unemployment, urban migration, and differences between rich and poor don't become big problems*

When China became a communist country in 1949, one of the greatest problems the government faced was extreme poverty. China's leaders decided that the best economic policy was one in which all farms, factories, and businesses were owned by the

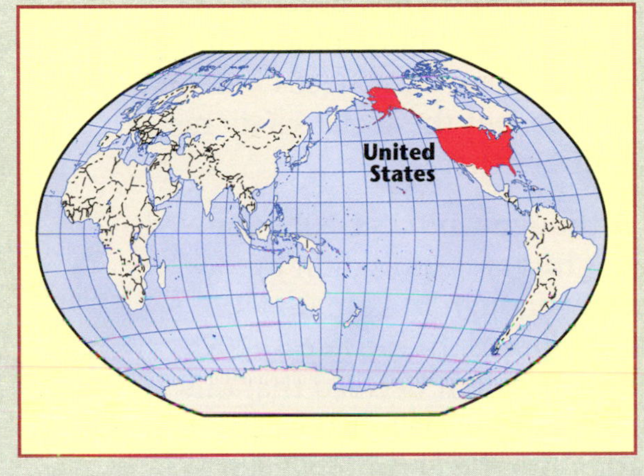

The flag has 50 stars, one for each of the 50 states. The 13 stripes represent the number of states there were when the country was created in 1776.

CAPITAL CITY
Washington, DC

LARGEST CITY
New York, population 16 390 000

LOCATION
North America
40°76′N 73°96′W
(based on the location of New York, the largest city)

HEAD OF GOVERNMENT
Elected president

MAIN LANGUAGE
English, with many Spanish speakers

CURRENCY
American dollar ($)

CLIMATES
Continental, coastal, Mediterranean, desert, tropical, high mountain

Americans are proud of their tradition of democratic government. This is Mount Rushmore, in the north-central US. From 1927 to 1941, the faces of four American presidents were carved into the mountainside. They are George Washington, Thomas Jefferson, Theodore Roosevelt, and Abraham Lincoln.

government. The government could then set prices for basic goods to make sure that everyone could afford them. This meant, for example, that vegetables from government-owned farms would cost the same for everyone. It was illegal for any Chinese individual to set up his or her own business.

In China's centrally planned economy, everyone was guaranteed work and basic needs such as food, clothing, and shelter. Because the country did not have a lot of money to spend, these basic needs were not luxurious, but the social safety net was always there.

Although China's GNP improved under this system, it didn't grow quickly enough to keep up with China's needs. In the late 1970s, the government decided that one solution might be to have a more market-oriented economy. Since then, China has changed its laws and it now encourages private businesses. These may range from a factory building aircraft parts to a family noodle-making operation. Farmers are also now allowed to rent land from the government and to grow extra produce and sell it at any price they can get at the market.

As a result of this change in economic policy, China's GNP has grown. But this growth has caused big changes in people's lives. In the past, Chinese people were guaranteed jobs, but they did not have much freedom to move around. Now they have the freedom to move, but often find that they can't get work. Since most of the benefits from these economic changes are happening in the cities, **urban migration** is becoming a problem. In the countryside, some landowners are becoming wealthy while others are facing hardships because they are no longer guaranteed certain prices for their produce.

Cities such as Shanghai are experiencing economic growth as China moves towards a more market-oriented system. But many small family businesses find it more difficult to meet their basic needs in the new economy.

Canada

Trend: *To become more market oriented*

Challenges for the future: *Finding ways to keep the social safety net strong in a market-oriented economy*

Canada has a strong economy. Our GNP is one of the highest in the world and unemployment is low compared to most other countries. In addition, we have lots of natural resources and skilled workers to make sure we continue to do well in the future.

Canada's basic economic system is market oriented, but it has some features that are not always found in market-oriented economies. Canadians place a high value on a strong social safety net, so taxes are high to make sure these services are provided. These include:

- free or low-cost medical care for everyone
- Employment Insurance Benefits (or income) for people who have lost their jobs and are looking for work, and programs to train people to help them find work
- government assistance for people who can't meet their basic needs of food, shelter, and clothing
- government pensions for Canadians over age 65 to help support them once they have retired from the workforce.

There is an increasing trend towards private business. In the past, the provincial and federal governments owned many of the businesses that provide important services, such as road maintenance and a national airline. In recent years, more and more of these services are being provided by private companies.

Canada still has quite a few regulations and policies that help businesses, though. In agriculture, for example, the government allows **marketing boards** to set prices for some farm products, such as milk, eggs, and wheat. The marketing boards make sure that prices remain high enough for farmers to earn a profit and stay in business. The federal government also sets rules for other important businesses, such as banks.

Many Canadians are concerned that as the country becomes more market oriented, the social safety net will become weaker. For example, if the government reduced taxes to help businesses, there might be less money to pay for social services. In addition, most of the benefits of a strong economy go to those people who already have higher incomes. The difference between rich and poor in Canada is not as great as it is in the United States, but some people fear it might become worse, especially if the social safety net becomes weaker.

Why do you think the Canadian government continues to make sure that wheat farmers are guaranteed a certain amount of money for their wheat?

Try This

Think about these questions to check that you understand the trends discussed in this section. Answer the questions for yourself, then check with a partner to see if you reached the same conclusions.

- *Based on the information in this section, what type of economic system is becoming the most common in the world today?*
- *What is the main benefit of this type of economic system?*
- *What problems does this type of system cause?*
- *What can be done to solve these problems?*

Think For Yourself

Imagine you are the MP for your local riding. The House of Commons is debating how to make sure next year's budget is balanced. The choices are: (a) to cut back on spending for job-creation programs or (b) to raise taxes. Prepare an oral presentation expressing your opinion. Discuss both the cultural and economic reasons for your opinion. (You might want to check back to pages 174 to 175.)

Looking Back

This chapter described different types of economic systems and how they meet people's needs and wants.

Why is understanding how economic systems work an important part of being a responsible global citizen?

Chapter 11

The Ties of Trade

Imagine what your life would be like if you had been working 10 hours a day since the age of four. What would you have missed in your life? How do you think working would have affected your health?

This is the reality of life for at least 250 million children around the world today. "But not in Canada!" you might say, and you'd be right. Although there is some child labour in Canada, it isn't very common. There are laws to protect children, and these laws are usually enforced. Things aren't the same in all parts of the world, though. Some families have such trouble meeting their basic needs that even the youngest children must help out. The laws either do not protect children or they are not enforced.

Of course, as a global citizen, child labour is your problem, even if it isn't common in Canada. To find out how to solve the problem, you need to know how global trade works. That's where this chapter starts.

Global Trade

You've seen how the strength of a country's economy depends on the buying and selling of goods. **Global trade** is the buying and selling of goods between countries. In the world today, this is often the most important part of a country's economy.

Most of us don't think about global trade when we go shopping. After all, we do most of our shopping at the local store or mall—not in Mumbai or Singapore! If they could talk, though, the products we buy would have interesting stories about their global adventures. What do the parts of Sarah's new computer tell you about their world travels?

Sarah's New Computer

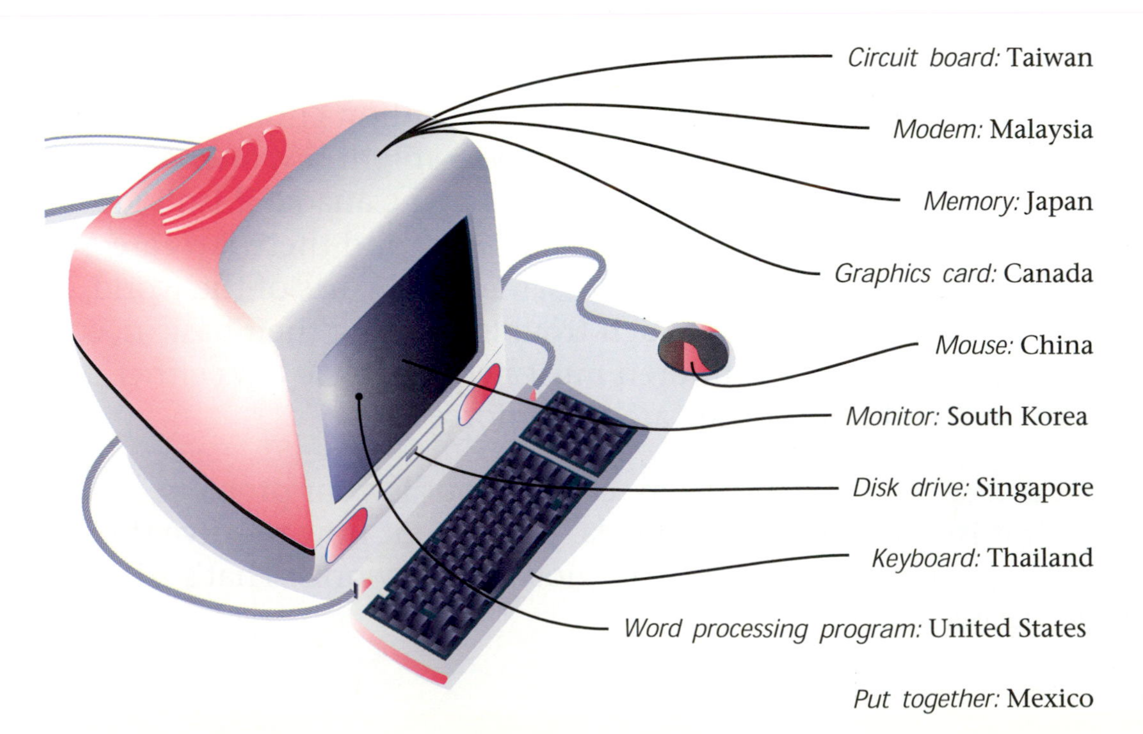

If Sarah needs help, she'll be connected to a friendly technician in Bangalore, India!

The World Labour Force

Why are the parts of Sarah's computer and so many other things we use made in different parts of the world?

The answer is, "Because it makes good business sense!" Many large companies today build factories in several countries around the world. These **transnational corporations** do this so they can buy resources where they are cheap and hire people where wages are low. Cutting costs this way increases the company's profits. It also makes the products cheaper for the consumer to buy.

Eighty-one per cent of the head-quarters of large transnational corporations are in the high-income countries of the North, such as the United States. These countries already have strong economies, so the businesses have the money to set up factories in other parts of the world. Most of the profits go back to the headquarters.

The World Market

Transnationals also want to have **branches** in other countries because it helps them sell their products all over the world. Of the largest 100 transnational corporations in the world, 31 have branches in more than 50 countries. Nine companies have branches in over 75 countries.

What benefits might there be for low-income countries when a transnational company sets up a factory? What drawbacks might there be?

Investigate

You might not be buying a new computer soon, but there is probably evidence of global trade all around you, starting with the clothes you wear.

As a group project, collect data on where your clothing is made. Use these questions to organize your project:

- *What questions do we want the data to help us answer?*
- *What are our hypotheses about the answers?*
- *What categories of information will we gather?*
- *From where will we get the information?*
- *How many examples do we want to collect?*
- *How will we record the information?*
- *What will we do to draw conclusions?*

Partners in Trade

International trade is a two-way arrangement. Goods that one country sells to another are its **exports**. Goods a country buys from another country are its **imports**. Most goods can be classed as either **raw materials** (for example, wheat, oil, and timber) or **manufactured consumer goods** (for example, appliances, clothing, and computers). When two countries exchange imports and exports they are called **trading partners**. Today, changes in laws and **trade agreements** are making it easier for many countries to trade with each other.

Almost all the parts of Sarah's new computer are imports. If we only imported goods, though, all of Canada's money would end up in other countries. So to be part of the global economy, we have to export goods as well. This brings money into Canada.

International trade is a big part of the Canadian economy. Statistics Canada estimates that 25 per cent of income for all businesses in Canada is in some way connected to international trade.

Canada in the Global Economy

Main Exports *(in order of importance)*	Main Imports *(in order of importance)*
• motor vehicles and parts • newsprint • wood pulp • timber • crude petroleum • machinery • natural gas • aluminum • telecommunications equipment	• machinery and equipment • crude oil • chemicals • motor vehicles and parts • a variety of consumer goods
Where They Go	**Where They Come From**
• United States 79.1% • Japan 4.5% • England 1.7% • Plus small amounts to many other countries	• United States 76% • Japan 3% • England 2.3% • Plus small amounts from many other countries

Who is Canada's main trading partner? What kind of a graph would best show this?

Time to Do Business

One of the practical matters that people have to think about when it comes to doing global business is **time zones**. With modern communications technologies we can easily phone, fax, and e-mail another place. But the question is, *will anybody be there to answer your message?* It might be the middle of the work day for a business in Vancouver, but because of different time zones, the customer in New York might have gone home for the day.

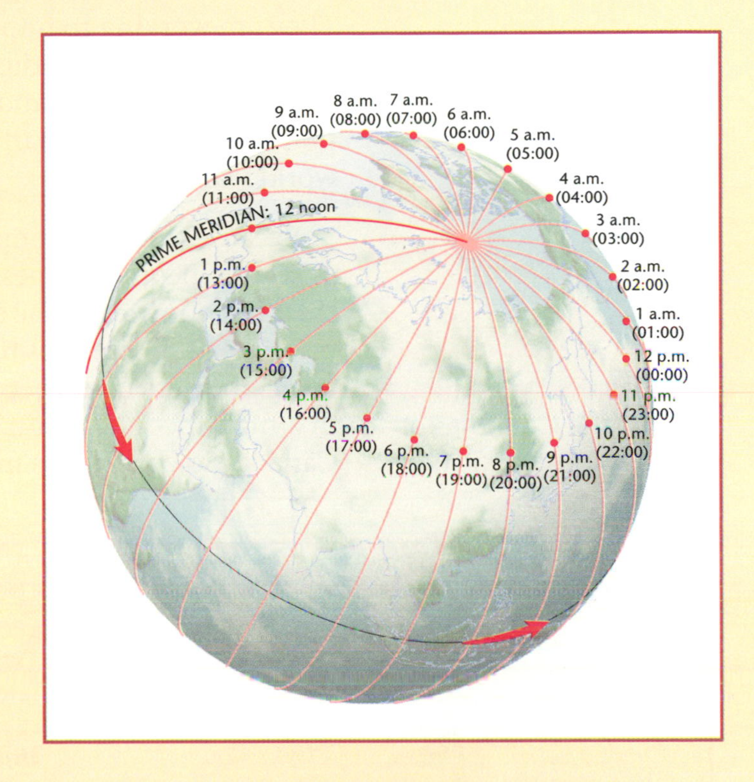

Time Zones

As the earth rotates, it takes about one hour for 15 degrees (°) of longitude to pass by the sun. So the entire surface of the earth can be divided into 24 time zones, one for every 15° of longitude. Every place in the time zone has the same time. In the next time zone to the east it is one hour later.

Time is counted from an imaginary north-south line called the **Prime Meridian**, which passes through Greenwich, England. The time there is called **Greenwich Mean Time**. Every time zone on earth is calculated as being *plus* (+) or *minus* (–) Greenwich Mean Time.

On the other side of the world from the Prime Meridian is the **International Date Line**. This is an imaginary north-south line that passes through the middle of the Pacific Ocean. This is an interesting place because it's where you actually change from one day to the next. If you travel from east to west you move ahead a day. If you travel from west to east you go back one day.

Making It Work

To make time zones work, though, people had to alter some of the borders. Think of the problems that would be caused if a time zone changed right in the middle of a big city! The map on the inside front cover of this book shows you the world's time zones.

The Pacific Rim

Turn back to page 182 and look again at the places where the parts of Sarah's computer are made. Notice that all of the countries are in the **Pacific Rim**—the countries that circle the Pacific Ocean.

This isn't a coincidence. Except for Japan, Canada, and the United States, the countries of the Pacific Rim have low or middle incomes. They are working to improve their GNPs by becoming industrialized and providing goods and services that people in other parts of the world want.

Because their economies are not as strong, people's wages are lower than in countries of the North. This means that it costs less to produce goods in these countries than it does in a high-income country such as Canada. So companies make the goods in places where costs are lower, then sell them in other parts of the world where people can afford to pay a lot of money for them.

Importance in Global Trade

Economists—people who study economics—predict that the Asian countries of the Pacific Rim will become more and more important in global trade. In 2000, these countries already contained 60 per cent of the world's population—from a business point of view, that's 60 per cent of the world's customers!

Economists also predict that these countries will continue to increase their ability to produce goods that the rest of the world wants. For these reasons, Canada is working hard to create strong trade ties with the Asian countries of the Pacific Rim.

The Countries of the Pacific Rim

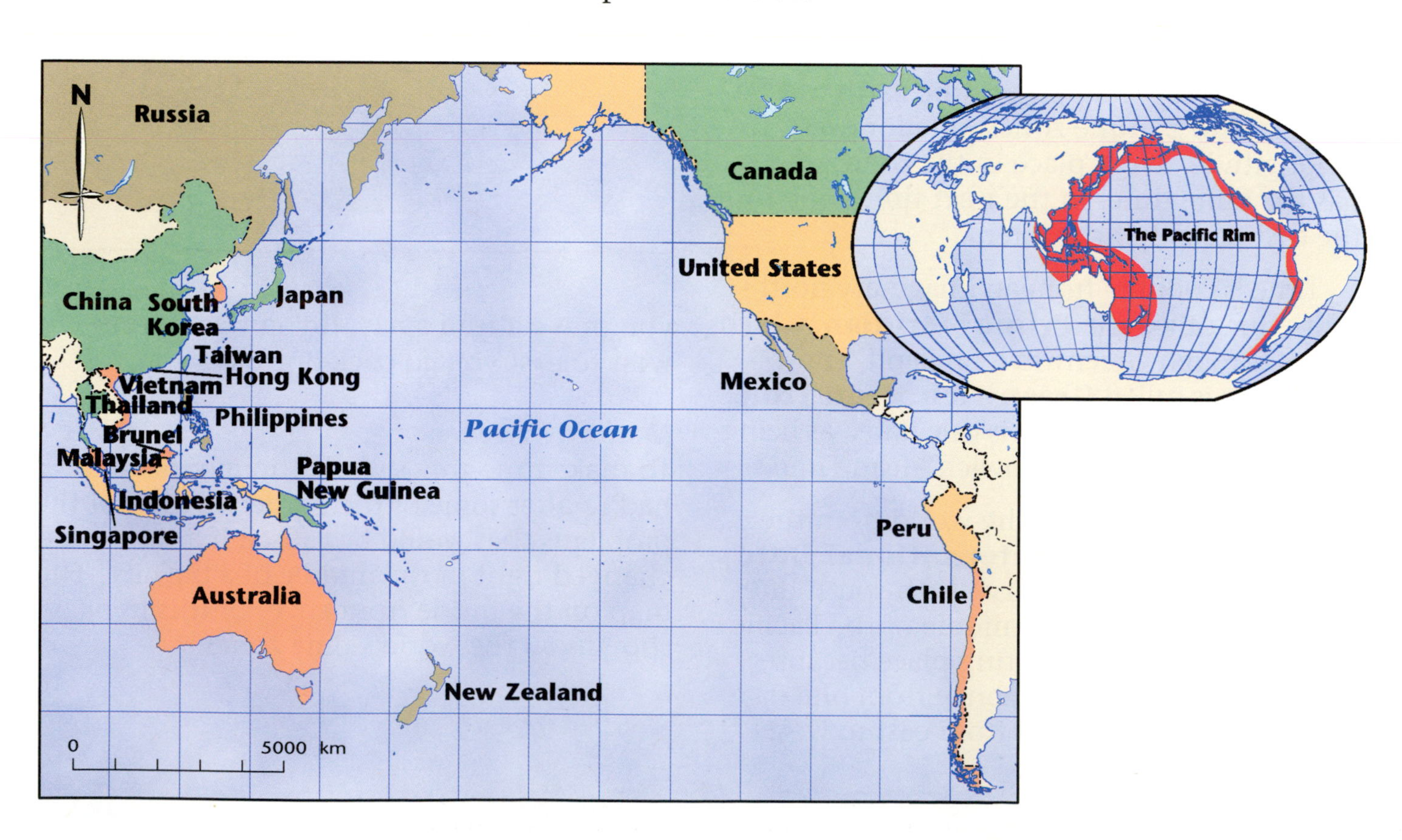

Trade with Japan

Main Exports to Japan *(in order of importance)*	Main Imports from Japan *(in order of importance)*
• lumber • wood pulp • coal • fish and seafood • metals such as copper and aluminum • canola (a grain used to make cooking oil)	• automobiles • power turbines • auto parts • office machinery (including computers) • complex tools • iron and steel

Source: Embassy of Japan in Canada Web Site, November 1999.

Japan is Canada's second most important trading partner.

Think For Yourself

Here are some questions to help you think about what the statistics in this section tell you about Canada's international trade.

- *When countries trade with each other they agree to certain laws and regulations to make sure trade is fair. The trade agreements between Canada and the United States favour a market-oriented system rather than a centrally planned system. Why do you think this is so? What do you predict would happen if Canada didn't agree to be part of a market-oriented system? How would this affect Canadians?*
- *Patterns of imports and exports can tell you a lot about a country's resources. What pattern do you see in the types of goods we import from Japan and the types of goods we export? What do you know about Japan that could explain this? What does this pattern tell you about Canada?*

Reading Hint

If you need to review information about Japan, use the index at the back of this book to help you find the right page numbers.

Try This

Here are some questions to check that you understand time zones. Work with a partner to answer these questions, based on the map on the inside front cover of this book.

- *How many time zones are there in Canada?*
- *When it is noon in Greenwich, England, what time is it in:*
  (a) Vancouver, Canada
  (b) Hong Kong, China (located on China's south coast)
  (c) Sydney, Australia (located on Australia's east coast)?
- *You have a company in Vancouver that imports dresses from India. You want to phone the manufacturer in Mumbai at 5:30 p.m., Mumbai time, on June 15th. What time and day will you have to place your call? (Mumbai is located on India's west coast.)*

The Real Cost of Global Trade

Most of us like to get a bargain. One thing global trade has given us is the chance to buy many different goods at low prices. What could be wrong with that?

Well, some people think that the price you pay in dollars is only a small part of the price the global village is paying for these goods. In this section, you can think about the *real* cost of global trade.

Environmental Costs

Sometimes we make decisions that make money in the short term but harm the environment in the long term. These are the **environmental costs** of doing business. Two important issues concerning global trade and the environment are the transportation of goods around the world and environmental regulations.

Transportation

In global trade, goods are shipped long distances around the world. This consumes a lot of non-renewable resources such as oil and contributes to air and ocean pollution.

People who have studied imports of agricultural products estimate that the food we eat in Canada travels an average of 2400 kilometres to get to our plates! This means you can eat grapes from South Africa in the middle of winter—but is shipping grapes around the world the best use of some of the world's *other* resources?

The Real Cost of Global Trade

This equation is one way to think about the real cost of global trade.

Many goods traded between Canada and the United States and Mexico are shipped by truck. For example, fruit and vegetables from California and Mexico are shipped this way. What resources does this use?

Environmental Regulations

In a global economy, the competition is fierce. This creates a great deal of pressure on companies to produce goods in the cheapest way possible. This might mean using a lot of pesticides to produce more crops for sale or saving money by not installing pollution controls in factory smokestacks.

While no country in the world has a perfect record when it comes to taking care of the environment, some countries have stricter regulations than others. Many countries of the South want businesses to locate there and create much-needed jobs. Having fewer regulations is one way to attract these businesses because the

Paint company threatens to relocate

St. Adelaide, Quebec

André Benoit of Colour Brite Paints announced today that the company is considering shutting down its main factory in St. Adelaide, as well as the smaller plant in Trois Lacs.

The issue is the requirement to put in back-up systems to handle an accidental paint spill into the St. Adelaide River. M. Benoit explains, "We have complied with every environmental regulation that has come along, but the equipment to do this would cost us $1 million. We just can't afford it."

M. Benoit says that if they are forced to make these changes, then they will relocate to Mexico, where this type of equipment is not required. This would mean the loss of 280 jobs in the two small communities.

This mock newspaper article is based on a real event. If you lived in St. Adelaide, which side of the issue would you support? Why?

companies don't have to spend extra money on environmental protection. Choosing to have fewer regulations gets jobs for people and helps companies make higher profits. But what is the cost to the environment?

In 2000, workers in Mexico making brand-name jeans to be sold in Canada made about $5.00 for a 10-hour work day. Even though the cost of living is lower in Mexico, it is hard to survive on this wage.

Human Costs

The **human costs** of global trade are the effects that trade has on people. Two things we need to think about are working conditions and culture.

Working Conditions

Many people in countries of the South who work for transnational corporations or local companies work under conditions that are illegal in Canada. In Canada, we have regulations to ensure that our workplaces are safe, don't cause illness, respect human rights, and don't take advantage of children. Although not every workplace is perfect, most regulations are usually enforced.

You can find out more about child labour in the next section.

This isn't always the case in the South, though. Often there are no regulations or they are not enforced. This is not because the people of the South don't care about their workplace, but because they need jobs. They are willing to work under very poor conditions to earn enough money to meet their basic needs. The lack of regulations saves the companies money, but it harms the lives of the workers. Wages are also low, which means people have to work long hours just to meet their basic needs. In some places, children as young as four years old work at some jobs.

In recent years, Canada has signed trade agreements with the United States and Mexico that have made it easier for goods made in these countries to be imported into Canada. Because of this, many American and Canadian clothing and car manufacturers now have factories in Mexico. Luisa works in one of the clothing factories. Here's what she says about conditions there:

There are a lot of problems. There's no ventilation, no exhaust fans—even though there's a lot of dust in the factory, the dust came from the fabric we were sewing. At the end of the day you would walk out there covered with dust all over your body. It caused a lot of illness. Headaches, sore throats, eye infections—all caused by dust.

Source: *The Global Factory* (Philadelphia: American Friends Service Committee, 1990).

Global Culture

Another effect of global trade is that along with products from different countries come different ideas about culture. These can influence what people wear, eat, and drink. Sometimes this can help us understand others. But it can also mean that a country with a strong economy can spread its culture around the globe.

Young people are often interested in new ideas from other cultures. In 1998, children between the ages of 7 and 18 in the Pacific Rim countries of Asia and Oceania were surveyed about their opinions on many things, including these two questions:

- *What's your favourite fast-food restaurant?*
- *What's your favourite soft drink?*

The map on page 191 shows the results.

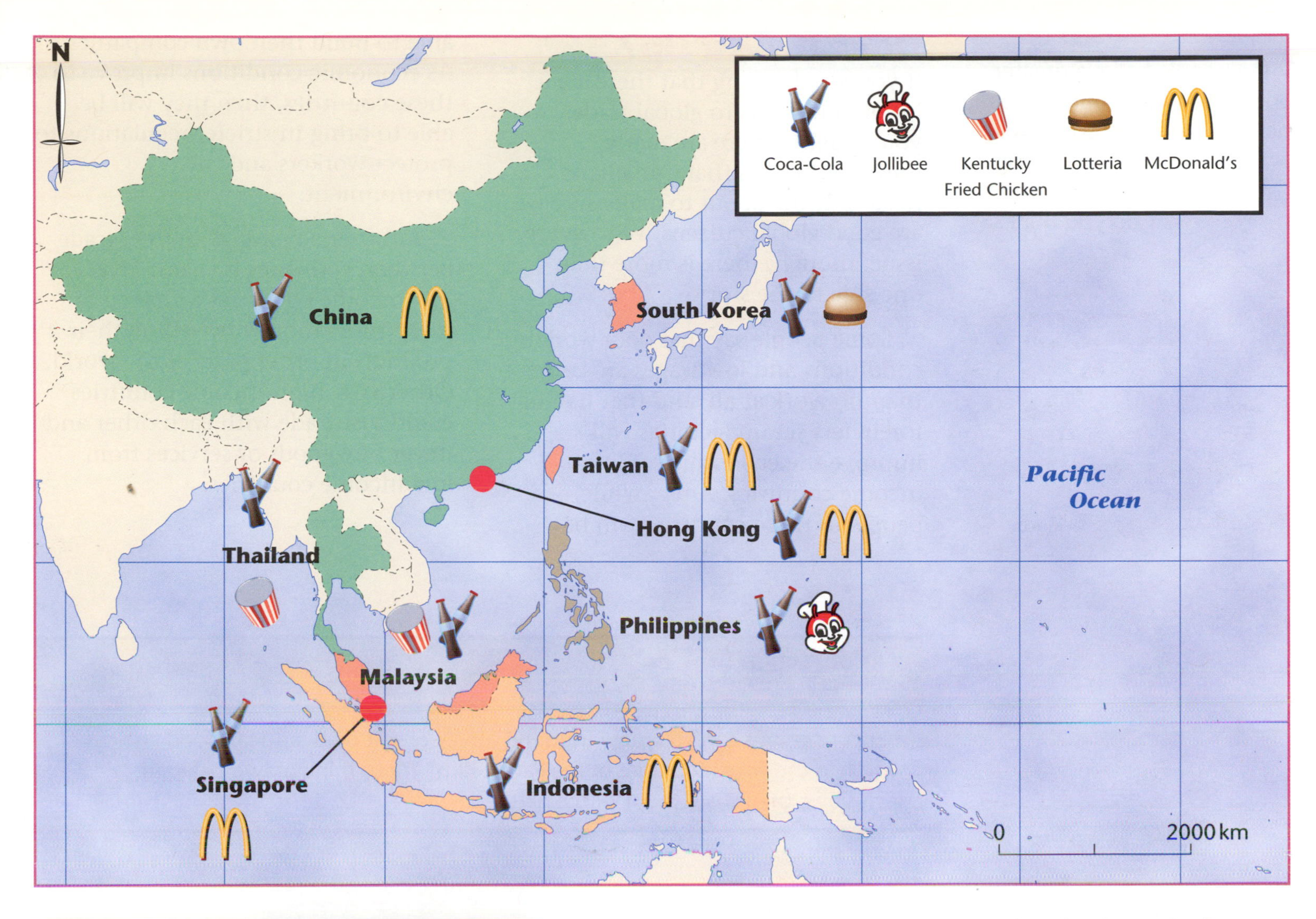

Fast-food and Soft Drink Choices in Some Pacific Rim Countries

McDonald's originally began in the United States. By 1997, the company had more than 23 000 restaurants in 113 countries. On average, McDonald's opens five new restaurants somewhere in the world every day. Coca-Cola and Kentucky Fried Chicken are also American products.

Some people believe greater contact between countries of the North and the South will help to improve human rights around the world. What do you think?

Does It Add Up?

If you are thinking that there are a lot of drawbacks to global trade, you're right. There are many important issues that Canadians need to think about to make sure we are good global citizens. With every issue, though, there is more than one side to the story.

Some people say that poor working conditions and low wages are better than no work at all, and that having foreigners set up factories will improve the economies of low-income countries. After awhile, people in these countries will be able to build their own companies. As economic conditions improve in these countries, then they will be able to bring in stricter regulations to protect workers and the environment.

Another advantage to freer trade between countries is that it gives low-income countries a chance to make more money by selling their products in other parts of the world. Otherwise, high-income countries could just trade with each other and never buy goods or services from low-income countries.

Try This

What conclusions can you draw from the survey of soft drink and fast-food choices of children in the Asian countries of the Pacific Rim? Try to think of two different conclusions, then share them with a partner.

Think For Yourself

Form two groups and debate this topic:

- Increased global trade is good for the world.

Here are some questions to help you think of arguments for and against this statement:

- *What are the benefits of global trade?*
- *What are the drawbacks of global trade?*
- *How does global trade affect the way we share the world's resources?*
- *How does global trade affect world cultures?*
- *Do some people benefit more from global trade than others?*

When you do research for facts and ideas to support your point of view, think about how to make sure the information you use is reliable and includes different perspectives. What biases should you look for?

Child Labour

You've discovered in the last section that some workers in countries of the South are children. In this section, you can find out more about **child labour**.

What Is Child Labour?

In many families, children make valuable contributions. This might be helping on the farm, hunting or fishing, doing the dishes, or working in the family store for a few hours. As children get older and stronger, they may be expected to help out more. Sometimes children also work for pay, such as mowing lawns in the neighbourhood, delivering papers, and babysitting.

This kind of work helps children feel part of the community and prepares them for life as adults. As long as children still have time to go to school, to play, and to get enough rest and exercise so that they can grow into healthy adults, this type of work is okay.

Child labour, on the other hand, is work that is not okay for children to do. According to the Convention on the Rights of the Child, children have the right to be protected from work that **exploits** them or is **hazardous**. Work that exploits children benefits others but does not benefit the child. Hazardous work is work that is too dangerous for children to do. Signs of child labour include:

- the work is too hard for a child
- working conditions are unsafe or unhealthy
- there is no time for play or social time with friends and family
- the child does not go to school or is too tired to learn
- the work doesn't pay fairly

In what ways do you contribute to your family? How do you feel about this?

Where Is Child Labour the Most Common?

Child labour happens, legally or illegally, in all countries of the world. For example, in the United States many children work picking crops. They must move during the year as different crops become ripe, so they often miss out on getting a proper education. In Canada, UNICEF estimates that there are 8000 child labourers working on farms and in clothing factories. This is illegal, but it still happens. Why do you think this is so?

According to the United Nations, however, child labour is most common in the countries of Asia, except for Japan. (In Japan, it is even unusual for teenagers to have part-time jobs—time for school is considered much more important.) There are also high numbers of child labourers in Africa and Latin America.

What do you know about the economies of the Asian countries of the Pacific Rim that might help explain this pictograph? How does global trade connect Canadians to this issue?

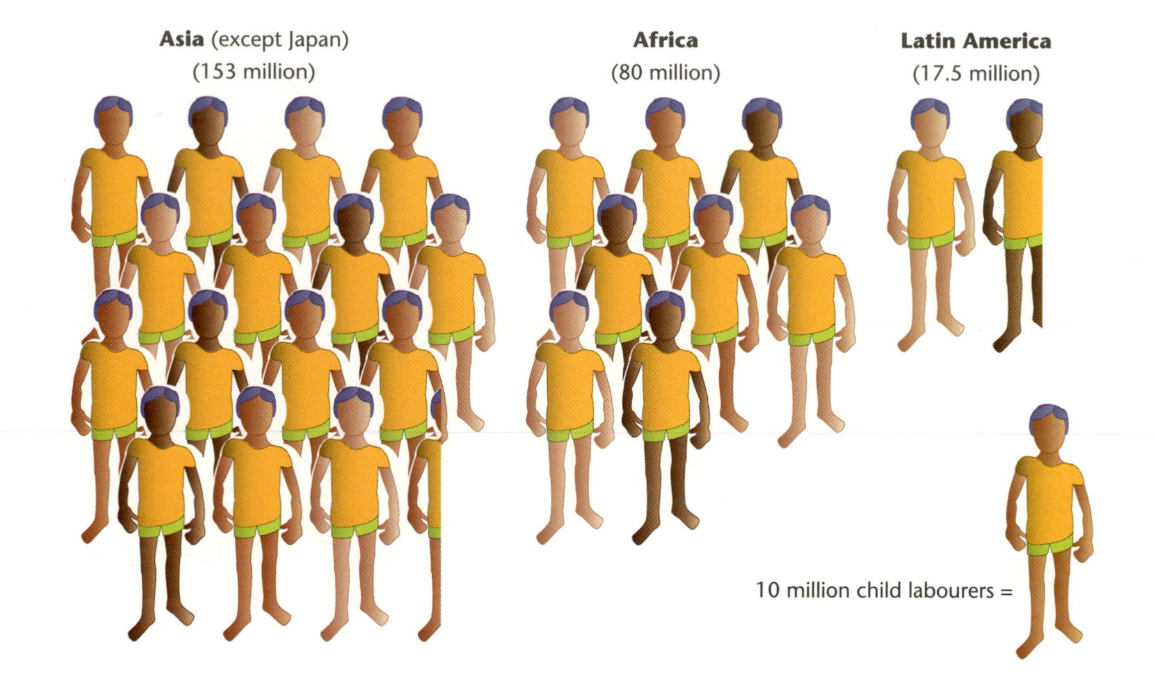

Try This

With a partner, read and look at the examples of child labour in A Closer Look on pages 195 to 196. Decide for yourselves why the work is not suitable for a child.

A Closer Look

Types of Child Labour

Child labour can be found in almost any kind of work. According to UNICEF, however, children mostly work:

- on the streets, selling goods or offering services
- in agriculture—on big farms owned by others
- in their own homes or on their family farms

Some children—about 5 per cent of all child labourers—work in industries making consumer goods.

Children who work on the streets work wherever they can find customers. Profits are low because there is so much competition. Some children live on the street, while others go home at night. Weather, traffic, and beatings from other street children are hazards all children who work on the street face. In some countries, they also face beatings by police and other adults who want to keep the streets clear for other businesses. What kind of problems do you think squeegee kids living on the streets in Canada might face?

Farm work is very hard and it often means working with poisonous chemicals in pesticides. Children often begin by going to the fields with their parents because there is no one else to look after them. As soon as they are old enough, they start working as much as they can. This young girl and her family work on farms in the southern United States. They move from place to place to work where they're needed.

Most kids help out around the home, but in some families children are needed so much that they don't get a chance to go to school. Children might be needed to care for younger children, help with farm chores, or gather fuel and water. This type of work is usually done by girls. This young girl in a village in Bangladesh takes care of her brother while her parents work.

Children who produce consumer goods don't usually work in big factories. Instead, they work for small businesses. Some of these businesses sell goods such as baseballs or clothing to larger companies that export them. Other companies make things such as bricks for local use. Wages are low, and there is no safety equipment. Many children work six or seven days a week and may work more than 10 hours a day. These girls are working in a clothing factory in Malaysia.

Changing the World

When we work to find solutions to problems, we sometimes find that the issues are more complicated than they might seem at first. One issue like this is child labour.

Some people think that we should **boycott** goods produced by children. Boycotting is when people agree not to buy something to show that they disagree with something the company is doing. Because boycotting affects the profits a company makes, it can be a powerful way to get companies to change the way they do things.

Is boycotting the best solution to the problem of child labour? In this section, you can investigate the issue and find out why it's not so simple.

Iqbal Masih's Story

For centuries, children around the world have worked in conditions that have ruined their health, shortened their lives, and deprived them of the chance to get an education and to lead a normal life as adults. People have always known about this. Some people have even tried to do something to improve the situation for children. In our times, though, one 10-year-old boy made the world really pay attention to this problem. His name was Iqbal Masih.

Iqbal Masih was born to a low-income family in Pakistan. When he was four years old his father needed money. In exchange for a loan of approximately $12, Iqbal went to work for the local carpet manufacturer. The idea was that Iqbal would

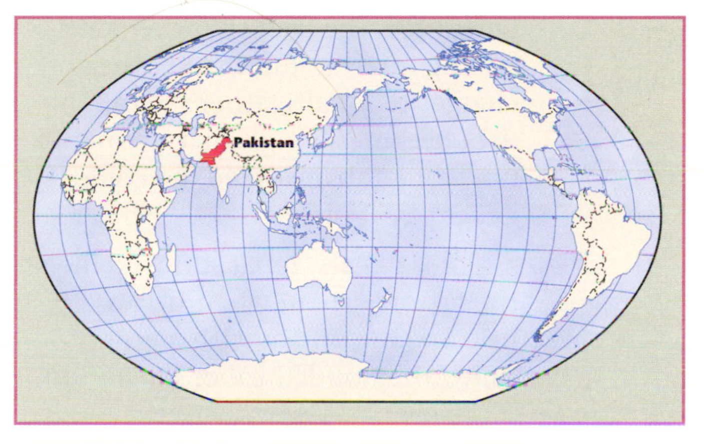

Pakistan is a low-income country in Asia. What does this photo show you about life for some people in Pakistan? What do you need to remember when you see only one photograph of a country?

The life Iqbal led as a bonded labourer is not unusual. The International Labour Organization estimates that there are 15 million bonded child labourers in India alone.

Some of the goods made by children that are imported into Canada are running shoes, sports equipment (soccer balls, baseballs), carpets, and clothing.

work to pay off the loan. This is called **bonded** labour—the worker is not free to leave the job.

In the factory, Iqbal joined other children working in harsh conditions. He was chained to a loom where he made carpets. The air he breathed was filled with dust from the carpet wool. Often, his fingers were cut by the sharp tool used to trim the wool. When this happened, the cut finger was dipped in hot oil to stop the bleeding.

Iqbal worked six days a week, 13 hours a day. He was given just enough food to keep him alive. If he made a mistake, he was beaten. Over time, the factory owner kept adding interest, fines, and other charges to Iqbal's father's loan. The debt became so high that no matter how long Iqbal worked, he could never pay it off.

For six years, Iqbal survived life at the factory. Then, when he was 10, he came in contact with a group called the Bonded Labor Liberation Front (BLLF). The group helped him get away from his owner. Because of his difficult life, Iqbal was small for his age, and he had trouble breathing and pain in his fingers. None of these things stopped him from working with the BLLF, though, and he helped at least 3000 children forced into labour in Pakistan to gain their freedom.

Eventually Iqbal travelled around the world, speaking to groups about the life of child labourers. One of the most important things he talked about was the need for all children to get an education. Iqbal became a well-known spokesperson for children's rights and won awards for his work.

Tragically, when he was 12, Iqbal was shot and killed while riding a bicycle near his home. Some people believed he was murdered by factory owners who were against his work, although there was no evidence to prove this. Iqbal's death touched the hearts of people all over the world.

This photograph shows a child working in a carpet factory similar to the one Iqbal worked in. Pakistan has a tropical climate, so it's very hot in a factory like this. Usually there are no windows to open for fresh air—this is to keep bugs from getting in and damaging the carpets. Can you imagine what it would be like to work in a factory like this?

In 1994, Iqbal received a "Youth in Action" award for his work in human rights. In his speech when he received the award he said, "I appeal to you that you stop people from using children as bonded labourers because the children need to use a pen rather than the instruments of child labour." What do you think he meant?

No Easy Answers

Iqbal inspired many people to take action on the issue of bonded child labourers. Politicians in the governments of the United States and Germany spoke out and began working to make it illegal to import goods made by child labourers. Many people started boycotting products made by children.

The carpet manufacturers decided they'd better pay attention. They started firing child workers. For many children, though, this didn't solve the problem. Instead, they were forced to look for other jobs. Many of these jobs, such as crushing stone and working with metal, were worse than the jobs in the factories and paid even lower wages. So while people had good intentions, the results often made matters worse.

Better Understanding

In time, people realized that they had to look at the reasons why children need to work in the first place. Families don't make their children work because they don't love them or don't want them—they make their children work because they need the income. People interviewing child labourers found that some children were proud to be helping their families. For many, life in the factory was better than staying home and starving.

It turned out that this was a complicated problem that needed more solutions than just stopping child labour. One solution was for organizations to provide families with a small income or loan to replace the income of a child who stops working. Another solution was to provide schools to educate children so that they could get jobs in the future. So far, these solutions have had good results in communities where they have been tried.

UNICEF reports that about 50 000 children in Pakistan lost their jobs because of threats of boycotts, while about 1.5 million families in India no longer receive income from their children.

Kids in Action!

This school for freed bonded labourers in Pakistan was planned and built by local people with money raised by Grade 7 students in the United States. Iqbal Masih had visited the American school. When he died, students decided to raise money for a school in his memory.

Investigate

If reading this chapter has made you think you'd like to do something about child labour, think about how you can make a difference. Sometimes the best way to make a difference is to come up with your own ideas and act on them. When it is a complicated issue, though, it is sometimes better to join others who have already learned about the issue and have figured out what works.

Do some research to find information on organizations that are working to help improve the conditions of child labourers. You could write to UNICEF for information, or you could do some Internet research. Free the Children International is one organization you might want to look into. It was started by a 12-year-old Canadian boy named Craig Keilburger, and it is especially for young people.

Once you have gathered information about different organizations and their projects, plan a way for you or your class to participate.

Looking Back

This chapter showed you how trade connects us in many ways with people all around the world.

What do you think is the biggest drawback to Canada being involved in global trade? What is the biggest benefit?

Chapter **12**

Your Voice, Your Actions

Your **voice** is what you have to say about your ideas, opinions, and feelings. Your **actions** are what you do about them.

All through this text there are examples of "*Kids in Action*"—young people who have found their voices and taken action to make the world a better place. Reading about these people might have helped you find your voice and decide to take action yourself.

In this short chapter, you can think about the topics, issues, and problems you've investigated this year. Then you can have fun thinking of a creative way to show what's most important to you about being a good global citizen.

Now You Know

At the beginning of this book, we listed some powerful questions about topics we were going to investigate this year in social studies. Here's a reminder of what some of those questions were and some of the main ideas presented in the chapters you've read.

Cultures

How can we make sure that solutions to global problems work for people of all cultures?

Ideas and Issues

- *Learning About Others*
- *Stopping Stereotypes*
- *Respecting Indigenous Cultures*

Environments

How do our actions and technologies affect our environments? How can we make sure everyone takes care of the environment?

Ideas and Issues

- *Sustainable Management*
- *North/South Sharing*
- *Urban Migration*
- *Industrialization*

Governments

What are the different systems of government in the world? Do people have the same rights and responsibilities in all countries?

Ideas and Issues

- *Democracies*
- *Dictatorships*
- *Human Rights*
- *Children's Rights*

Economies

What are the economic systems we use to share resources? How can we share more equally?

Ideas and Issues

- *Market-oriented Economies*
- *Centrally Planned Economies*
- *Global Trade*
- *Social Safety Nets*

Think For Yourself

1. With a partner, look over page 202 and discuss:
   - your opinion of the most important idea you learned about each topic this year
   - one hope you have for the future for each topic
   - any important questions you still have.
2. Choose one of these activities to do on your own, with a partner or in a group.
   - Pick the topic that matters to you the most. Present your ideas on why it is important and what you plan to do about it. Be creative—you could sing a song, write a poem, do a skit, make a video . . . well, you get the idea!
   - Describe what it takes to be a good global citizen. This is another chance to be creative. For example, you could write a Recipe for a Good Global Citizen, make a giant Global Citizen Charm Bracelet, make Good Global Citizen flashcards . . . or? Include at least eight ideas about global citizenship—think of words and pictures.

Taking care of the environment is one way young people can be good global citizens.

Looking Back

And looking ahead!

What advice would you give to next year's Grade 6 class to help them enjoy social studies and learn as much as they can? What do you want to remember for yourself for next year?

Maps

Reading maps and making maps are important parts of social studies. Maps can help us locate and understand many things about the global village, including borders between countries, landforms, environments, and climates. In your reports, you can also use maps to show what you know to others.

This special section of *Global Citizens* includes some tips on how to read maps and how to find your place in the world using latitude and longitude. It also has a map of British Columbia and four different maps of the world. You'll need to use these maps to do some of the activities in this text. You may also find the maps useful when you do research.

What's in This Section

Maps

Reading Maps

Here are some tips on how to read maps.

1. Look for a **title**. It tells you what the map is about.

World Climates

2. See if there is a **directional symbol** on the map. It tells you which direction is North. Once you know that, you can figure out East, West, and South.

3. Find the **scale**. It compares the distance on the map to the actual distance in a real place.

0 1000 2000 3000 km
Scale at the Equator

4. Look for a **legend**. It tells you what the symbols and colours on the map mean.

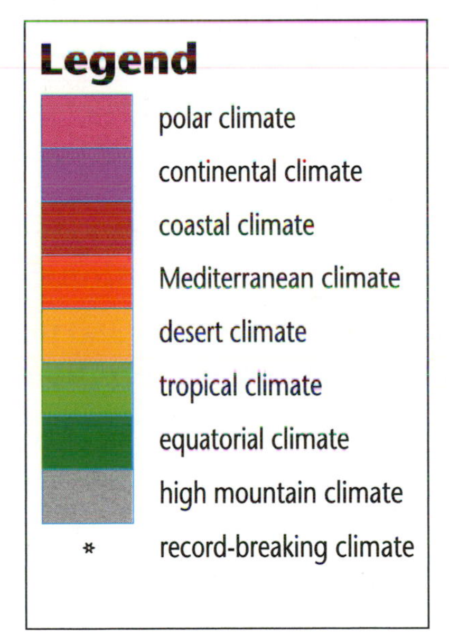

5. See if the map has a **grid**. It gives you co-ordinates you can use to find a specific location. For example, the house on this grid is B3.

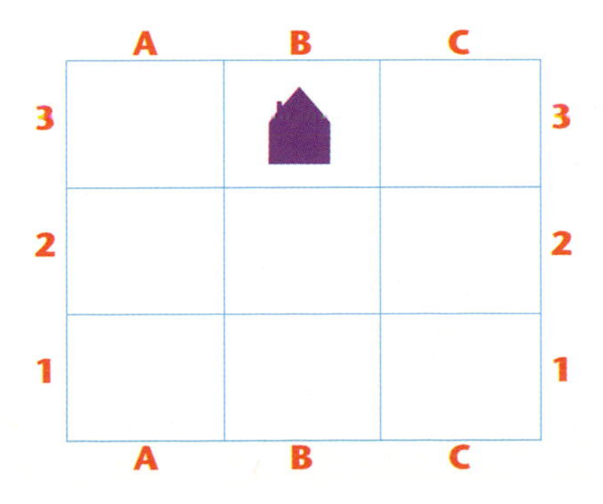

Finding Your Place

Latitude and **longitude** are imaginary lines that are used to create a grid for the world. They are measured in **degrees**, which are shown by this symbol: °.

Parallels of Latitude

Parallels of latitude are the lines that go around the earth. Each line is marked N (north) or S (south) to show whether it is in the **Northern** or **Southern hemisphere**. The Equator is at 0° latitude. The two poles are at 90°N latitude (the North Pole) and 90°S latitude (the South Pole).

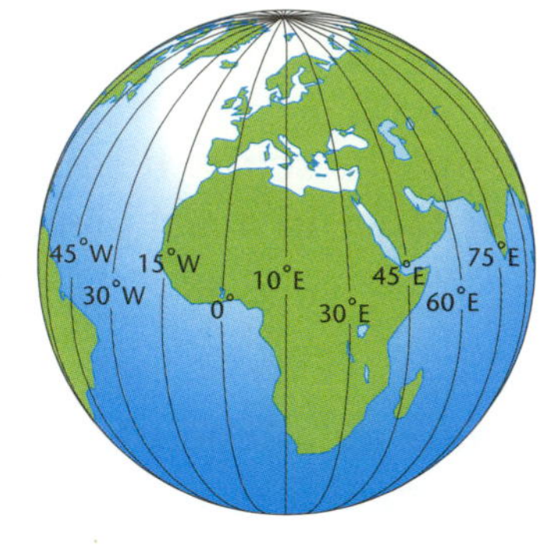

Meridians of Longitude

Meridians [muh-RID-ee-unz] of longitude are lines that go from the North Pole to the South Pole. There isn't a natural "middle" for these lines, like the Equator is for parallels of latitude. So some time ago mapmakers decided a place called Greenwich in England would mark 0° for meridians of longitude.

Mapmakers called this first meridian of longitude the **Prime Meridian**. The other meridians measure distances in degrees east or west of the prime meridian, up to 180°E and 180°W. Directly opposite the Prime Meridian, on the other side of the world, the east meridians meet up with the west meridians. This point is called the **International Date Line**.

Together, the Prime Meridian and the International Date Line divide the world into **Eastern** and **Western hemispheres**.

The World Grid

Combining parallels of latitude and meridians of longitude creates a grid that covers the world. To describe a location in the world, you give the latitude first, then the longitude. If a place isn't exactly where two lines cross, you can still give a close approximate location.

British Columbia

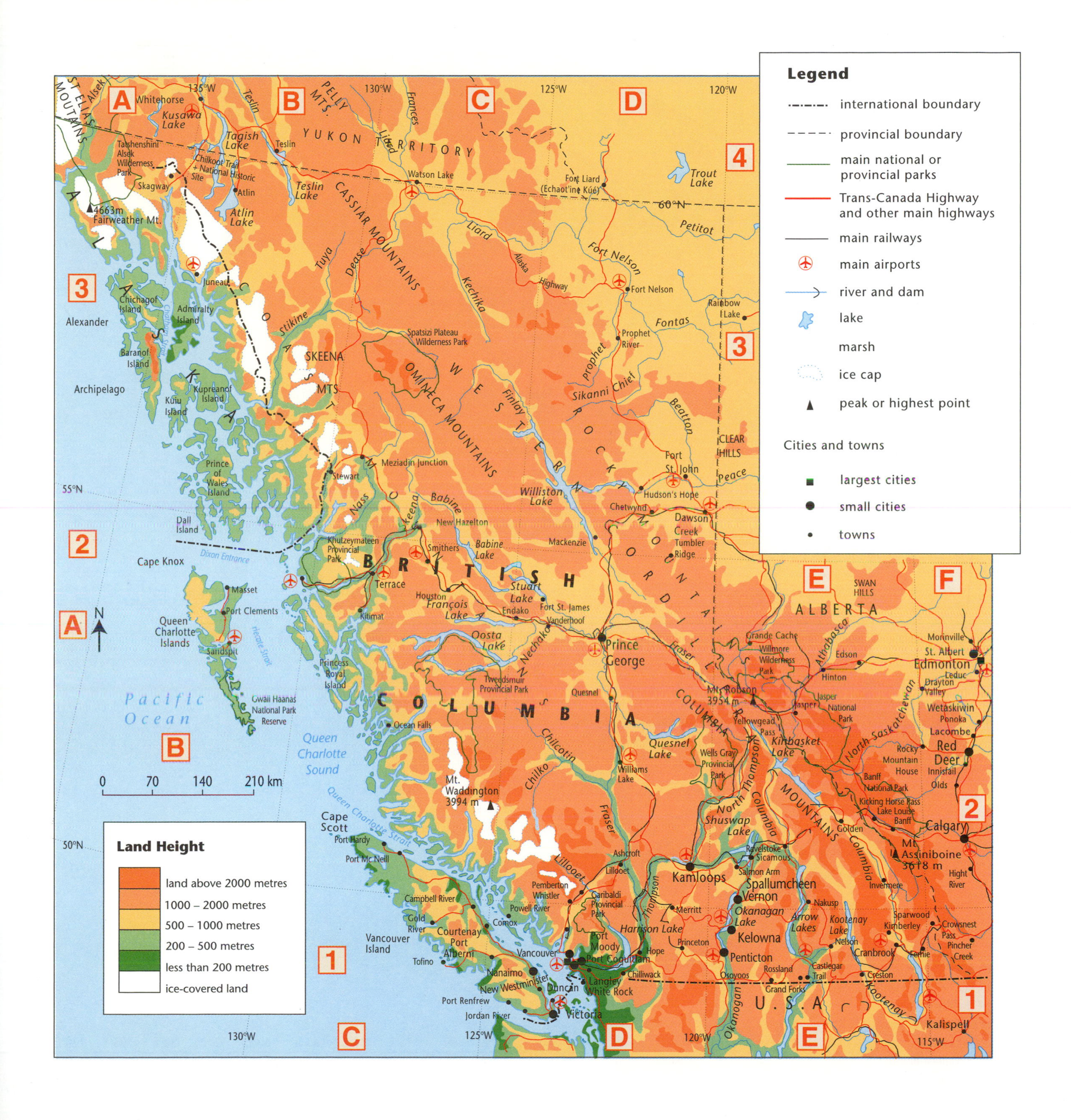

Countries of the World

5°E
180°
165°W
150°W
135°W
120°W
105°W
90°W
75°W
60°W
45°W
Greenland
75°N
Arctic Circle
66°33'N
60°N
Canada
45°N
United States
of America
Atlantic
Ocean
Bermuda
30°N
Tropic of Cancer
The
Bahamas
23°27'N
Hawaiian
Islands (US)
Mexico
Cuba
Haiti
Jamaica
D.R. P.R.
St. Kitts & Nevis
Antigua & Barbuda
Belize
Honduras
Do
St. Lucia
15°N
Guatemala
S.V.
Barbados
Nicaragua
Grenada
T.&T.
El Salvador
Pacific Ocean
Costa Rica
Venezuela
Guyana
Panama
Suriname
French Guiana
Colombia
Equator
0°
Galapagos Islands
Ecuador
lomon
lands
Brazil
Peru
Samoa
15°S
Vanuatu
Bolivia
Fiji
Tonga
New Caledonia
23°27'S
Paraguay
Tropic of Capricorn
Chile
30°S
Uruguay
Argentina
New
Zealand
45°S
Caribbean
Do Dominica
D.R. Dominican Republic
P.R. Puerto Rico
S.V. St. Vincent and
The Grenadines
T.&T. Trinidad and Tobago
60°S
66°33'S
Antarctic Circle
75°S

World Land Heights and Rivers

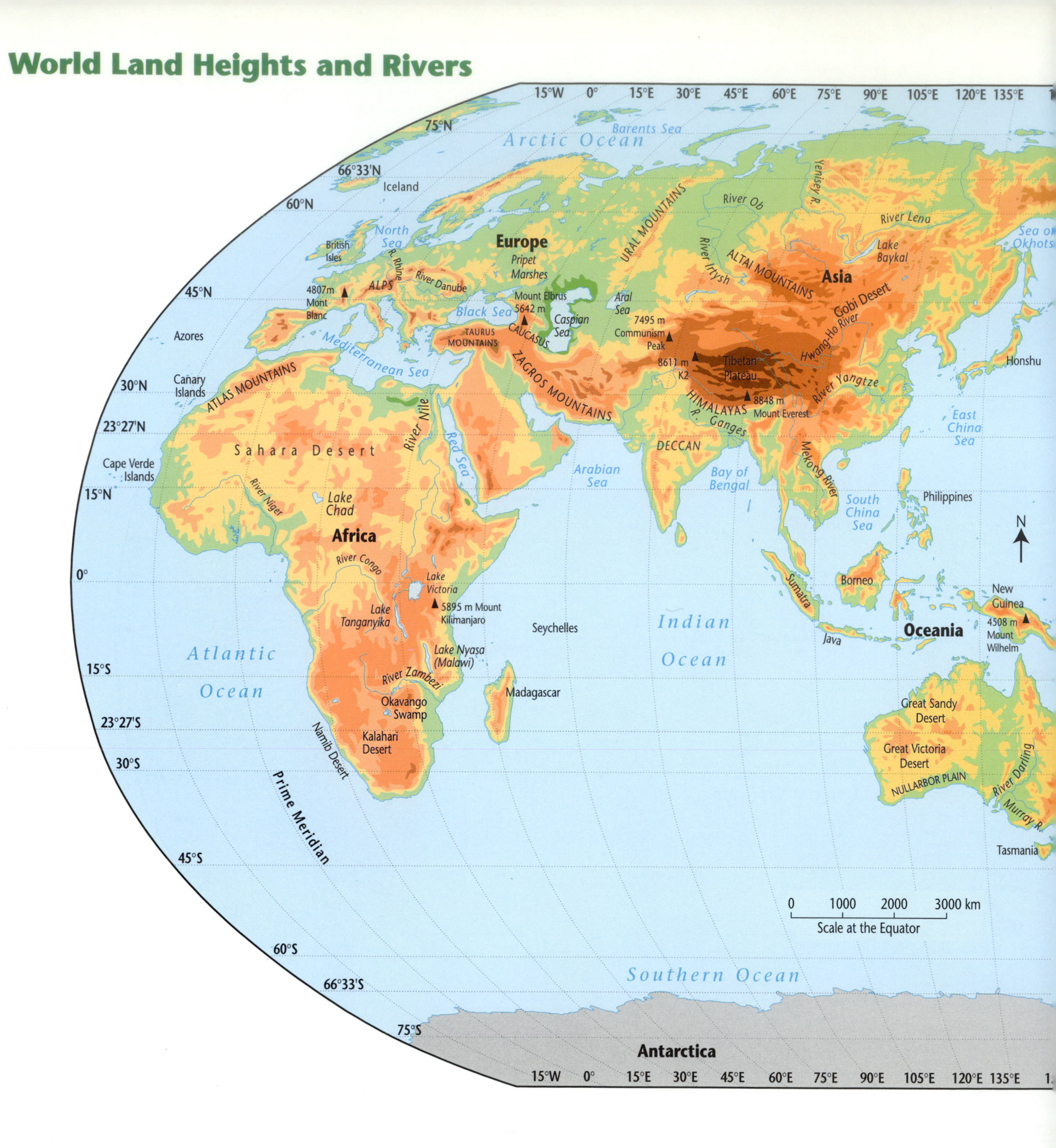

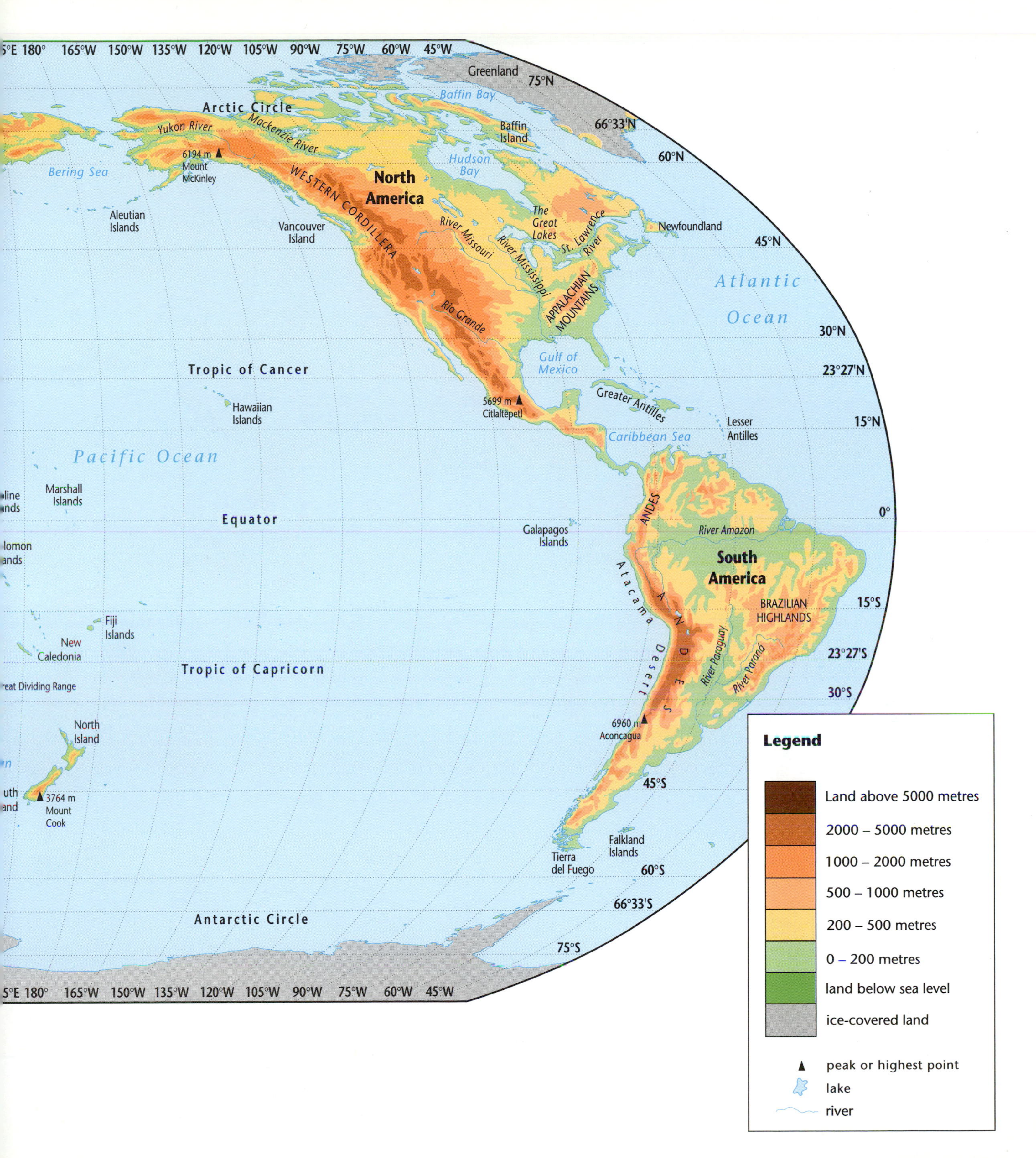

Greenland
Baffin Bay
Arctic Circle
Yukon River
Mackenzie River
Baffin Island
Hudson Bay
6194 m
Mount McKinley
Bering Sea
North America
WESTERN CORDILLERA
Aleutian Islands
Vancouver Island
River Missouri
River Mississippi
The Great Lakes
St. Lawrence River
Newfoundland
APPALACHIAN MOUNTAINS
Rio Grande
Atlantic Ocean
Gulf of Mexico
Tropic of Cancer
Greater Antilles
5699 m
Citlaltépetl
Hawaiian Islands
Lesser Antilles
Caribbean Sea
Pacific Ocean
Marshall Islands
Equator
ANDES
Galapagos Islands
River Amazon
South America
Atacama Desert
BRAZILIAN HIGHLANDS
Fiji Islands
New Caledonia
River Paraguay
River Paraná
Tropic of Capricorn
Great Dividing Range
6960 m
Aconcagua
North Island
3764 m
Mount Cook
Falkland Islands
Tierra del Fuego
Antarctic Circle
75°N
66°33'N
60°N
45°N
30°N
23°27'N
15°N
0°
15°S
23°27'S
30°S
45°S
60°S
66°33'S
75°S
180°
165°W
150°W
135°W
120°W
105°W
90°W
75°W
60°W
45°W
Legend
Land above 5000 metres
2000 – 5000 metres
1000 – 2000 metres
500 – 1000 metres
200 – 500 metres
0 – 200 metres
land below sea level
ice-covered land
peak or highest point
lake
river

World Environments

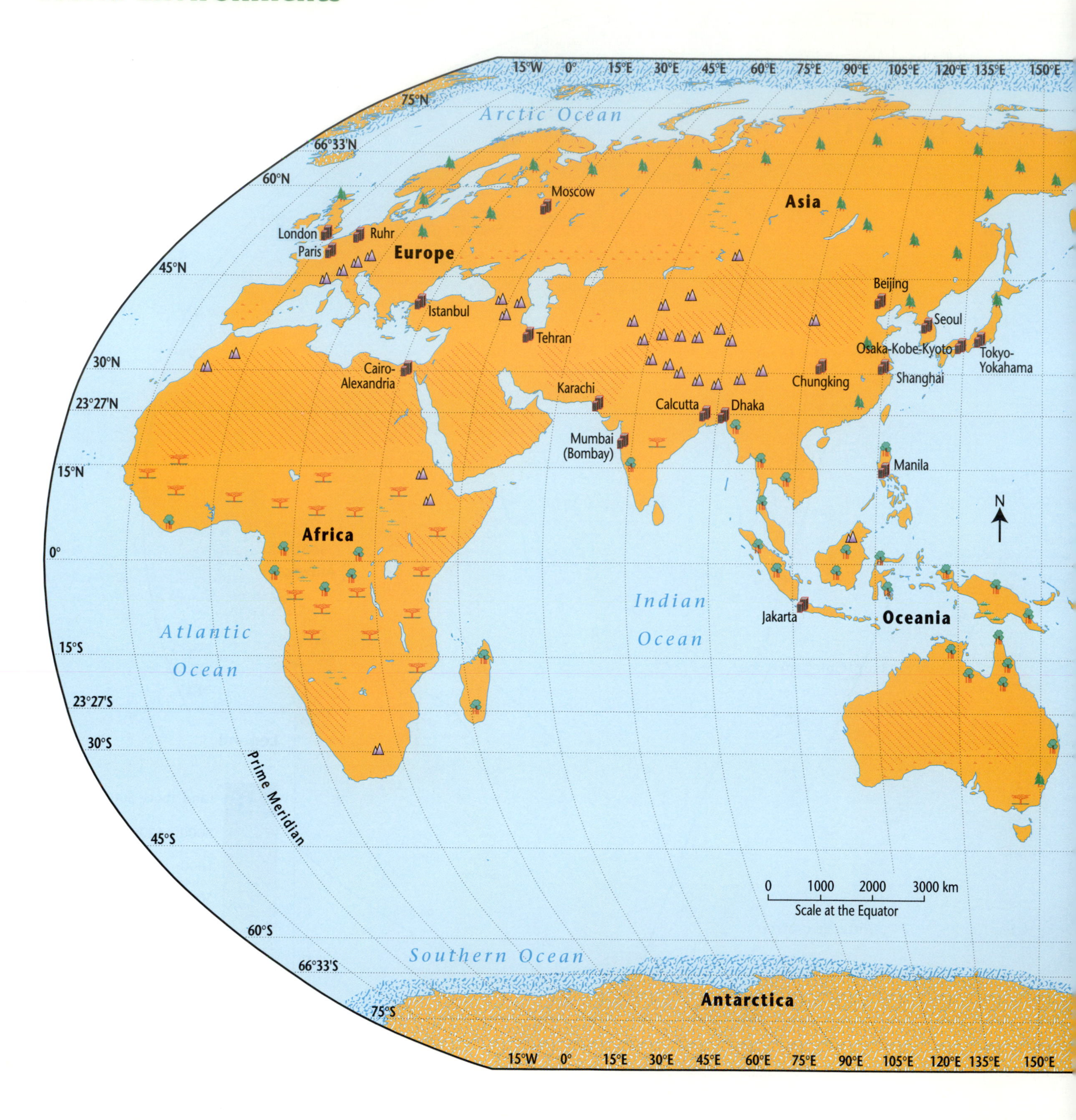

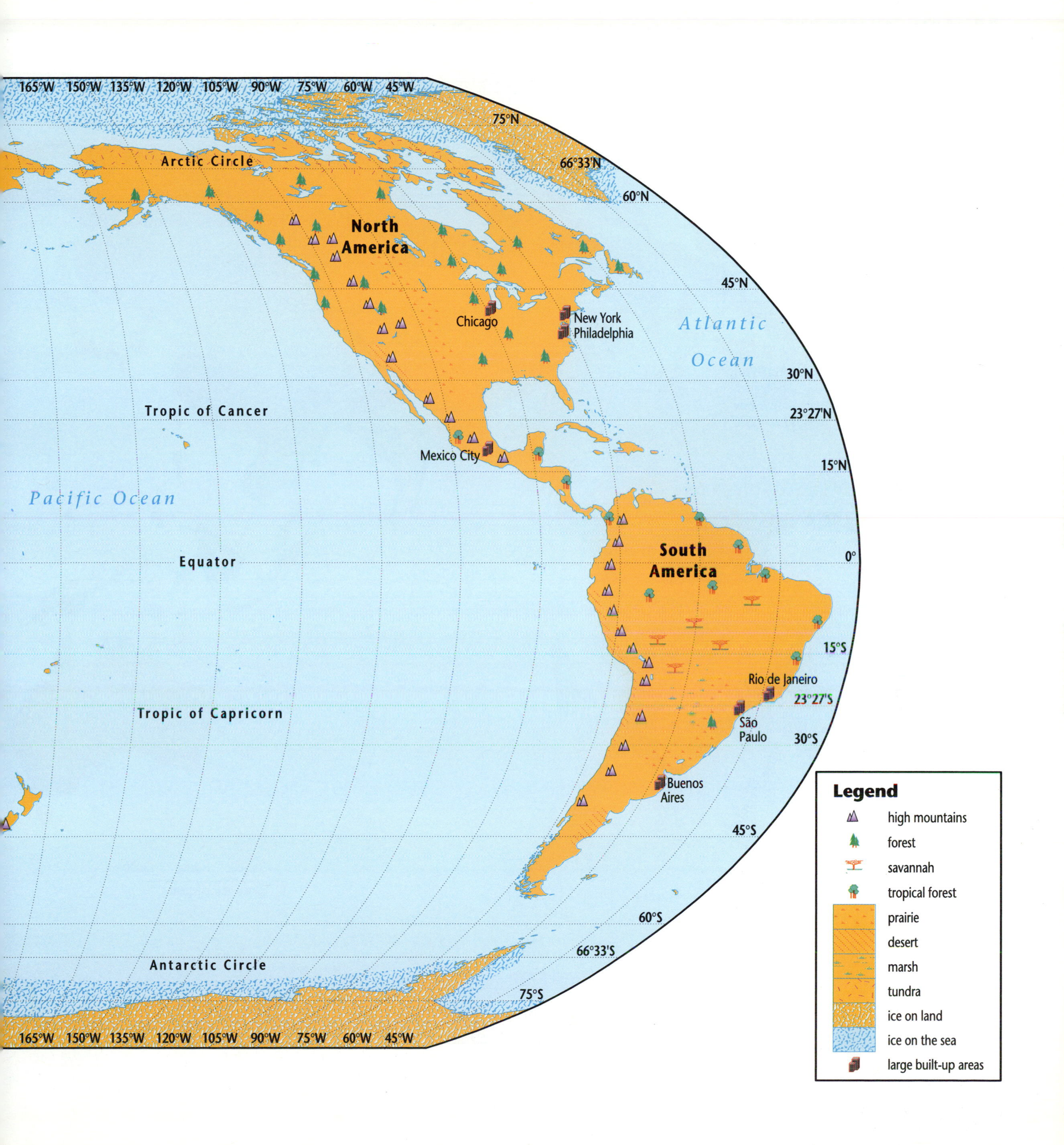
165°W 150°W 135°W 120°W 105°W 90°W 75°W 60°W 45°W
75°N
66°33'N
60°N
45°N
30°N
23°27'N
15°N
0°
15°S
23°27'S
30°S
45°S
60°S
66°33'S
75°S
Arctic Circle
North America
Chicago
New York
Philadelphia
Atlantic Ocean
Tropic of Cancer
Mexico City
Pacific Ocean
Equator
South America
Rio de Janeiro
São Paulo
Buenos Aires
Tropic of Capricorn
Antarctic Circle
Legend
high mountains
forest
savannah
tropical forest
prairie
desert
marsh
tundra
ice on land
ice on the sea
large built-up areas

World Climates

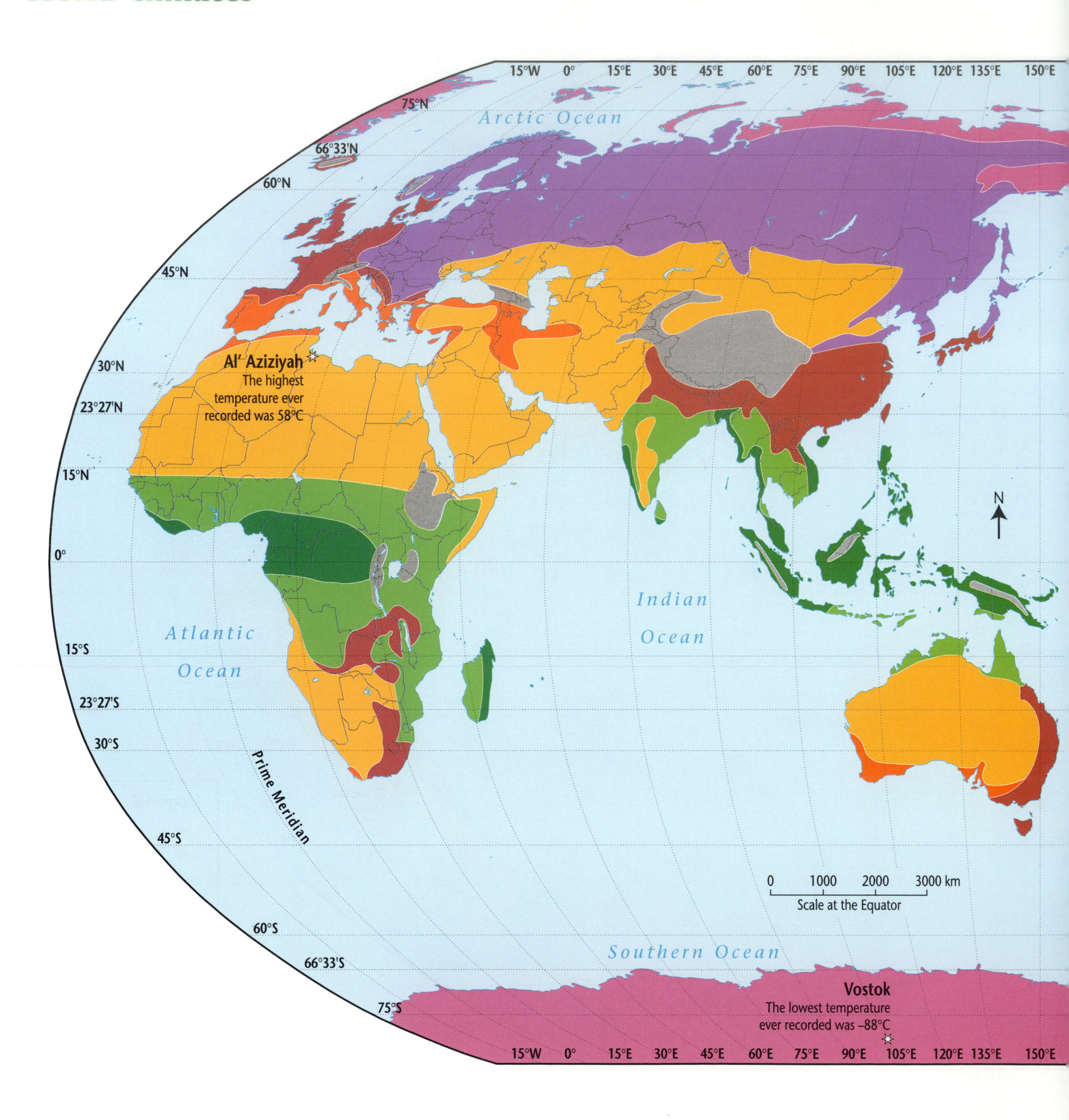

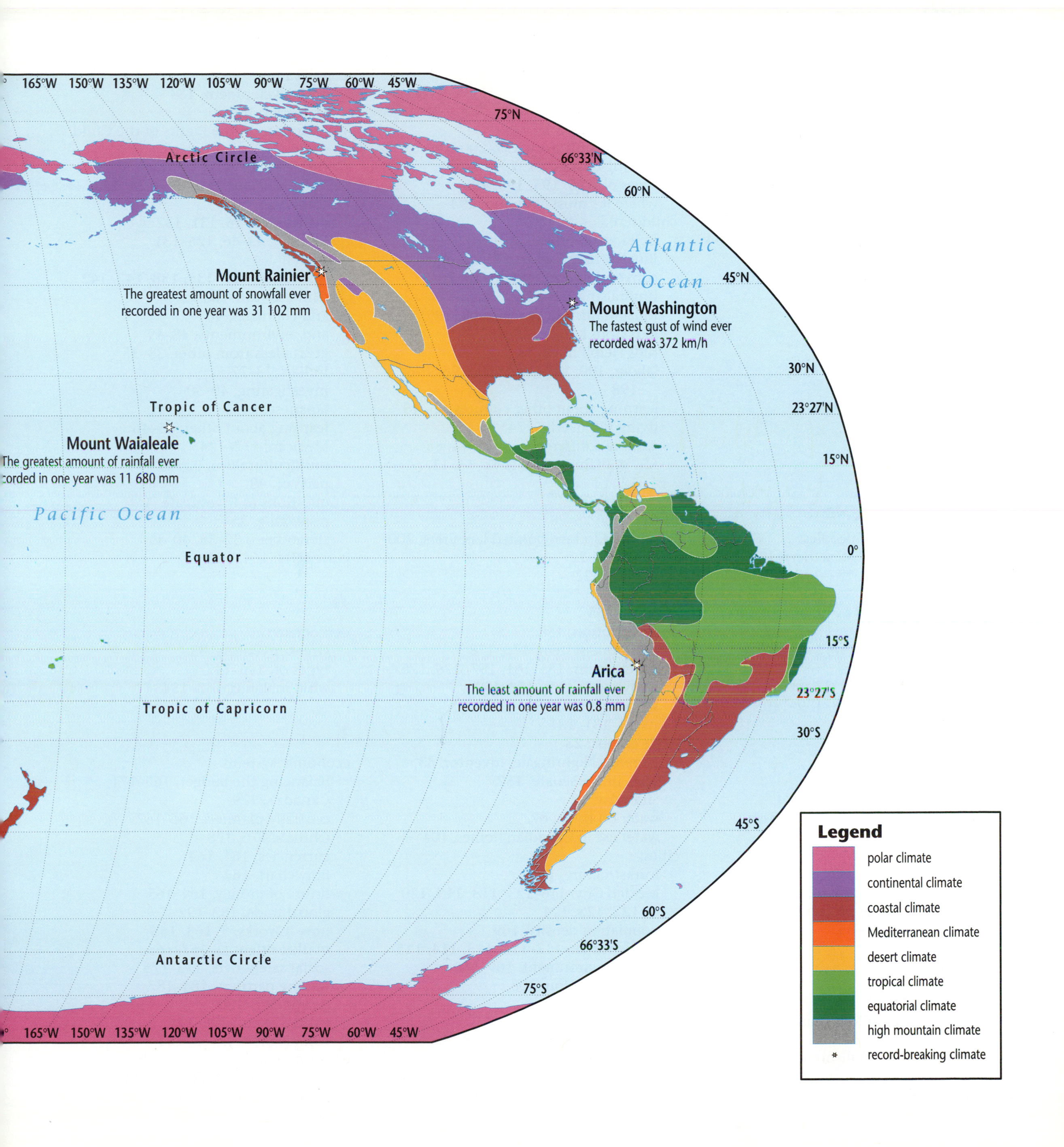
165°W 150°W 135°W 120°W 105°W 90°W 75°W 60°W 45°W
75°N
Arctic Circle
66°33'N
60°N
Atlantic
Ocean
45°N
Mount Rainier
The greatest amount of snowfall ever recorded in one year was 31 102 mm
Mount Washington
The fastest gust of wind ever recorded was 372 km/h
30°N
Tropic of Cancer
23°27'N
Mount Waialeale
The greatest amount of rainfall ever corded in one year was 11 680 mm
15°N
Pacific Ocean
Equator
0°
15°S
Arica
The least amount of rainfall ever recorded in one year was 0.8 mm
23°27'S
Tropic of Capricorn
30°S
45°S
60°S
66°33'S
Antarctic Circle
75°S
165°W 150°W 135°W 120°W 105°W 90°W 75°W 60°W 45°W
Legend
polar climate
continental climate
coastal climate
Mediterranean climate
desert climate
tropical climate
equatorial climate
high mountain climate
record-breaking climate

Index

Numbers in **boldface** indicate an illustration

U

W

Y

Photo Credits

p. 4 (t) Kennon Cooke/Valan Photos, (b) CP Archives;
p. 5 (t) Dick Hemingway, (b) Valan Photos;
p. 12 (b) Oshawa/Whitby This Week;
p. 16 (t) Courtesy United Nations, (b) Joseph Sohm; ChromoSohm Inc./CORBIS;
p. 17 From *A World In Our Hands*, Tricycle Press;
p. 19 Courtesy UNICEF Canada/Richard Ponsonby;
p. 22 Tony Makepeace Photography;
p. 26 Al Harvey/The Slide Farm;
p. 28 (l) Dick Hemingway, (r) CP Archives;
p. 33 (bl) Bettmann/CORBIS;
p. 34 (tr) Wolfgang Kaehler/CORBIS, (bl) Neal Preston/CORBIS, (br) Bettmann/CORBIS;
p. 44 (t) Eagle Dancer Enterprises, (b) Michael Tickner;
p. 45 Al Harvey/The Slide Farm;
p. 50 (b) Robert Holmes/CORBIS;
p. 53 Michael S. Yamashita/CORBIS;
p. 55 (t) John Dakers; Eye Ubiquitous/CORBIS;
p. 56 Michael Boys/CORBIS;
p. 58 Roger Ressmeyer/CORBIS;
p. 59 (b) Catherine Karnow/CORBIS;
p. 68 David Cumming; Eye Ubiquitous/CORBIS;
p. 69 (l) Toronto Sun, (r) Valan Photos;
p. 73 CP Archives;
p. 74 (b) David Cumming; Eye Ubiquitous/CORBIS;
p. 76 Valan Photos;
p. 81 David H. Wells/CORBIS;
p. 84 Courtesy St. Elizabeth School, Ottawa;
p. 90 Dorset Fine Arts;
p. 93 PictureQuest;
p. 94 (l) Dick Hemingway;
p. 97 James L. Amos/CORBIS;
p. 98 Superstock;
p. 99 Liba Taylor/CORBIS;
p. 104 Spectrum Stock;
p. 105 Al Harvey/The Slide Farm;
p. 108 Associated Press;
p. 110 Al Harvey/The Slide Farm;
p. 113 Courtesy Dept. of Library Services, American Museum of Natural History, photo by Rota, neg. no. 326597;
p. 114 Newberry Library, Edward E. Ayer Collection;
p. 115 Charles & Josette; Ecoscene/CORBIS;
p. 116 Associated Press;
p. 118 NASA – Goddard Space Flight Center, Scientific Visualization Studio;
p. 120 Stephanie Maze/CORBIS;
p. 122 Woodfin Camp;
p. 123 (t) Doug Bryant, (b) Stephanie Maze/CORBIS;
p. 124 Doug Bryant;
p. 126 Paul Harris/Survival International;
p. 127 Nik Wheeler/CORBIS;
p. 129 (l) David Neel Photography, (r) Na na kila Institute;
p. 130 (t) Victor Englebert/Survival International, (b) Dennison Berwick/Survival International;
p. 131 Paul Harris/Survival International;
p. 132 CP Archive;
p. 134 Courtesy Inuit Circumpolar Conference;
p. 136 Barb & Ron Kroll;
p. 137 Ales Fevzer/CORBIS;
p. 138 Christine Osborne Pictures;
p. 141 Paul A. Souders/CORBIS;
p. 142 David Moore, Black Star Publishing/PictureQuest;
p. 145 Dick Hemingway, Al Harvey/The Slide Farm;
p. 148 CP Archives;
p. 150 Dick Hemingway;
p. 152 CP Archives;
p. 155 (t) Tiziana and Gianni Baldizzone/CORBIS, (b) Keren Su/CORBIS;
p. 156 John Corbett/CORBIS;
p. 159 Joseph Sohm; ChromoSohm/CORBIS;
p. 160 Kevin R. Morris/CORBIS;
p. 170 CP Archives;
p. 173 Dick Hemingway; Al Harvey/The Slide Farm;
p. 175 CP Archives;
p. 176 Superstock;
p. 177 Associated Press;
p. 178 (t) Todd Gipstein/CORBIS, (bl) Ponopresse, (br) Kevin R. Morris/CORBIS;
p. 179 (t) Superstock, (b) Paul A. Souders/CORBIS;
p. 189 CP Archives;
p. 191 Ponopresse;
p. 193 Dick Hemingway;
p. 195 (l) Dick Hemingway, (r) Associated Press;
p. 196 (t) Associated Press, (b) Catherine Karnow/CORBIS;
p. 197 Associated Press;
p. 198 Associated Press;
p. 199 Courtesy Reebok Human Rights Foundation;
p. 200 Courtesy Ron Adams;
p. 203 Stone Images